First World War
and Army of Occupation
War Diary
France, Belgium and Germany

1 DIVISION
Divisional Troops
23 Field Company Royal Engineers
4 August 1914 - 30 April 1918

WO95/1252

The Naval & Military Press Ltd
www.nmarchive.com
Published in association with The National Archives

Published by

The Naval & Military Press Ltd

Unit 10 Ridgewood Industrial Park,

Uckfield, East Sussex,

TN22 5QE England

Tel: +44 (0) 1825 749494

www.naval-military-press.com

www.nmarchive.com

This diary has been reprinted in facsimile from the original. Any imperfections are inevitably reproduced and the quality may fall short of modern type and cartographic standards.

© Crown Copyright
Images reproduced by permission of The National Archives, London, England, 2015.

Contents

Document type	Place/Title	Date From	Date To
Heading	B.E.F. France & Flanders. 1 Division. Troops. 23 Field Coy Royal Engineers. 1914 Aug To 1919 Apr.		
Heading	1st Division 23rd Field Company Royal Engineers Aug-Dec 1914		
Heading	1st Divisional Engineers Disembarked ROUEN 19.8.14. 23rd Field Company R.E. August & September 1914.		
Heading	23rd Field Coy RE 1st Division Vol. I & II 4.8-4.10.14		
War Diary	Aldershot	04/08/1914	14/08/1914
War Diary	Farnboro Stn. Southampton	15/08/1914	18/08/1914
War Diary	Havre Roven	19/08/1914	03/09/1914
War Diary	Bridge Across R. Aisne On The Soissons-paisley Noad about 1/2 Mile N. G 2nd. O In Soissons On The 1/80,000 O.S. Map.	31/08/1914	31/08/1914
War Diary	Marolles Near La Ferte Milon River Ourcq	01/09/1914	01/09/1914
War Diary	Sammeron River Marne	03/09/1914	03/09/1914
War Diary	Demolition of Bridge at St Jean Les 2 Jumeaux	03/09/1914	04/10/1914
Heading	1st Divisional Engineers 23rd Field Company R.E. October 1914		
War Diary	Vendresse And Bourg	01/10/1914	15/10/1914
War Diary	Perles	16/10/1914	17/10/1914
War Diary	In Train	18/10/1914	18/10/1914
War Diary	Hazebrouck	19/10/1914	19/10/1914
War Diary	Poperinghe	20/10/1914	20/10/1914
War Diary	Pilitem	21/10/1914	21/10/1914
War Diary	N. Ypres	22/10/1914	25/10/1914
War Diary	Ypres	26/10/1914	26/10/1914
War Diary	Hooqe	27/10/1914	02/11/1914
Diagram etc	Medium Bridge Constructed Over Canal 1 Mile N.W. Of Ypres. By 23rd Fd Coy. R.E.		
Heading	1st Divisional Engineers 23rd Field Company R.E. November 1914.		
War Diary	Hooge	01/11/1914	01/11/1914
War Diary	Rly Cussing Near Ypres	02/11/1914	15/11/1914
War Diary	Westoutre	16/11/1914	16/11/1914
War Diary	Barre	17/11/1914	17/11/1914
Heading	1st Divisional Engineers 23rd Field Company R.E. December 1914.		
War Diary	Borre	18/11/1914	20/12/1914
War Diary	Borre-Locon	21/12/1914	21/12/1914
War Diary	Locon	22/12/1914	23/12/1914
War Diary	Beuvray	24/12/1914	24/12/1914
War Diary	Beuvray Cambrain	25/12/1914	25/12/1914
War Diary	Cambrain	26/12/1914	31/12/1914
Heading	1st Division Roy. Engineers 23rd Field Coy. Jan-Dec 1915.		
Heading	1st Division 23rd Field Coy. R.E. Vol V 1-31.1.15.		
War Diary	Combrain	01/01/1915	31/01/1915
Heading	1st Division 23rd Field Coy. R.E. Vol VI 1-28.2.15		
War Diary	Cambrin	01/02/1915	03/02/1915

War Diary	Hurionville	04/02/1915	16/02/1915
War Diary	Rambert	17/02/1915	27/02/1915
War Diary	Oblinghem	28/02/1915	28/02/1915
Heading	1st Division 23rd Field Coy. R.E. Vol VII 1-31.3.15		
War Diary	Les Glautignies Near Le Touret	01/03/1915	31/03/1915
Heading	1st Division 23rd Field Coy R.E. Vol VIII 1-30.4.15		
War Diary	Le Touret	01/04/1915	30/04/1915
Heading	1st Division 23rd Field Coy. R.E. Vol IX 1-31.5.15.		
War Diary	Le Touret	01/05/1915	10/05/1915
War Diary	M Bernechon	11/05/1915	12/05/1915
War Diary	Beuvry	13/05/1915	31/05/1915
Heading	1st Division 23rd Field Coy R.E. Vol X 1-30.6.15		
War Diary	Beuvry	01/06/1915	01/06/1915
War Diary	Fontenelle Fmc	02/06/1915	23/06/1915
War Diary	Raimbert	24/06/1915	27/06/1915
War Diary	La Bourse Vermelles	28/06/1915	30/06/1915
Heading	1st Division 23rd Field Coy. R.E. Vol XI From 1st To 31st July 1915		
War Diary	Labourse Vermelles	01/07/1915	31/07/1915
Heading	1st Division 23rd Field Coy. R.E. Vol XII 1-31 August. 15		
War Diary	Labourse Vermelles	01/08/1915	31/08/1915
Heading	1st Division 23rd F. Co. RE. Vol XIII Sep-Oct 15		
War Diary	Labourse Vermelles	01/09/1915	05/09/1915
War Diary	Drouvin Labourse Vermelles	06/09/1915	27/09/1915
War Diary	Mazingarbe Les Brebis Noeux Les Mines Mazingarbe	28/09/1915	08/10/1915
War Diary	Mazingarbe	09/10/1915	13/10/1915
War Diary	Lozinghem	14/10/1915	31/10/1915
Miscellaneous	A Form Messages And Signals.		
Miscellaneous		27/09/1915	27/09/1915
Miscellaneous	A Form Messages And Signals.		
Miscellaneous		25/09/1915	26/09/1915
Miscellaneous	A Form Messages And Signals.		
Miscellaneous			
Miscellaneous	A Form Messages And Signals.		
Miscellaneous			
Miscellaneous	A Form Messages And Signals.		
Miscellaneous		25/09/1915	25/09/1915
Miscellaneous	A Form Messages And Signals.		
Miscellaneous		24/09/1915	24/09/1915
Heading	1st Division 23rd F. Coy. RE. Nov. Vol. XIV		
War Diary	Lozinghem	01/11/1915	13/11/1915
War Diary	Mazingarbe Philosophe	14/11/1915	19/11/1915
War Diary	Mazingarbe Philosophe Fort Glatz	20/11/1915	30/11/1915
Heading	23rd Field Coy R.E. Dec. Vol. XV		
War Diary	Mazingarbe Philosophe Fort Glatz	01/12/1915	05/12/1915
War Diary	Mazingarbe Philosophe	06/12/1915	31/12/1915
Heading	1st Division Divl. Engineers 23rd Field Company R.E. Jan-Dec 1916.		
Heading	1st Divisional Engineers 23rd Field Company R.E. January 1916.		
War Diary	Philosophe Mazingarbe 58 Metre Point	01/01/1916	05/01/1916
War Diary	Philosophe Mazingarbe	06/01/1916	13/01/1916
War Diary	Lillers	14/01/1916	15/01/1916
War Diary	Lillers Allovagne	16/01/1916	30/01/1916
War Diary	Lillers	31/01/1916	31/01/1916

Heading	1st Divisional Engineers 23rd Field Company R.E. February 1916		
Heading	War Diary of 23rd (Field) Co. R.E. For February, 1916, Forwarded for retention		
War Diary	Lillers	01/02/1915	14/02/1915
War Diary	Les Brebis Loos	15/02/1915	29/02/1915
Heading	1st Divisional Engineers 23rd Field Company R.E. March 1916.		
Heading	War Diary of 23rd Field Co. R.E. For March 1916 forwarded Herewith VOl XVIII		
War Diary	Les Brebis Loos	01/03/1916	31/03/1916
Miscellaneous	Appendix A		
Heading	1st Divisional Engineers 23rd Field Company R.E. April 1916.		
Heading	War Diary, 23rd (Field) to the for month of April 1916 herewith.		
War Diary	Les Brebis Loos	01/04/1916	30/04/1916
Heading	1st Divisional Engineers 23rd Field Company R.E. May 1916.		
War Diary	Les Brebis Loos	01/05/1916	14/05/1916
War Diary	Les Brebis Loos Colonne	15/05/1916	31/05/1916
Heading	1st Divisional Engineers 23rd Field Company R.E. June 1916.		
War Diary	Les Brebis Calonne	01/06/1916	30/06/1916
Heading	1st Divisional Engineers 23rd Field Company R.E. July 1916		
War Diary	Les Brebis Calonne	01/07/1916	04/07/1916
War Diary	Ruitz	04/07/1916	06/07/1916
War Diary	Wargnies	07/07/1916	07/07/1916
War Diary	Molliens Au Bois	08/07/1916	08/07/1916
War Diary	Baisieux	09/07/1916	11/07/1916
War Diary	Albert & Becourt Wood	12/07/1916	21/07/1916
War Diary	Albert And Becourt	21/07/1916	21/07/1916
War Diary	Albert Becourt And Quaorangle Trench Approx. X22b50	22/07/1916	26/07/1916
War Diary	Baizieux	27/07/1916	31/07/1916
Heading	1st Divisional Engineers 23rd Field Company Royal Engineers August 1916		
War Diary	Baizieux	01/08/1916	14/08/1916
War Diary	Fricourt Albert	15/08/1916	26/08/1916
War Diary	Albert Fricourt Bazentin	27/08/1916	29/08/1916
War Diary	Albert Fricourt Bazentin Le Grand	30/08/1916	31/08/1916
Heading	1st Divisional Engineers 23rd Field Company R.E. September 1916		
War Diary	Albert Fricourt And Bazentin Le Grand	01/09/1916	04/09/1916
War Diary	Albert Fricourt (Hd Qrs)	05/09/1916	13/09/1916
War Diary	Behencourt	14/09/1916	15/09/1916
War Diary	Bresle Wood	16/09/1916	19/09/1916
War Diary	Fricourt Bazentin Le Grand	20/09/1916	28/09/1916
War Diary	Fricourt	29/08/1916	30/08/1916
Heading	1st Divisional Engineers 23rd Field Company R.E. October 1916.		
War Diary	Fricourt	01/10/1916	25/10/1916
War Diary	Bazentin & Fricourt	26/10/1916	31/10/1916
Heading	1st Divisional Engineers 23rd Field Company R.E. November 1916.		

War Diary	Fricourt F3bo9 & Bazentin F 15 B 58	01/11/1916	30/11/1916
Heading	1st Divisional Engineers 23rd Field Company R.E. December 1916		
War Diary	Fricourt F. G09 Bazentin S.15 B.6.8	01/12/1916	31/12/1916
Heading	1st Division Roy. Engineers 23rd Field Company, R.E. Jan-Dec 1917		
Heading	War Diary 23rd. Field Coy. R.E. 1st. Division. January. 1917.		
War Diary	Fricourt F 3 G 09 & Bazentin S 15 B 58	01/01/1917	25/01/1917
War Diary	Warloy	26/01/1917	31/01/1917
Heading	War Diary 23rd. Field Coy. R.E. 1st. Division. February. 1917.		
War Diary	Warloy	01/02/1917	02/02/1917
War Diary	Warloy & Merricourt Sur Somme	03/02/1917	03/02/1917
War Diary	Merricourt Sur Somme	04/02/1917	04/02/1917
War Diary	Merricourt Moulin De Becquincourt M 6 D 51 Fontaine De Cappy M9 D 27. Map references Sheet B 2 C. S.W. 1/20000	05/02/1917	05/02/1917
War Diary	Becquincourt G S De Boulogne & Fontrine De Cappy	06/02/1917	06/02/1917
War Diary	Map 62 C. S.W. 1/20.000	07/02/1917	09/02/1917
War Diary	Becquincourt M6 D 53 Bois De Boulogne N16a 8.3. Fontaineles Cappy M9 D 2.8.	10/02/1917	25/02/1917
War Diary	Chuignolles	26/02/1917	28/02/1917
Heading	War Diary 23rd. Field Coy. R.E. 1st Division. March.1917.		
War Diary	Chuignolles	01/03/1917	04/03/1917
War Diary	Chuignolles Becquincourt Dump. M6 Central Bois De Boulogne N 16a 83 & Fontaine Les Cappy. M9c 58.	05/03/1917	06/03/1917
War Diary	Fontaine les Cappy. M 9 C 58.	06/03/1917	06/03/1917
War Diary	Becquincourt Dump M6 Central Bois Pe Boulogne N16 a 83 Fontaine Les Cappy M9C 58.	07/03/1917	12/03/1917
War Diary	Becquincourt Dump M6 Central-Coy H.Q. Bde Boulogne N16.a.83-adv. Sects Bulltts Fontaine Le Coppy M9 C. 5. 8-Tramport Linse	13/03/1917	19/03/1917
War Diary	Eterpigny O 20.3. 6.7 H.Q.s With Tramport Line at Fontaine Le Cappy Official Becquincourt as before	20/03/1917	21/03/1917
War Diary	H.Q. Eterpigny O 20 b 67 Office Becquincourt M b Transport Lines M9 C 58	22/03/1917	24/03/1917
War Diary	HQ= Eterpigny O 20 b 67 Transport Lines Fontaine le Cappy. M9 C 5.8	25/03/1917	27/03/1917
War Diary	Eterpigny O 20.3.6.7 & as before.	28/03/1917	31/03/1917
Heading	War Diary 23rd. Field. Coy. R.E. 1st. Division. April.1917.		
War Diary	Eterpigny 4000 S. Of Peronne On R. Somme. Horse Lines At Fontain Les. Cappy.	01/04/1917	17/04/1917
War Diary	Mericourt Sur Somme	18/04/1917	18/04/1917
Heading	War Diary 23rd Field Coy R.E. 1st Division May. 1917.		
War Diary	Mericourt Sur Somme	01/05/1917	19/05/1917
War Diary	Bayonvillers	20/05/1917	27/05/1917
War Diary	On The Move Map 27 1/40,000 W. 5 A Central	28/05/1917	28/05/1917
War Diary	Thieushouck	29/05/1917	31/05/1917
Heading	War Diary 23rd. Field Coy. R.E. 1st. Division. June 1917.		
Miscellaneous	1st Division.	01/07/1917	01/07/1917
War Diary	Thieushouk Sheet 27 1/40.000 W 5.a. Central	01/06/1917	10/06/1917
War Diary	On The Move	11/06/1917	11/06/1917

Type	Description	Start	End
War Diary	Queue De Bavinchove	12/06/1917	18/06/1917
War Diary	Wormhoudt 27 C. 10.3 (1/40.000)	19/06/1917	19/06/1917
War Diary	Tleegervelt 19.I. 11.C (1/40.000)	20/06/1917	20/06/1917
War Diary	11. R 35 A. C. Coxyde Les Bains	21/06/1917	21/06/1917
War Diary	Carnh Le Fevre R. 35 A. D. C. Or R 32 Coxyde (1/20.000)	22/06/1917	22/06/1917
War Diary	M13 D.63.	23/06/1917	23/06/1917
War Diary	Nieuport bain M 13 D 63	24/06/1917	24/06/1917
War Diary	HQ at Nieuport Bains M 13 d 63 Transport R 32	25/06/1917	26/06/1917
War Diary	HQ at Nieuport Bains M 13 d 63 Transport Oost Dunkerque Bains	27/06/1917	30/06/1917
Heading	War Diary 23rd. Field Coy., R.E. 1st. Division. July. 1917.		
Miscellaneous	A Form. Messages And Signals.		
War Diary	Nieuport Bains M 13 D.63 Transport Lines Oost Dunkerque Bains	01/07/1917	03/07/1917
War Diary	Nieuport Bains M 13 D.6.3.	04/07/1917	06/07/1917
War Diary	Comp Le Fevre Coiyde Les Bains	07/07/1917	07/07/1917
War Diary	Camp Le Fevre Coxyde Bains Le Clippon	08/07/1917	13/07/1917
War Diary	Le Clippon	14/07/1917	31/07/1917
Heading	War Diary 23rd. Field Coy., R.E. 1st. Division. August. 1917.		
War Diary	Le Clipon Camp St Pol-Sur-Mor	01/08/1917	01/08/1917
War Diary	Suburb of Dunkerque	02/08/1917	31/08/1917
Heading	War Diary 23rd. Field Coy., R.E. 1st. Division. September. 1917.		
War Diary	Le Clipon Camp	01/09/1917	14/09/1917
War Diary	On The Move	29/09/1917	29/09/1917
War Diary	Villa Juliette X. 4.a.2.7.	30/09/1917	30/09/1917
Heading	War Diary 23rd. Field Coy., R.E. 1st. Division. October. 1917.		
War Diary	Oost Dunkerque Villa Juliette X 4.a.2.6.	01/10/1917	09/10/1917
War Diary	Oost Dunkerque X 4.a.2.6.	10/10/1917	17/10/1917
War Diary	Ghyvelde Map 19 1/40.000 II 15.b.7.6	18/10/1917	21/10/1917
War Diary	Arneke Map 27 1/40.000 H.6.3.9.3	22/10/1917	25/10/1917
War Diary	Herzeele Sheet 27 1/40.000 D. 15.a.3.3.	26/10/1917	30/10/1917
War Diary	Hospital Farm Camp Sheet 28 1/40.000 B. 19 D.central	31/10/1917	31/10/1917
Heading	War Diary 23rd. Field Coy., R.E. 1st. Division. November. 1917.		
War Diary	Hospital Farm Camp Sheet 28 1/40.000 B.19 D Central	01/11/1917	01/11/1917
War Diary	Hill Top Farm Camp C21d. 3.8. 28 1/40.000	02/11/1917	05/11/1917
War Diary	Hill Top Farm C 21 D. 38 Hospital Farm B 19 D Camp	06/11/1917	07/11/1917
War Diary	HQ. K Canal Bank No 47 N. Bank	08/11/1917	09/11/1917
War Diary	Gdu Sec Hill Top Form H.Q. Canal Bank Horse Lines Hospital Form	10/11/1917	13/11/1917
War Diary	HQ. East Bank Of Canal Gow. Bilets Hill Top Farm. C 21 D. 37 (nissen Huts) Transport Hospital Farm B 19 D.	14/11/1917	16/11/1917
War Diary	Goh Bllits Colforning Trench C 22 D.5.2.	17/11/1917	19/11/1917
War Diary	HQ At Canal Bank No 63 East Adv. Blliks 3 Section. in Caliporaia Trench C 22 D. 52 Transport. Hospital Farm B 19 D.	20/11/1917	28/11/1917
War Diary	Pardo Camp W. Cuthove	29/11/1917	29/11/1917
War Diary	Proven Poperinghe Road	30/11/1917	30/11/1917
Heading	War Diary 23rd. Field Coy., R.E. 1st. Division. December. 1917.		
Heading	CRE 1st Dvn War Diary for December herewith		

War Diary	Pardo Camp N Cuthove Chan. On The Proven To Poperinghe Road.	01/12/1917	03/12/1917
War Diary	Paratonnere Farm	04/12/1917	07/12/1917
War Diary	Paratonnere Camp N Woeston & Het Sas	08/12/1917	31/12/1917
Heading	1st Division Roy. Engineers 23rd Field Company R.E. Jan-Dec 1918		
War Diary	Paratonnere Farm Near Hetsas Woestan	01/01/1918	23/01/1918
War Diary	Bank Of Ypres Dixmude Canal Near Bridge 3 Horse Lines Near Salvation Corner	24/01/1918	21/02/1918
War Diary	Horse Lines Moued To Reigerborg Chatead	22/02/1918	28/02/1918
War Diary	Bank Of Yser Canal Near Bridge 3	01/03/1918	01/03/1918
War Diary	Horse Lines Regersburg Chateau	02/03/1918	09/03/1918
War Diary	Kempton Park Sheet 28 N W Horse Camp Reigersburg Chateau	10/03/1918	31/03/1918
Heading	1st Divisional Engineers 23rd Field Company R.E. April 1918.		
War Diary	Ilminster Camp Sheet 28. C.27.b.2.3 Horse Lines At Reigersburg Chateau	01/04/1918	05/04/1918
War Diary	Ilminster Camp. & Reigersburg chateau.	05/04/1918	07/04/1918
War Diary	Elverdinghe B.15.c.5.4. Ricour Farm And Caestre	07/04/1918	08/04/1918
War Diary	Ricour Farm near Caestre	08/04/1918	08/04/1918
War Diary	Annezin Sheet 36b E.3a.5.2.	08/04/1918	10/04/1918
War Diary	Sailly Labourse L.4.a.2.6.	10/04/1918	11/04/1918
War Diary	Fouquiers E.21.a.5.8.	12/04/1918	15/04/1918
War Diary	Fouquiers N. Annequin F.24. C.0.3.	16/04/1918	18/04/1918
War Diary	N. Annequin Marais Keep F. 11.a.4.2.	18/04/1918	20/04/1918
War Diary	N. Annequin F.24. C.0.3	21/04/1918	24/04/1918
War Diary	Transport Noeux Les Mines L 13d.4.6.	24/04/1918	28/04/1918
War Diary	N. Annequin	29/04/1918	29/04/1918
War Diary	Transport Lines Noeux Les Mines	30/04/1918	30/04/1918
War Diary	N. Annequin (F.23.d.9.2) Horse Lines	01/05/1918	01/05/1918
War Diary	Noeux-Les-Mines	02/05/1918	07/05/1918
War Diary	Horse Lines	08/05/1918	08/05/1918
War Diary	Moved To Maisnil Les Ruitz	09/05/1918	09/05/1918
War Diary	N Annequin Horse Lines	09/05/1918	09/05/1918
War Diary	N Annequin	18/05/1918	18/05/1918
War Diary	Horse Lines	19/05/1918	19/05/1918
War Diary	Maisnu-les-Ruitz.	20/05/1918	24/05/1918
War Diary	N Annequin Horse Lines	24/05/1918	24/05/1918
War Diary	Maisnu-les-Ruitz.	25/05/1918	31/05/1918
Miscellaneous	Copy of Messages Received from G.O.C. 2nd Bde on the Subject of the Raid Period out on 24th inst.	24/05/1918	24/05/1918
War Diary	Tourbieres	01/06/1918	01/06/1918
War Diary	F.29.d.9.2 (Gorre Sheet)	01/06/1918	01/06/1918
War Diary	Horse lines	01/06/1918	01/06/1918
War Diary	Maisnil-Les-Ruitz.	01/06/1918	02/06/1918
War Diary	Sailly Labourse L.3.d 37. house Lues	02/06/1918	03/06/1918
War Diary	Unchanged	04/06/1918	06/06/1918
War Diary	Sailly la Bourse l.3.a.3.7 transport lues	07/06/1918	07/06/1918
War Diary	Maisnil-Les-Ruitz	08/06/1918	11/06/1918
War Diary	Sailly-Labourse	11/06/1918	11/06/1918
War Diary	Transport at Maisnil-Les-Ruitz.	12/06/1918	17/06/1918
War Diary	Sailly-Labourse	18/06/1918	18/06/1918
War Diary	Transport at Maisnil-Les-Ruitz	19/06/1918	24/06/1918
War Diary	Tourbieres F.23. d Central	25/06/1918	25/06/1918
War Diary	Transport Lines	25/06/1918	25/06/1918

War Diary	Maisnil-Les-Ruitz		26/06/1918	27/06/1918
War Diary	Tourbieres F.23.d. Cen		28/06/1918	30/06/1918
War Diary	Tourbieres. F.23.d.c. Cen Gorre. Sheet Horse Lines Maisnil. Les Ruitz.		01/07/1918	01/07/1918
War Diary	Gorre. Sheet.		01/07/1918	01/07/1918
War Diary	Horse Lines.		01/07/1918	01/07/1918
War Diary	Maisnil. Les Ruitz.		02/07/1918	05/07/1918
War Diary	Tourbieres F29.d Cent.		05/07/1918	05/07/1918
War Diary	Horse Lines.		05/07/1918	05/07/1918
War Diary	Maisnil Les Ruitz.		06/07/1918	10/07/1918
War Diary	Tourbieres		11/07/1918	11/07/1918
War Diary	Horse Lines		11/07/1918	11/07/1918
War Diary	Maisnil-Les-Ruitz.		11/07/1918	14/07/1918
War Diary	Tourbieres		15/07/1918	15/07/1918
War Diary	Horse Lines		15/07/1918	15/07/1918
War Diary	Maisnil-Les-Ruitz.		15/07/1918	18/07/1918
War Diary	Tourbieres		19/07/1918	19/07/1918
War Diary	Horse Lines		19/07/1918	19/07/1918
War Diary	Maisnil-Les-Ruitz.		19/07/1918	24/07/1918
War Diary	Tourbieres		25/07/1918	25/07/1918
War Diary	Horse Lines		25/07/1918	25/07/1918
War Diary	Maisnil-Les-Ruitz.		25/07/1918	28/07/1918
War Diary	Tourbieres		29/07/1918	29/07/1918
War Diary	Horse Lines		29/07/1918	29/07/1918
War Diary	Maisnil-Les-Ruitz.		29/07/1918	31/07/1918
War Diary	Tourbieres		01/08/1918	01/08/1918
War Diary	Horse Lines		01/08/1918	01/08/1918
War Diary	Maisnil-Les-Ruitz.		01/08/1918	05/08/1918
War Diary	Sailly Labourse		06/08/1918	07/08/1918
War Diary	Transport		07/08/1918	07/08/1918
War Diary	Maisnil-Les Ruitz		07/08/1918	12/08/1918
War Diary	Sailly Labourse		13/08/1918	13/08/1918
War Diary	Transport		13/08/1918	13/08/1918
War Diary	Maisnil-Les Ruitz		14/08/1918	19/08/1918
War Diary	Sailly Labourse		20/08/1918	20/08/1918
War Diary	Transport		20/08/1918	20/08/1918
War Diary	Maisnil-Les Ruitz		20/08/1918	22/08/1918
War Diary	Boyaval. G.14.d.8.1.		23/08/1918	23/08/1918
War Diary	Boyaval. Sheet 44 B.G.14.d.8.1.		24/08/1918	31/08/1918
War Diary	Arras		01/09/1918	07/09/1918
War Diary	Arras Sector.		08/09/1918	10/09/1918
War Diary	St.Quentin Sector.		11/09/1918	14/09/1918
War Diary	Sheet 62c SE. W.4.a.2.3		15/09/1918	20/09/1918
War Diary	Caulincourt W.6.d. 3.8 Sheet 62c		20/09/1918	23/09/1918
War Diary	Marteville		24/09/1918	29/09/1918
War Diary	Berthaucourt		30/09/1918	30/09/1918
War Diary	Berthaucourt		01/10/1918	01/10/1918
War Diary	Transport At Marteville		02/10/1918	05/10/1918
War Diary	Marteville		06/10/1918	08/10/1918
War Diary	Bellicourt		09/10/1918	11/10/1918
War Diary	Mericourt		12/10/1918	16/10/1918
War Diary	Vaux-Andigny Transport At Bohain		17/10/1918	18/10/1918
War Diary	La Vallee Mulatre		19/10/1918	25/10/1918
War Diary	Vallee Mulatre		26/10/1918	04/11/1918
War Diary	La Vallee Mulatre		01/11/1918	04/11/1918
Miscellaneous	Awards for Bridging Canal-November 4th 1918			

War Diary	Le Vallee Mulatre	05/11/1918	06/11/1918
War Diary	Fresnoy Le Grande	07/11/1918	13/11/1918
War Diary	Grande Fayt	14/11/1918	15/11/1918
War Diary	Sars Potteries	16/11/1918	16/11/1918
War Diary	Grandraeu	17/11/1918	17/11/1918
War Diary	Castillon	18/11/1918	18/11/1918
War Diary	Fraire	19/11/1918	19/11/1918
War Diary	Yves Gomezee	20/11/1918	23/11/1918
War Diary	Coreene	24/11/1918	24/11/1918
War Diary	Rostenne Summiere	25/11/1918	01/12/1918
War Diary	Lavys	02/12/1918	02/12/1918
War Diary	Furzee	03/12/1918	09/12/1918
War Diary	Noiseux Narre Ozo	10/12/1918	13/12/1918
War Diary	Khout-St Plout Bech	14/12/1918	16/12/1918
War Diary	Thommen	17/12/1918	17/12/1918
War Diary	Andler	18/12/1918	18/12/1918
War Diary	Kronenburg	19/12/1918	19/12/1918
War Diary	Blankenheimerdorf	20/12/1918	21/12/1918
War Diary	Eicherscheid	22/12/1918	22/12/1918
War Diary	Stotzheim	23/12/1918	23/12/1918
War Diary	Niederdrees	24/12/1918	28/02/1919
War Diary	Ipplendorf (Wormersdorf)	01/03/1919	24/03/1919
War Diary	Wormersdorf Germany	25/03/1918	30/04/1918

B.E.F. FRANCE & FLANDERS.

1 DIVISION. TROOPS.

23 FIELD COY ROYAL
ENGINEERS.
1914 AUG TO 1919 APR.

B.E.F. FRANCE & FLANDERS

1 DIVISION. TROOPS.

23 FIELD COY ROYAL
ENGINEERS.
1914 AUG TO 1919 APR.

1252

1ST DIVISION

23RD FIELD COMPANY
ROYAL ENGINEERS

AUG - DEC 1914

1st Divisional Engineers

Disembarked ROUEN 19.8.14.

23rd FIELD COMPANY R. E.

AUGUST & SEPTEMBER 1914.

Army Form C. 2118.

WAR DIARY
or
INTELLIGENCE SUMMARY.
(Erase heading not required.)

a 99

23rd Field Coy: RE

$\frac{121}{1363}$

1st Division.

Vol. I & II. 4.8 – 4.10.14

Army Form C. 2118.

Page 1.

WAR DIARY
or
INTELLIGENCE SUMMARY.
(Erase heading not required.)

Instructions regarding War Diaries and Intelligence Summaries are contained in F.S. Regs., Part II. and the Staff Manual respectively. Title pages will be prepared in manuscript.

Hour, Date, Place	Summary of Events and Information	Remarks and references to Appendices
6.5 p.m. 4-8-14 ALDERSHOT	Order for mobilization received.	
5-8- "	Had already completed Medical Inspection, Vet⁹ Insp⁹ & Arms insp⁹. Cart wagons also mostly packed	
1st Day of mob⁹	1. Capt⁹. 2 Subalterns + 120 rank & file joined. Making up & issuing of equip. as per mob⁹ scheme. All working smoothly & ahead of time. Propor⁹ report rendered accordingly at 5 p.m.	
6 "	All rank & file joined except one. Making up + issue as per scheme.	
2nd Day		
7 "	All horses except 11 ridden drawn, also brigden. Stables fitting harness	
3 "	Route march for dismounted men. Mounted section training. Implements drawn	
4th "		
9.30 a.m. 10 "	Same as yesterday — duties by M.O. Stables, inoculating men	
11 " (Last day of mob⁹)	Inspection by C.R.E. R.T.E. march. Completion attained and Inspection by H.M. The King soon after mid day.	
12 "	Route march & drills	
13 "	" "	
14 "	" "	
3.27 p.m. 15 " FARNBORO' STN.	"Company paraded complete ready for entrainment. Warped all vehicles Company entrained at L. & S.W. R⁹ Stn. will with⁹. The hour allowed and arrived at S'ton in under 2 hours. There being no ship available, Company went into Rest Camp.	
5.15 " " SOUTHAMPTON	C. standing by ready to embark at short notice	
16 "		
10.0 a.m. 17 "	Received message No. 61 ordering 4 Sections of 23rd F.C. to embark at once Capt. Addison + 4 Sections arrived at S'ton dock ptl. about mid⁹ day and embarked on S.S. Mellifont about 3 p.m. Capt Addison was O.C. Troops on board.	
4.25 p.m. "	Rec⁹ message No. 72 ordering H.Q.⁹ & Co (with portion to) to embark on the S.S. Bazil at 8.15 p.m. This boat did not arrive till later and the Vehicles & horses of H.Q.⁹ were not aboard until about 3.0 a.m. 18th inst.	
3.0 a.m. 18 "	" "	
7.0 " "	Left Southampton on S.S. Bazil with H.Q. 23rd F. and a Cav. Capt.	
8.0 p.m. " HAVRE.	arrived Havre + went slowly up the R. Seine during the night arriving at ROUEN. Orders to wait & man Gangway cranes. The	
8.30 a.m. 19 " ROUEN	portion requn⁹ had to be off loaded from wagons + its kept + ordn until the G. officer arrvd H.Q. & portion & 4 Sections & Co in Rest Camp where they had arrived this morning.	

WAR DIARY
or
INTELLIGENCE SUMMARY.
(Erase heading not required.)

Army Form C. 2118.

Page 2.

Hour, Date, Place	Summary of Events and Information	Remarks and references to Appendices or Special order
8/14	at ROUEN	
19.	4 sections rest in camp.	
20. "	Paraded 9.30 a.m. to leave camp. Train left ~~camp~~ gare du nord about 3.45 p.m.	C.J. 1/20/3/14
21. "	~~Arrived at~~ arrived at ROUVION at 4.30 p.m. Orders Received to join column at 12.0 noon and ~~train~~ follow into billets at DOMPIERRE.	
22. "	Marched to billets at VILLERS-SIRE-NICOLE. ~~Arrived~~ in billets 10 a.m. 22/8/14	
23. "	4.0 a.m. under 3rd Bgde orders marched to ROUVEROY. ~~Under orders~~ from 1st D.E. ~~proceeded~~ to LISEROEUX to prepare a defensive position facing N.W & W between FAUROEULX + PEISSANT. At 3.0 p.m. an attack was expected from the west, + the works were occupied by the Welsh Regt. About 8.0 p.m. orders were received to join R. Highlanders at GRAND RENG. The company proceeded to billets in GRAND RENG.	
24. "	8.0 a.m. company marched to VILLERS-SIRE-NICOLE + awaited 1st Gds. Bgde. to prepare a rearguard position on E. of village facing west. Afterwards the company marched into billets at LA LONGUEVILLE with ~~...~~ movement ~~...~~ today. N⁰ 1 + 2 sections ~~...~~ Bgde ~~...~~ H.Q. 2.& 3.& 4 sections with ~~...~~ reported to 1st Bgde ~~...~~ movement + bivouacked at DOMPIERRE. H.Q. with 3 & 4 sections billeted at HUGUEMENT.	
25. "	A wet march. The personnel with the train were fired on, one officer slightly wounded.	
26. "	Marched to CAMBRESIS. N⁰ 1 & 2 sections beginning on the march.	
27. "	The company was attached to 1st Gds. Bgde. as part of rearguard, and awaited to put bridge at CAMBRESIS into a state of defence to cover retirement. ~~...~~ The company also ~~...~~ a position just N of ETREUX + one were ~~received~~ not to blow up the bridge. On completion of work the company marched via ETREUX from the main body + came under fire South of that village, but escaped without	

Army Form C. 2118.

WAR DIARY
or
INTELLIGENCE SUMMARY.
(Erase heading not required.)

Page 3

Instructions regarding War Diaries and Intelligence Summaries are contained in F.S. Regs., Part II. and the Staff Manual respectively. Title pages will be prepared in manuscript.

Hour, Date, Place	Summary of Events and Information	Remarks and references to Appendices
28. 8.14	Any casualties, and proceeded via LA GUISE ETABLIN & FONQUEUSE. Nos. 1 & 2 sections arrived 2nd Rgde in outskirts a rearguard position at ORIGNY, afterwards rejoined the company, marching to WEST of BERTAUCOURT.	
29. "	Rest at BERTAUCOURT. Replenished complete rations, marched at dusk, and joined column at ST GOBAIN; advanced guard 1/c of convoy. 12.0 a.m.- 3.0 a.m. halt.	
30. "	3.0 a.m. Moved off again to MARGIVAL. The French are in bivouac here, to the Company bivouac with 1st gds Rgde at ALLEMANT.	
31. "	Left ALLEMANT, forming part of rearguard & went into bivouac just east of Wood near MISSY-AUX-BOIS. No. 4 Section demolished a bridge over river Aisne at SOISSONS	See page 3a. for special report by this demolition
1. 9.14	Left MISSY-AUX-BOIS, with rearguard & marched via VILLIERS-SUR-COTERETS to temporary bivouac near LA FERTE MILON. Nos. 1 & 2 sections assisted 2nd Brigade in preparation of an outpost position N. of river. About 7.0 p.m. orders were received to move to the S. side of LA FERTE MILON, and the Company moved off. Nos. 1 & 2 sections remained in LA FERTE, blowing up two road bridges, & destroying barges, & foot bridges.	
2. "	After blowing up bridges, Nos. 1 & 2 proceeded to join the company at 2.30 a.m. in time to meet Nº with rearguard on the march from to VERREDES. Nos. 2 & 3 sections assisted in preparing a rearguard position in rear of at VERREDES where they bivouacked.	See page 3b. for special report on the demolitions
3. "	Marched with A.G. to JOUARRE. Nos. 2 & 3 sections demolished bridges at ST TEAM and SAMMERON over the R. MARNE. No. 4 Section marched to R. 9 of Coldstream Guards and rejoined the company at JOUARRE.	See page 3c. for special report of the demolitions

Army Form C. 2118.

WAR DIARY
or
INTELLIGENCE SUMMARY.
(Erase heading not required.)

Instructions regarding War Diaries and Intelligence Summaries are contained in F.S. Regs., Part II. and the Staff Manual respectively. Title pages will be prepared in manuscript.

Page 3 a.

Hour, Date, Place	Summary of Events and Information	Remarks and references to Appendices
About 3.30 to 5.0 p.m. 31st Aug '14. Bridge across R. AISNE on the SOISSONS — PAISLEY road about 1½ mile N. of 2″ O in SOISSONS on the 1/80,000 O.S. map.	Report on Rhone Lattice Girder Bridge destroyed N. of SOISSONS by No. 4 Sect. 23rd F. Co. R.E. 1. The bridge was of lattice girder type, with two spans of about 100 ft. each. The strong masonry piers in the centre had been specially prepared for demolition with gunpowder by the French some years ago, but no the keys of the demolition well must could not be obtained for half an hour & no gunpowder was available. 2. In case of an attempt a possible attack owing to the want of a covering party, it was decided to blow down one girder only and to barricade the far end of road + bridge with barbed wire. 3. The section of the main girders is approx. as shown in sketch. Between the two main girders were two small longitudinal girders and three cross girders at intervals of about 10 ft supporting the roadway of 1½" double planks. 4. Charges were placed so as to cut the two main girders at top & bottom flanges (3 sticks of gun cotton 9oz ONE each) also the two longitudinal girders (12 sticks ONE each ¾ wide) making a total charge of 4×12 + 2×3 = 54 lbs. of old pattern G.C. slabs, fired by 6 electric fuzes. The girders were cut close to the central pier on the S.E. side of same. The demolition was complete, the span S.E. span falling into the river 30 ft below, as shown.	[sketch of girder cross-section: 6" flange, cross girder, small longitudinal girder of which there were two, ½" angle iron, ½" lattice bracing, 12", 0'] [plan sketch: N.W. end of bridge — 100' — S.E. end]

Forms/C. 2118/10

Army Form C. 2118.

WAR DIARY
or
INTELLIGENCE SUMMARY.
(Erase heading not required.)

Page 3 F

Instructions regarding War Diaries and Intelligence Summaries are contained in F.S. Regs., Part II. and the Staff Manual respectively. Title pages will be prepared in manuscript.

Hour, Date, Place	Summary of Events and Information	Remarks and references to Appendices
① 11 P.M. 1st Sept. 1914 MAROLLES Nr LA FERTÉ MILON. RIVER OURCQ.	Demolition of Steel Girder Bridge by No.1 Section. Bridge. Steel Girders, 3 spans of 21 feet each, each span consists of 2 I type girders. Size 21 feet (long) x 1' (top flange) x 3' (web) x 2' (bottom flange). Charges. Works out to be 20 lb per girder. This was placed at the ends of the centre span, against the web & the flange in the arrow way for all 3 girders. Fired electrically. Result. All three girders cut through & the places and centre span cantilevers down into river.	Elevation. Section.
② 6.30 p.m. 3rd Sept. 1914 SAMMERON RIVER MARNE.	Demolition of Masonry Bridge. Bridge. Span 298 feet. Width of roadway 18 feet. 3 arches each 3 feet thick. Span of each 99 feet. Road material cemented down & narrowing of the crown of the arches not according to C.R.E.'s orders. Charges of 110 lb. guncotton laid along the newel tampens wet. Fired electrically. Whole bridge demolished, including both outer spans. In lieu of above demolition, arrow posts of gabions were provided.	Elevation. 29'0"

Army Form C. 2118.

WAR DIARY
or
INTELLIGENCE SUMMARY.
(Erase heading not required.)

Instructions regarding War Diaries and Intelligence Summaries are contained in F.S. Regs., Part II. and the Staff Manual respectively. Title pages will be prepared in manuscript.

Hour, Date, Place	Summary of Events and Information	Remarks and references to Appendices
Demolition of Bridge at ST JEAN LES 2 JUMEAUX at 6.30 pm on 3/9/14	**Preparation** A cut 18" wide was made through both the concrete sideways, the small brick supporting arches and stone facing at the crown of centre span and carried across the road. Commenced at 8.30 am ready by 10 pm A board bridge was prepared to carry traffic while ditch was being dug. The masonry was of an open pore somewhat like slag or lava A charge of 112 slabs of guncotton was tied to a board and placed downwards on the arch ring, the inequalities being packed with earth. Two primers were used with two electric detonators in series. The charge was then tamped with material dug out. Wires a exploder were first tested with an electric exploder. The wires were taken along the West handrail of the bridge to behind a house where the exploder was attached. The charge was fired at 6.30 pm. **Result** On exploding the charge two thirds of the centre span was blown away and the other spans were cracked right across near the haunches both at the piers and land ends. About 3 mins later the cracks in the far span opened out, the handrails burst, the pier toppled over into the river and dropped the far span into the stream, leaving it right-away from the shore. The near span was badly cracked, and likely to give way at any moment.	*(sketches: Plan of charge & wiring; Before Demolition; After Demolition; Masonry Arch Ring Crown diagram with rail, concrete sideway, metalling, asphalt layer, brick rubble, cement & sand, facing masonry, 22", 8", 15½" charge, 3' dimensions)*

Army Form C. 2118.

WAR DIARY
or
INTELLIGENCE SUMMARY.
(Erase heading not required.)

Page 4

Hour, Date, Place	Summary of Events and Information	Remarks and references to Appendices
4-9-14	March) to COULOMIERS. In the evening the company was ordered to road COULOMIERS - CHOISY, to support Black Watch. During the night No. 1 & 4 sections assisted flanking this road; No. 2 blocked bridge at PONT DAMMARIN. The right hand without incident.	
5.	The company moved at dawn, & joined the column on the road to MAUPERTHUIS. Arrived in bivouac near ROZOY. Nos. 1 & 2 sections assisted 1st Brigade to prepare outpost position and block roads.	
6.	Orders were received to advance. No. 2 section in Advanced guard with cold-stream gds came into action 1 mile S. of ROZOY. On the continuance of the advance, the company bivouacked at LE PLESSIS.	※ This was our first advance after a long retirement and the first time BEF a section came under shell infantry and artillery fire. No. 2 Section heroically under Lt. Bond carried out their manoeuvres with great steadiness on this occasion in spite of some chaff among neighbouring troops.
7.	Advanced across country & bivouacked at LE FRESNOIS.	
8.	Advanced and bivouacked at LA BOISSEROTIE.	
9.	Advanced across R. MARNE & bivouacked at LA NOUETTE FARM. The company came under shell fire on the march, for a short period.	
10.	Advanced & billeted at LATILLY.	
11.	Advanced & (billets) at BRUYERES.	
12.	Advanced & billeted at PAARS.	
13.	Advanced to passage of R. AISNE. The company was employed all day in improving temporary pontoon bridge at Bourg, constructed by 17th company RE for passage of transport. Bivouacked at PAISSY. At dawn, moved to VENDRESSE, which immediately was continuously under artillery fire.	
14.	Next position, E. of VENDRESSE. Bivouacked outside VENDRESSE. The company prepared a Second Int. ady 10.0 pm to dig trenches for Queens Regt. N. of CHEMIN DES DAMES.	

Forms/C. 2118/10

(9 29 6) W 3332-1107 100,000 10/13 H W V

Army Form C. 2118.

Page 5

WAR DIARY
or
INTELLIGENCE SUMMARY.
(Erase heading not required.)

Hour, Date, Place	Summary of Events and Information	Remarks and references to Appendices
15.9.14.	Company was sent to firing line N. of VENDRESSE, as reinforcement to 1st Gds. Bgde., returning at night to billets in MOULINS.	
16.9.14.	In billets in MOULINS. No 4 Section sent to assist 17th Sqdn. in repair of bridges at VILLERS.	
17.9.14.	Left MOULINS & marched to PARGNAN, commencing work on bridge - head position N. of PARGNAN. No 4 Section at work at VILLERS and beyond the cemetery at PARGNAN.	
18.9.14.	Worked on position at PARGNAN in afternoon.	
19. "	1.0 a.m. - 4.30 a.m. The company manned the defences at PARGNAN. Work continued till 10.0 p.m. when orders were received to proceed	
20. "	to PASSY to assist R. SUSSEX Regt. The company reached PASSY at 7.0 p.m. and dug a position on ridge above the village under fire till 2.0 a.m. next morning.	
21. "	5.0 a.m. Marched back to billets at VILLERS. In the afternoon, orders received to go to VENDRESSE to assist 8th Brigade. No 2 & 3 sections dug a flank position for S.W.B., returning at 2.0 a.m.	
22. "	5.0 a.m. returned to billets in VILLERS. 1.0 p.m. received orders to relieve trenches of 1st Inf.y Bgde. at CHEMIN DES DAMES, starting about 8.0 pm. The company marched out to carry out work in	
23. "	1.0 a.m. to billets in VENDRESSE. Remained in VENDRESSE by day. At night, the company employed with the 18th Inf.y Bde. in putting up entanglements and obstruction paths	
24.9.14.	In VENDRESSE by day. At night, carried on with work for 18th Inf.y Bde.	

WAR DIARY
or
INTELLIGENCE SUMMARY.

Army Form C. 2118.

Page 6

Hour, Date, Place	Summary of Events and Information	Remarks and references to Appendices
25.9.14.	In VENDRESSE. At night, the company carried on putting up barbed wire in front of the Trenches on near KAILEUR. (The 1st Bde had relieved by the 2nd Inf Bde.)	The O.C. CHEMIN DES DAMES.
26.9.14.	In VENDRESSE. At midday, the company started a Sap for the trenches of the Queen's Regt (3rd Bde). The object being to establish an observing station near the road. At night, the sap was carried on and 1 section constructed a M.G. emplacement with O.H.C. for Black Watch.	During period 25th onwards the O.C. carried on a detailed plane Table survey of the 1st Division area, on a 3" map, with a view to giving accurate information as to range & position of trenches to artillery, with the view of accurately locating the enemy front lines; also fixing the exact position of the Thies Koss observations overlooking the enemy position on the CHEMIN DES DAMES. Arranged with Capt Wilbraham R.E. 2/1st Printing Section to take a photographic panorama from this & then the observations locating which from support information as to the position of the enemy Trenches. Hereinaufter this 3" map mounted on a plane table were if put was in laying out a line of enfer from a machine gun a field for a horringer placed in the 1st Bde lines to enfilade the enemy trenches in front of own 2nd Bde position on the CHEMIN.
27.9.14.	In VENDRESSE. Erection of wire in front of 2nd Inf? Bgde.	
28.9.14.	In VENDRESSE. 1 section wiring. 2 sections making traverses on the CHEMIN DES DAMES.	
29.9.14.	2 sections wiring in front of 2nd Inf Brigade. No 1 section erected an observatory in Two trenches destroyed and N°1 Test cart damaged by shell fire	
30.9.14	Work in trenches for 2nd Inf. Bgde. No 1 section, ½ mill E g TROYON rear of the brigade	
1.10.14.	N° 1 section in VENDRESSE. Remainder of company proceeds after work (wiring) to billets in BOURG.	
2.10.14.	2 sections placing barbed wire & clearing long front of position running N° 4 S put N° of COURTONNE, Welsh Regt.	
3.10.14.	3 section at work with 2nd Bgde Putting up wire making communication trench across the CHEMIN DES DAMES & laying out new trenches for "enforcement" just south of existing trenches on CHEMIN. ½ plane table & staves for aligning trenches N° 1 section supplying list buildis & wall party erected an observatory North front of own 2nd Bde position on MOULINS.	

1st Divisional Engineers

23rd FIELD COMPANY R. E.

OCTOBER 1914.

Army Form C. 2118.

WAR DIARY
or
INTELLIGENCE SUMMARY
(Erase heading not required.)

of 23rd Fld. Coy R.E. 1st Div[ision]

Instructions regarding War Diaries and Intelligence Summaries are contained in F.S. Regs., Part II. and the Staff Manual respectively. Title pages will be prepared in manuscript.

Place	Hour, Date	Summary of Events and Information	Remarks and references to Appendices
VENDRESSE and BOURG	1-10-14	No.1 Section in VENDRESSE. Remainder of company proceed afterwards (mining) to billets in BOURG.	
	2-10-14	2 Sections placing barbed wire & clearing about front of positions running N.S. just N. of COURTONNE. Welsh Regt.	
	3-10-14	3 Sections at work with 2nd Brigade, putting up wire, making communication trenches across the Chemin des Dames & laying out new trench.	
	do		
	4-10-14	No.1 section sapping. Fired Molliere revolt party erects an observatory near MOULINS.	Rfmn Brown W. Hosp.
	5-10-14	2 Sections working with 2nd and 1st Brigades at VENDRESSE. after work at night. No.1 Section returned to BOURG & No.2 Section stopped at VENDRESSE. No. 3rd Sections sent to work on the bridge at VILLERS EN PRAYERES for the day. The work consisting of putting cribs from in the centre of the larger & planks to join.	
	6-10-14	No. 4 Section at work at VILLERS on the bridge. No.3 Section at work on position at OBSERVATION HILL, N. of MOULINS. No. 2 Section at work with 1st & 2nd Brigades.	
	7-10-14	No. 2 Section at work with 2nd Bgd. No.1 Section at work on OBSERVATION HILL. Remainder of company had innoculated.	

(9 29 6) W 3352-1107 100,000 10/13 H W V Forms/C. 2118/10

Army Form C. 2118.

WAR DIARY
or
INTELLIGENCE SUMMARY.
(Erase heading not required.)

Instructions regarding War Diaries and Intelligence Summaries are contained in F.S. Regs., Part II. and the Staff Manual respectively. Title pages will be prepared in manuscript.

Hour, Date, Place		Summary of Events and Information	Remarks and references to Appendices
VENDRESSE and BOURG	8.10.14	No 2 Section at work with 2nd Bde. To construct a line of advance under cover of "COCKED HAT WOOD" at spur S.E. of CHIVY, from the direction of BOURG. No 1 Section here inside wire.	W. Roth. Lieut R. A.A. H.R.E. reconnoitred
do.	9.10.14	No 2 Section returned from Vendresse and No 3 Section went there for duty. No 2 Sapping. During last four days company re-fitted with shick, socks, boots, caps etc.	2/Lt Morris Hosp R.
do.	10.10.14	No. 3 Section at Vendresse, sapping. Rest of Company Route March. No 3 section 200 were in front of Black watch at midnight.	
do.	11.10.14	No 3 Section carry on Sap and head cover on right of 2nd Bde. at night. Rest of Company Route March.	
do.	12.10.14	No 3 Section carry on Sap. Rest of Coy Route March. In the evening No 4 Section relieved No 3 at VENDRESSE.	
do.	13.10.14	No 4 Section carry on Sap. Rest of Company were on demolition pit with Black Watch at night. No 4 Section were in wood West of the BEAULNE spur. No 1 & 3 Sections were Route March.	
do.	14.10.14	No. 4 section at VENDRESSE. Nos. 2 & #1 Section wire on west of BEAULNE spur.	
do.	15.10.14	No. 4 Section return from VENDRESSE. During the night the French took over the line from 1st Division. 1-23rd Coy left in observation party on Trestle bridge at BOURG during the operation.	

(9-29-6) W 3332--1107 100,000 10/13 H W V Forms/C. 2118/10.

Army Form C. 2118.

WAR DIARY
or
INTELLIGENCE SUMMARY.
(Erase heading not required.)

Instructions regarding War Diaries and Intelligence Summaries are contained in F. S. Regs., Part II. and the Staff Manual respectively. Title pages will be prepared in manuscript.

Hour, Date, Place	Summary of Events and Information	Remarks and references to Appendices
FISMES. 16.10.14	March at 6.0 a.m. after the whole 1st Divⁿ had crossed bridge at BAZOCHES to billet at FISMES, leaving N° 3+4 sections to dismantle the bridges at PONT-ARCY. These sections rejoined about 8.30 p.m. at 4.0 p.m. N°s 1+2 section marched to PONT-ARCY to dismantle main road pontoon bridge.	Mr White. Hosp^l. L^t McDowell. Hosp^l 15/10/14.
" 17.10.14	4.30 a.m. N°s 1+2 sections rejoined in billets at FISMES. Company remain in billets.	
In Train 18.10.14	3.0 a.m. Entrain at FISMES, leaving 6.30 a.m.	
HAZEBROUCK. 19.10.14	Detrain CASSEL, 8.0 p.m. March to billets at HAZEBROUCK.	[Sgn. Clamp. Hosp^l.] [Sgt Uren. Hosp^l.]
POPERINGHE. 20.10.14	March at noon. Division to POPERINGHE.	
PILKEM 21.10.14	March to PILKEM.	
N. YPRES. 22.10.14	Company is ordered to construct a bridge across canal 1½ miles N by W of YPRES. Work commenced about 12.0 noon + continued day + night- till the bridge was ready for normal traffic.	Sketch of Bridge to be attached.
" 23.10.14	5.0 p.m. Bridge complete for traffic. Work on approaches + on hand rails etc. The company received a message from Major General Cuidley[?] D.n.a. congratulating it on the work carried out on the AISNE.	
" 24.10.14		L^t. R. Donnell 24.10.14 Hosp^l.

Army Form C. 2118.

WAR DIARY
or
INTELLIGENCE SUMMARY.
(Erase heading not required.)

Instructions regarding War Diaries and Intelligence Summaries are contained in F.S. Regs., Part II. and the Staff Manual respectively. Title pages will be prepared in manuscript.

Hour, Date, Place	Summary of Events and Information	Remarks and references to Appendices
Nr YPRES. 25.10.14	Rest.	
YPRES. 26.10.14	March to H of HAIG, 1 mile E. of YPRES. Assisted Flying Corps to level landing ground. Bivouac at this point.	
HOOGE. 27.10.14	9.30 a.m. moved to bivouac ½ mile E of HOOGE. 1.0 p.m – 6.0 p.m Company employed on improving wheel track to ZEHUWELT through woods on S. of YPRES–MENIN road. 11.30 p.m. Commence work in connection with 11 Gds. Bgde trenches at x roads 1 mile E of ZEHUWELT. 3.30 a.m. Return to bivouac. at night dug trenches & barricaded road	28th/10 Sapper Brown J. Wood ?
" 28.10.14	for 2nd Bgde at GHELUVELT.	
" 29.10.14 → 30.10.14	2.0 p.m. Return to bivouac. work with 2nd Bgde from 1.0 pm – 11.0 pm (trenches & wiring). 11.0 pm ordered to hold ZILLEBEKE till relieved.	30/10/14 {Sgt Donoghey } Hosp. {Cpl Ryan } Spr Plumner "
" 30.10.14	2.30 a.m. Relieved. During this day dug & manned trenches in rear position near HOOGE. In afternoon sent out to act as infantry to clear up situation & cleared the wood S.W. of VELDHOEK. Billet in Chateau grounds HOOGE.	II Cpl Mann slightly wounded. " Burbanks. missing. Pr Morrison. S.W. Wounded " Hanson. S⁄ll⁄14 Sg. Mees, slightly wounded of battn. Dr Blomfield wounded 1/11/14 Died 2/11/14 Smith W gasses wounded 1/11/14 Died 4/11/14 Ar Freeman wounded 1/11/14
" 1.11.14	CHATEAU Grounds. at night, work with 1st Brigade. Wire on E. side of Billet west of HOOGE. work on rear position.	
" 2.11.14	Billet west of HOOGE Construct huts for G.O.C. 1st Division. Work with 1st Gds Bgde. Wire, m.g. Platters it at VELDHOEK.	

MEDIUM BRIDGE CONSTRUCTED OVER CANAL 1 MILE N.W. OF YPRES.
BY 23RD FD COY. R.E.
TIME APPROX. 1000 MAN HOURS. MAXIMUM AXLE LOAD 1½ TONS.

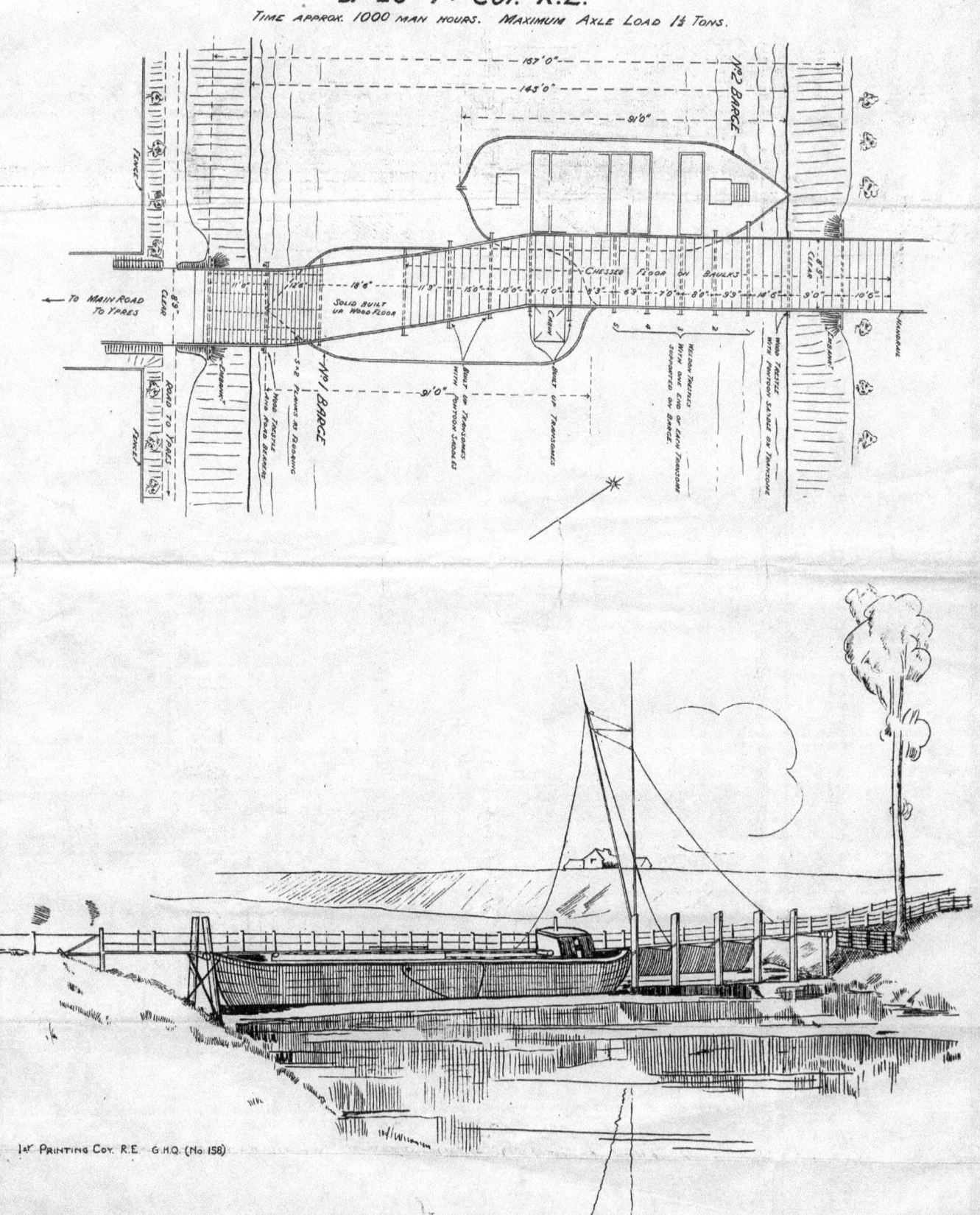

1st Divisional Engineers

23rd FIELD COMPANY R. E.

NOVEMBER 1914.

Army Form C. 2118

23rd (Field) Company R.E.

WAR DIARY
or
INTELLIGENCE SUMMARY

(Erase heading not required.)

Hour, Date, Place	Summary of Events and Information	Remarks and references to Appendices
HOOGE.		
1.11.14	Billet in CHATEAU grounds HOOGE. Work on new position on E. side of CHATEAU grounds. At night work with 1st Brigade, wiring at VELDHOOK.	
2.11.14 Rly Crossing near YPRES.	Billet west of HOOGE. Constructs Shelter for G.O.C. 1st Div 2 G.S. Shelters & n.g. Shelters etc at VELDHOOK. Work with 1st Gds Bde, wire, n.g. Shelters etc at VELDHOOK.	Pte Downes Hosp.

Army Form C. 2118

WAR DIARY
or
INTELLIGENCE SUMMARY.
(Erase heading not required.)

Instructions regarding War Diaries and Intelligence Summaries are contained in F.S. Regs., Part II. and the Staff Manual respectively. Title pages will be prepared in manuscript.

Hour, Date, Place	Summary of Events and Information	Remarks and references to Appendices
YPRES. 3.11.14	3 sections making defended localities in rear of 1st 9th Brigade. 1 section constructing shelter for H.Q. 1st Devon	
" 4.11.14	Further work on defended localities. Wire construction of O.H.C.	2/Lt. Brennan. Hosp.? Capt. Allen left & took up duty of A.A. Mt. F.
" 5.11.14	2 sections 1st R. Ryle. Dug out for G.O.C. & wire in front of trenches. 1 section 6th Cav. Byde. dug in for G.O.C.	
" 6.11.14	1 section tasked wire work for 1st Brigade. 2 sections tasked communications in woods for 6th Cavalry Brigade.	
" 7.11.14	Whole company for fighting in YPRES.	
" 8.11.14	Digging trenches & tasked wire work in VERDHOEK Chateau.	
" 9.11.14	Making fire trenches & erecting bombproof shelter in Chateau grounds.	
" 10.11.14	Company not required for work. Lieut Clifford conducted sqd F Coy over Chateau area.	2/Lt Rede. Hosp.?.
" 11.11.14	Whole Company digging & tasked wiring new firing line for 1st Brigade N. of VERDHOEK Chateau.	He had killed in action.
" 12.11.14	3 sections digging for 1st Ryle.	13/11 2/Lt McKay wounded.
" 13.11.14	2 sections digging + wire for 1st Ryle.	2/Lt. Donnell. Killed in action.
" 14.11.14	1 section digging & O.H.C. for 2d Ryle.	Allen, Brennan, Redmond, Vardon, Sandy, Kennedy
" 15.11.14	Bn billets. Billets shelled about 12.30 p.m. Parade 11.30 p.m. march to VERBRENDINGHE.	Capt. Parker, Griffin, Clarke & wounded.
WEST OUTRE 16.11.14	March to WESTOUTRE. Billets in & Byde area.	
BORRE 17.11.14	march to BORRE.	

1st Divisional Engineers

23rd FIELD COMPANY R. E.

DECEMBER 1914.

Army Form C. 2118.

WAR DIARY
or
INTELLIGENCE SUMMARY.
(Erase heading not required.)

Instructions regarding War Diaries and Intelligence Summaries are contained in F.S. Regs., Part II. and the Staff Manual respectively. Title pages will be prepared in manuscript.

Hour, Date, Place	Summary of Events and Information	Remarks and references to Appendices
BORRE.		
18.11.14	In billets at BORRE, received 17 remounts and made up horsed	Capt. Henning joined the company dated 16/11/14
19.11.14	In billets at BORRE. Route March and Exercise. Major Russell Brown	
20.11.14	Lt Bond & Mullins on leave to England.	
21.11.14	BORRE. Route March & Exercise	
22.11.14	BORRE. do.	
23.11.14	BORRE. do. Refit of Clothes & Jackets & Reinforcements	
	BORRE. handed up.	
24.11.14	Route march & making wind screen.	
25.11.14	Making wind screen for London Scottish & 26 Bde R.F.A.	
26.11.14	" " on reconnaissance to Indian Army H.Q.	Lt Bond
27.11.14	Making wind screen.	
28.11.14	Route march.	
29.11.14	Church parade.	
30.11.14	Inspection parade & route march. Major Russell Brown & Lieut Bond visit No. 6 & 7 sec. R.E. to test making.	

Forms/C. 2118/10.

Army Form C. 2118.

23rd (Field) Company R.E.

WAR DIARY
or
INTELLIGENCE SUMMARY.
(Erase heading not required.)

Instructions regarding War Diaries and Intelligence Summaries are contained in F. S. Regs., Part II. and the Staff Manual respectively. Title pages will be prepared in manuscript.

Hour, Date, Place	Summary of Events and Information	Remarks and references to Appendices
BORRE. 1.12.14.	Preliminary parade for C.R.E's inspection. 1 Section road making.	
" 2 "	C.R.E's inspection. 2 Sections road making. Making hurdles.	
" 3 "	Digging trenches. Road making. Visit of H.M. the King.	
" 4 "	Digging trenches. Pay. Visit of G.O.C. & officers 1st Cyclist Brigade, also inspection of officers & N.C.O.s of 1st & 2nd Cyclists in trench digging.	
" 5 "	Trenchwork, & work on trench guns.	
" 6 "	Sunday. Rest.	
" 7–11 "	Experimental work on trenches overhead cover, trench fronts, trench guns. Approaches etc. Frequent visits were paid by officers of 1st & 2nd Cyclist Brigades to see trenchwork. Visits also by C.R.E. & G.O.C. 1st Division with a view to determining the most suitable type of trench for use under present conditions.	
" 12.12.14. "	Route march. Road making. Visit by G.O.C. & officers 1st Cyclist Brigade. Instruction in the use of rifle grenades.	

(9 29 6) W 3332—1107 100,000 10/13 H W V Forms/C. 2118/10.

Army Form C. 2118.

WAR DIARY
or
INTELLIGENCE SUMMARY.
(Erase heading not required.)

Instructions regarding War Diaries and Intelligence Summaries are contained in F.S. Regs., Part II. and the Staff Manual respectively. Title pages will be prepared in manuscript.

Hour, Date, Place	Summary of Events and Information	Remarks and references to Appendices
BORRE. 13.12.14.	Sunday. Rest - Church Parade.	
" 14.12.14.	12.30 a.m. Orders received to be ready to move at 2 hours notice after 7.0 a.m. Cancelled later.	
" 15-19 "	Continued work on trenches, springs, gum, hippo-pots etc.	
" 20th "	Church parade. 3.30 pm Received orders to be prepared to move at once. Orders cancelled. Reason H.O. & WILLIS	
BORRE-LOCON. 21st "	7.0 a.m. Company ordered to march to LOCON. 5.0 pm Arrived at LOCON. Weather very bad.	
LOCON 22nd "	2 sections digging new trenches with F.R.R. near le TOURET.	
LOCON 23rd "	Machining trenches. 1 Section repairing houses Regt in trenches, 1 section carrying parcels for trenches.	
BEUVRAY. 24th "	March to BEUVRAY.	
BEUVRAY-CAMBRAIN 25th "	March to CAMBRAIN. 2 sections work in trenches. Point Thomas. 2 " repairs pontoon bridges over canal.	

Army Form C. 2118.

WAR DIARY
or
INTELLIGENCE SUMMARY.
(Erase heading not required.)

Instructions regarding War Diaries and Intelligence Summaries are contained in F. S. Regs., Part II. and the Staff Manual respectively. Title pages will be prepared in manuscript.

Hour, Date, Place	Summary of Events and Information	Remarks and references to Appendices
CAMBRAIN 26. 12. 14	Trench work at GIVENCHY.	
27. "	2 sections work at GIVENCHY digging new trench. 1 section working on road from pontoon bridge towards road.	
28. "	1 section laying mines & placing wire at GIVENCHY. 1 section supplying near GIVENCHY. 1 section placing wood down across canal near lock gates.	
29. "	1 section work on lock gates. 1 section drawing trenches at GIVENCHY.	
30. "	2 sections drawing trenches. 1 section bomb throwing, laying mines.	
31. "	3 sections drawing trenches. Attack on K.R.R. trenches. M.G. emplacement captured.	

1ST DIVISION
ROY. ENGINEERS

23RD FIELD COY.
JAN-DEC 1915.

$\frac{121}{4262}$

1st Division

26th Field Coy: R.E.

Vol V. 1 — 31.1.15.

Page 1

Army Form C. 2118.

WAR DIARY
or
INTELLIGENCE SUMMARY.
(Erase heading not required.)

23rd (Field) Co. R.E.

Instructions regarding War Diaries and Intelligence Summaries are contained in F.S. Regs., Part II. and the Staff Manual respectively. Title pages will be prepared in manuscript.

Hour, Date, Place	Summary of Events and Information	Remarks and references to Appendices
CAMBRIN. 1.1.15	2 sections draining trenches. 1 section making heaps.	
2.1.15	1 section draining trenches N. of canal. S. " " "	1 sec. tapping & digging new trench
3.1.15	" " " S. " " " N.	1 sec. sapping. 1 sec. making trench heaps
4.1.15	" " " N. " " " S.	1 sec. making heaps.
5.1.15	" " " N. " " " S.	1 sec. making heaps at GIVENCHY
6.1.15	" " " S.	2 sections digging new trench by night
7.1.15	" " " S. of canal.	
8.1.15	" " " S. " " working on heaps & " "	1 sec. canal & preparing stores & ?hurdles

Page (2)

Army Form C. 2118.

WAR DIARY
or
INTELLIGENCE SUMMARY.
(Erase heading not required.)

Instructions regarding War Diaries and Intelligence Summaries are contained in F. S. Regs., Part II. and the Staff Manual respectively. Title pages will be prepared in manuscript.

Hour, Date, Place	Summary of Events and Information	Remarks and references to Appendices
CAMBRIN 9.1.15	1 section draining trenches S. of canal. 1 " " " N. " . 1 Section Hennessy's	
10.1.15	a house & workshop on defences at GIVENCHY.	
11.1.15	4 sections avoid rapidly to make 4 captured post, on railway line, together with 1st 2nd good located Field C.J. R.E. (T).	Sapper Bell killed. " Elvin) seriously wounded " Taylor)
12.1.15	Work on captured post continued.	Lce Cpl Vans wounded
13.1.15	Work carried on portion until left about 2.30 p.m. Drawing main communication trenches. New trench dug on left of fifteen A.	Sapper Bucknam killed.
14. "	" "	
15. "	" "	
16. "	" "	
17. "	" " Work on keeps.	
18. 19. 20.	" "	
21. "	" " Keep completed. Mine commenced near THE BRICK STACK.	
22. "	" " Mine continued.	

Page 3

Army Form C. 2118.

WAR DIARY
or
INTELLIGENCE SUMMARY
(Erase heading not required.)

Hour, Date, Place	Summary of Events and Information	Remarks and references to Appendices
CAMBRIN		
23.1.15	Drainage work carried on in OLD KENT RD & WEST Com Trench. Mine continued.	
24.1.15	Drainage same place. Mine continued.	
25.1.15.	First line taken by Germans and mining party missing. New Trench dug by 2 Sections on right by main road.	Night Raid. Sapr Lowrie } missing 25.1.15 Lapr Kate } Cantwell
26.1.15.	Communication Trench to new Trench dug from CUINCHY. Inner walls added to Keep	Sapr Burke } wounded 25.1.15 Kirby " Thurgood 29.1.15 " Johnson 28.1.15 Dr Reardijah killed 28.1.15
27.1.15.	Another Trench dug in front of New Trench on right.	
28.1.15	Sap work carried on on 2nd line and Com Trench to same. Sap commenced at Keep.	
29.1.15"	Work on 2nd line at CUINCHY. Sap carried on in Keep.	
30.1.15	Strengthening position at CULVERT on railway embankment. Sap carried on	
31.1.15	Wire obstacle round 2nd line supporting point. Making pavers across the LA BASSÉE road.	

R L Reid Lieut RE
for O.C. 23rd F.P. Co - R.E.

121/4657

1st Division

23rd Field Coy: R.E.

Vol I. 1 - 28.2.15

Army Form C. 2118.

WAR DIARY
or
INTELLIGENCE SUMMARY 23rd F.D. Co. Y. R.E.
(Erase heading not required.)

Instructions regarding War Diaries and Intelligence Summaries are contained in F.S. Regs., Part II. and the Staff Manual respectively. Title pages will be prepared in manuscript.

Hour, Date, Place		Summary of Events and Information	Remarks and references to Appendices
CAMBRIN	1.2.15	2 sections strengthening advanced position. 1 section trenchwork on right of 2nd line. 1 section sandbag barrier across railway entrenchment (sentry)	On night of 1st–2nd shell burst in billets, 2 killed 15 wounded. Names J. Lovett 17418 pm. Moran to pieces 20735 Malone & [illegible] + 15 wounded
"	2. "	4 sections desayning & manning 3rd line.	
"	3. "	7.30 a.m. Company marched to reserve billet at HURIONVILLE.	
HURIONVILLE	4.2.15	Camp fatigues cleaning equipment.	
"	5.2.15	Drill & route march.	
"	6.2.15	Drill & route march.	
"	7.2.15	Church parade.	
"	8. "	a.m. Drill & route march. p.m. Machine boats. Practise with searchlight. Musketry.	
"	9.2.15	Drill & route march. Practise with searchlight. Musketry.	
"	10.2.15	Drill & route march. Practise with searchlight. Musketry.	
"	11.2.15	Drill & route march. Pay.	

Army Form C. 2118.

WAR DIARY
or
INTELLIGENCE SUMMARY.
(Erase heading not required.)

Instructions regarding War Diaries and Intelligence Summaries are contained in F.S. Regs., Part II. and the Staff Manual respectively. Title pages will be prepared in manuscript.

Hour, Date, Place	Summary of Events and Information	Remarks and references to Appendices
HURIONVILLE. 12.2.15	Drill & platoon drill. Musketry. Battn.	Inf? instructed in trench throwing.
" 13. "	Roadmaking, making horse shelters.	
" 14. "	Sunday. Divine by G.O.C. 1st Div:	
" 15. "	Musketry. Repairing about thawing.	15.2.15 Maj. Rennie + Gason returned from a/att. Proceeded some a/att. to find new billets to RAIMBERT & LILLERS. Started from the right with Adv. party & making final arrangements 15-2-15 — return 9.15-2.15 Billets E.O.D. in details at RAIMBERT belonging to C". Maire de MARLES 5.
" 16. "	Musketry. Repairing hedges + barn. Repairing road. Company marched to new name billets in REMBERT. A Capt Herring whilst instructing a party 7 infantry in bomb throwing met with a serious accident, May Herring & a sergeant of the A.S.D. watch were killed.	
RAIMBERT. 17.2.15	Repairing barn at HURIONVILLE. Making up parade ground. Battn. in two platoons, followed by drill. A course of beacons will arrived on the 16th inst. Lt. J.F. Pugh M.O. & Capt. T. Lee attending.	
18.2.15	8.30 - 12.30 a.m. 2.0 - 4.0 p.m. Mining fatigues.	
19.2.15	Battn. making parade ground.	

Army Form C. 2118.

WAR DIARY
or
INTELLIGENCE SUMMARY
(Erase heading not required.)

Instructions regarding War Diaries and Intelligence Summaries are contained in F.S. Regs., Part II. and the Staff Manual respectively. Title pages will be prepared in manuscript.

Hour, Date, Place	Summary of Events and Information	Remarks and references to Appendices
RAMBERT. 20. 2. 15	Preliminary inspection parade. Packing up.	
" 21. 2. 15	"	
" 22. 2. 15	C.R.E.'s inspection. Fieldworks.	
" 23. 2. 15	Fieldwork. Parties out searchlight.	
" 24. 2. 15	Fieldworks. Company joined by 1 Officer 50 men of R.W.F. & 9 horses	
" 25. 2. 15	Fieldworks. " for mining.	
" 26. 2. 15	Packing up stores & removing material from mines.	
" 27. 2. 15	March to Lillers & Oblinghem.	
OBLINGHEM 28. 2. 15	March to Lillers & Les Glauteries, near Le Touret.	

R.N.Bond.
Lieut. R.E.
for O.C. 23rd F.D. Co. R.E.

1st Division

23rd Field Coy: R.E.

Vol VII 1 – 31.3.15

Confidential

23rd (FIELD) Company R.E.

Army Form C. 2118.

WAR DIARY
or
INTELLIGENCE SUMMARY.
(Erase heading not required.)

Instructions regarding War Diaries and Intelligence Summaries are contained in F.S. Regs., Part II. and the Staff Manual respectively. Title pages will be prepared in manuscript.

Hour, Date, Place	Summary of Events and Information	Remarks and references to Appendices
R.E.'s GLAVIGNIES. 1.3.15 from LE TOURET	Cleaning up Billets. Reconnaissance of positions.	
2.3.15	Work at CHOCOLAT MENIER CORNER (supporting point) SNIPERS &c. (improving barricades). S. of Home A.1. putting up farm line breastwork.	Spr Lendrie } killed Shott
3. "	Section D.1. Work Breastwork cont.? Section D.2. Breastwork on B line heightened	Mining commenced at Home A.
4. "	"	Spr H Gay (slightly) wounded Pre Russell (mine dust?) 2/3/15 transferred
5. "	Section D.2. Parados on B line commenced	M.K.T. begin boreholes at Home A. completed
6. "	"	
7. "	Work on Keep at Indian Village. Making traverses in front line.	
8. "	Work on Keep at Richeban Village. Making traverses in front line. Wire details in front of main firing line.	
9. "	Breastwork of Keep continued.	mine shaft full spate.

Army Form C. 2118.

WAR DIARY
or
INTELLIGENCE SUMMARY.
(Erase heading not required.)

Instructions regarding War Diaries and Intelligence Summaries are contained in F. S. Regs., Part II. and the Staff Manual respectively. Title pages will be prepared in manuscript.

Hour, Date, Place		Summary of Events and Information	Remarks and references to Appendices
LES GLAUTIGNIES			
10.3.15	Section D.	Breastwork in C line heightened to 4'6" for empty yards (no strutting material party available).	
11.3.15	"	Breastwork in C line heightened for 40" front work in Indian Village. Breastwork raised to 3'6" for 30'.	
12.3.15	"	Work in trenches continued. Work in C line near BREWERY.	
13.3.15	"	Work in trenches & portion of C line in Indian Village also heightened. Breastwork of C line S of BREWERY.	
14.3.15	"	Work in trenches continued. Breastwork to make 2 butt entered. 66" wired communication between trenches & running path completed.	

WAR DIARY
or
INTELLIGENCE SUMMARY.

(Erase heading not required.)

Army Form C. 2118.

Instructions regarding War Diaries and Intelligence Summaries are contained in F.S. Regs., Part II. and the Staff Manual respectively. Title pages will be prepared in manuscript.

Hour, Date, Place	Summary of Events and Information	Remarks and references to Appendices
BEAUTIGNIES		
15.3.15	Section D. Breastwork at front line near Lett 2 continued. Work on Indian Village keep continued.	
16.3.15	" Breastwork at Bott 2 completed. B'with ys of Brewery continued. Indian village, Bistro continued, also tubed wire entanglement.	Water level observed 3½" mean 15/3/15
17.3.15	" Wire entanglement in front of Botts 1 & 2. Work on C line continued. Indian village Breastwork continued, Traverses erected. Comm" Breastwork between Brewery & house A continued.	
18.3.15	" Work on C line S.G. Brewery continued. Indian village Breastwork on N. & W sides of Keep completed. 120ˣ wire entanglement round Keep.	Water gauge 1½" below datum.
19.3.15	" 100ˣ low wire entanglements at S. end of C line. 50ˣ " " " Indian village Keep. Breastworks continued at S. end of C line, & portion of C line between Indian village & post 14.	Water gauge 1½" below datum.

Army Form C. 2118.

WAR DIARY
or
INTELLIGENCE SUMMARY.
(Erase heading not required.)

Instructions regarding War Diaries and Intelligence Summaries are contained in F.S. Regs., Part II. and the Staff Manual respectively. Title pages will be prepared in manuscript.

Hour, Date, Place	Summary of Events and Information	Remarks and references to Appendices
LES CLAUTICHES		
20.3.15	Section D. Work on C line S. of Brewery + N. of Rohin Village continued. Wire round N. end of C line continued round N. of Rohin Village. Keep completed.	Water level 3¾' below datum.
21.3.15	" Work on C line between Rohin village + Post 14. " at S. of Brewery. Wire entanglement across gap between 1st + 2nd Ryles. Thin ground reconnoitred + thickened. Traverse at S end of C line + breastwork modified. Reconnaissance of new section of line.	
22.3.15	new Section D.	
23.3.15	" Section between CHOCOLAT MENIER CORNER to E. of ORCHARD KEEP taken over. Work on reclaimed trench S. of ORCHARD, + making dug out in rear of R.E. Store. Wires established ① behind ORCHARD KEEP, ② RUE DU BOIS, ③ at CHOCOLAT MENIER corner.	
24.3.15	Section D3. Communication trench from COPSE to P2 completed + deepened.	

WAR DIARY
or
INTELLIGENCE SUMMARY.
(Erase heading not required.)

Army Form C. 2118.

Hour, Date, Place	Summary of Events and Information	Remarks and references to Appendices
LES GLAOTIGNIES		
25.3.15	Section 3g. 60' of new breastwork erected behind water, sketch in rear of P₂	Sketch of breastwork erected section.
26.	" 60' " " " "	
27.	" 60' " " " "	
28.	" 70' " " " "	
29.	" +5' " " " "	Canvas made up in 18' lengths
	+15' communication trench to join up with P₄.	
30.	" Work on rear line, improving communication of RUE DU BOIS. Reconnaissance of drainage	
31.	" Futon D₂. 60' breastwork from cinder track Pb, to west.	R.E. Alexander R.E. proceed from the Base.

R.W.Bond
Lieut R.E.
for O.C. 23rd F.D.Co. R.E.

121/5294

1st Division

23rd Field Coy RE.

Vol VIII 1.— 30.4.15

Confidential

23rd (Field) Company R.E.

Army Form C. 2118.

WAR DIARY
or
INTELLIGENCE SUMMARY

(Erase heading not required.)

Instructions regarding War Diaries and Intelligence Summaries are contained in F.S. Regs., Part II. and the Staff Manual respectively. Title pages will be prepared in manuscript.

[Stamp: 23RD FIELD COMPANY, APRIL 1915, ROYAL ENGINEERS]

Hour, Date, Place	Summary of Events and Information	Remarks and references to Appendices
LE TOURET 1.4.15	Section D3. Blinding communication Trench with hurdlework.	
2.4.15	" D2. Making new front line breastwork at P6	
3.4.15	" "	
4. "	Section D2. Making new front line breastwork.	
5. "	" E1. Reclaiming old trench.	
6. "	" "	
7. "	Section D3. Making new front line breastwork.	
8. "	" E1. Reclaiming old trench.	
9. "	Section D3 } Erecting dug out for H.Q. 1st Bde. Bridging ditch in front of copse with E1. } fascines.	Sapper R. Goodwin seriously wounded.
10. "	Section D3. Breastwork continued.	
	" E1. New breastwork commenced.	

Army Form C. 2118.

WAR DIARY
or
INTELLIGENCE SUMMARY.
(Erase heading not required.)

Instructions regarding War Diaries and Intelligence Summaries are contained in F. S. Regs., Part II. and the Staff Manual respectively. Title pages will be prepared in manuscript.

Hour, Date, Place	Summary of Events and Information	Remarks and references to Appendices
LE TOURET		
11.4.15	Section D3. 60' of com" trench part w. of P5 revetted + heightened. 30' breastwork completed from P. to P2. 2 hidg. renewed	
12.4.15	Section D2. 40' new breastwork completed W. of Redt 6. 25' com" trench in rear of Redt 6. defences renewed.	
13.4.15	Section D2. 35' new breastwork completed between Redts 5 + 6. 60' com" trench revetted revewed in rear of Redt 6. 70' wire placed in front of Redt 6. Infantry manned in further up traverses in rear of Redt 5.	
14.4.15	Section D2. 70' com" trench revetted / prof. 40' renewed. 35' new breastwork completed between Redts 5 + 6. work on observation station in RUE DU BOIS.	
15.4.15	Section D2. 25' new breastwork completed between Redts 5 + 6. 40' of com" trench revetted / prof. work on observation station in RUE DU BOIS.	
16.4.15	Section D2. 35' new breastwork E. of Redt 6 completed. work on obs" station + splinter proofs continued.	

Army Form C. 2118.

WAR DIARY
or
INTELLIGENCE SUMMARY.
(Erase heading not required.)

Hour, Date, Place		Summary of Events and Information	Remarks and references to Appendices
LE TOURET	17.4.15	Section D₃. Splinter proof erected in C line. Communication trench east of CINDER TRACK commenced. Work on full nightwork "Comm" track that 6 carried on.	
	18.4.15	" C line. Splinter proofs & traverses continued. Comm. trenches. (a) ½ to hutt 6 continued. (between D₂) (b) Just E of CINDER TRACK continued. Front line. Breastwork completed, & bridge made over drain.	
	19.4.15	" Comm. trenches. (a). Just E of CINDER TRACK continued, revetted. (b). To hutt 6 without cost. 4 people Relieved. (c) ½ w of some dugouts traversed & thickened. Splinter proofs continued. Breastwork continued.	
	20.4.15	" C line. between breastwork commenced. Wash pits & platform completed. Comm. trenches (a). Part W of CINDER TRACK cont'd. (b) " " E " " cont'd.	

Army Form C. 2118.

WAR DIARY
or
INTELLIGENCE SUMMARY.
(Erase heading not required.)

Instructions regarding War Diaries and Intelligence Summaries are contained in F. S. Regs., Part II. and the Staff Manual respectively. Title pages will be prepared in manuscript.

Hour, Date, Place	Summary of Events and Information	Remarks and references to Appendices
LE TOURET 20.4.15 cont?	letter D3 Con. trenches (c) W/Corps cont?	
21.4.15	Con. trenches (c) - w/Corps (cont?)	
22.4.15	Con. Trenches (c) W/Corps (cont?) C line trenches created westerly sphere prop widened	
23.4.15	D line 120° new headwork + trench widened A line Breastwork raised + lid raised Con. trench W/Corps continued D line 290° new breastwork completed 120° old	
24.4.15	Con. trench W/Corps cont? D line 140° new trench dug 70° old breastwork completed	
25.4.15	Con. trench (a) Post F. W/Corps under trench cont? F-1 W/Corps enfilade D line completely enfilade 1 + post filled	

Army Form C. 2118.

WAR DIARY
or
INTELLIGENCE SUMMARY.
(Erase heading not required.)

Instructions regarding War Diaries and Intelligence Summaries are contained in F. S. Regs., Part II. and the Staff Manual respectively. Title pages will be prepared in manuscript.

Hour, Date, Place	Summary of Events and Information	Remarks and references to Appendices
LE TOURET. 26.4.15	Section D3. Com. trenches (a) Junt W. of COPSE improved	Lieut Matthew + 2 yd N.mon. moved not to build a new cannon ditches in front of a line.
	(b) " = Gavouse Rocure	
27.4.15	D line completed with loom. completed	
	C line. Breastwork thickened Com. to RUE DU BOIS improved Got new old RE store filled up side	N° Donaldson wounded. 4" copying "
28.4.15	Front line C line H.Q. D3	{ Parapets continued E end heightened. 15'x lined unfilled 70' continued erected
29.4.15	H.Q. D3. Breastwork + parados continued	
30.4.15	A line. Parados continued New breastwork commenced Hea. qrs line. Breastwork + parados continued H.Q. D3.	

R.W. [signature]
[signature] O.C. 23 & F.Co.
O.C. 23 R.E.

131/5543

1st Division

23rd Field Coy: R.E.

Vol IX 1 — 31.5.15.

A97
A74

Army Form C. 2118.

WAR DIARY
or
INTELLIGENCE SUMMARY.
(Erase heading not required.)

23rd Field Company R.E. 1st Divn

May 1915

Hour, Date, Place	Summary of Events and Information	Remarks and references to Appendices
LE TOURET		
1. 1.5.15	Section D3 . Rue J. Blin.. Breastwork redoubt & parados commenced.	
	H.Q. D3 . O.H.C . traverse & parados continued	
2. "	Rue J. Blin.. Breastwork & parados continued	Lieut Boyd on leave till 9th.5/15
	RUE DU BOIS. Work on dug outs	
	H.Q. D3 . O.H.C . in breastwork.	
3. "	Rear J/5 line Breastwork & parados continued Forms expected	
	H.Q. D3 . O.H.C . continued for breastwork	
4. "	As for 3/5/15	
5. "	As for 3/5/15	
	also dug outs in RUE DU BOIS continued	

Forms/C. 2118/10.

Army Form C. 2118.

WAR DIARY
or
INTELLIGENCE SUMMARY.
(Erase heading not required.)

Instructions regarding War Diaries and Intelligence
Summaries are contained in F. S. Regs., Part II.
and the Staff Manual respectively. Title pages
will be prepared in manuscript.

Hour, Date, Place	Summary of Events and Information	Remarks and references to Appendices
LE TOURET.		
6.5.15	Section D3. Work on D line, + shelter headwork in pat of horse X.	Lieut Bond returns from leave.
7.5.15	Section D3. Stores transported to Rue Du Bois. Packing wagons.	
8.5.15	Section D3. Bridges placed across stream in front of front line in preparation for attack. Track for guns from Rue Du Bois to Ferme Du Bois commenced when possible.	
9.5.15	1st Division attack on Rue Du Bois front. Attack failed + only work carried out was clearance of CINDER TRACK + EDWARD ROAD.	Killed. Jupper, McClean, Standler. Wounded Lie Cpt Lee, Dellbridge, Copps, Lake, Sinclair.
10.5.15	Marched to billets a Mont Bernechon.	
Mt BERNECHON. 11.5.15	REST. Cleaning wagons + tools.	
12.5.15	March to billets at BEUVRY. One section to billets in CAMBRIN. 3rd Bde at CUINCHY.	

Army Form C. 2118.

WAR DIARY
or
INTELLIGENCE SUMMARY.
(Erase heading not required.)

Instructions regarding War Diaries and Intelligence Summaries are contained in F. S. Regs., Part II. and the Staff Manual respectively. Title pages will be prepared in manuscript.

Hour, Date, Place	Summary of Events and Information	Remarks and references to Appendices
BEUVRY 13.5.15	Cleaning billets, & erecting shelters. Drill parade	142nd London Bde at CUINCHY. 3rd Bde to Z Section
14.5.15	No. 3 section at CAMBRIN, working on A section. Making well. No. 1 " " " " " " Z " " "	
15.5.15	A section. Making well. Sapping. Z section. Collecting stores, reconnaissance of line.	
16.5.15	A section. Sapping. No 4 section to CAMBRIN to B to BEUVRY in evening. Z section. Maintenance of front line trenches.	
17.5.15	A section. Sapping for trenches. Making chevaux de frise. Z section. Revetting " " barbed wire belts.	
18.5.15	A section. Construction of trench across entanglement in second line of defence. Z section. Barbed wire entanglements in CAMBRIN line, & at CAMBRIN KEEP. Clearing & making communication trench. Wire in front of centre lottaken.	
19.5.15	R Section. Repairs to MILLION LINE, work on Trench across Embankment 2nd Line Z Section Assisting infantry with wire. Comn Trench cleared & wire in front of CAMBRIN KEEP	2nd Bde take over from 3rd Bde in Z

9 29 6) W 3332—1107 100,000 10/13 H W V Forms/C. 2118/10.

Army Form C. 2118.

WAR DIARY
or
INTELLIGENCE SUMMARY.
(Erase heading not required.)

Instructions regarding War Diaries and Intelligence Summaries are contained in F. S. Regs., Part II. and the Staff Manual respectively. Title pages will be prepared in manuscript.

Hour, Date, Place	Summary of Events and Information	Remarks and references to Appendices
BEUVRY 20.5.15	A. Section Work on Embankment continued Breaking out under parapet to starting new sap hole 11. to new sap. No 3 relieved No 9 in evening Z Section Finishing the mason work & communication trench. Reconnaissance of position.	
21.5.15	A section New sap No 11 continued. Cleaning out & repairing trench over entrenchment, & Z section cutting railway line. Mason Rouge trench continued.	
22.5.15	A section Continuing trench over entrenchment. Z section aeroplane Mason Rouge trench continued. Z3 Keep commenced.	

WAR DIARY
or
INTELLIGENCE SUMMARY.
(Erase heading not required.)

Army Form C. 2118.

Hour, Date, Place	Summary of Events and Information	Remarks and references to Appendices
BEUVRY. 23.5.15	A section. Carrying on Sap No. 11. Carrying on work at STAFFORD REDOUBT. Z section. Starting M.G. emplacement at CAMBRIN KEEP.	
24.5.15	Z section. Keep on Trench Mortar continued. Z_3 Keep on Madow Range trench connected. Z_1 Work on intermediate line continued. A section. No. 11 Sap carried on. Kitchen well in A1. Completing M.G. emplacement CAMBRIN Keep. Z_1 keep completed. Z_3 " continued.	
25.5.15	A section. Sap No. 11 continued. M.G. emplacement completed. Cleaning up part of WILLOW LANE. Z_3 keep continued. Z_2 keep recommenced.	Work on intermediate line continued. No. 4 Section allied to 3.

Army Form C. 2118.

WAR DIARY
or
INTELLIGENCE SUMMARY.
(Erase heading not required.)

Instructions regarding War Diaries and Intelligence Summaries are contained in F.S. Regs., Part II. and the Staff Manual respectively. Title pages will be prepared in manuscript.

Hour, Date, Place		Summary of Events and Information	Remarks and references to Appendices
BEUVRY. 26.5.15	A section	No 11 n/p continued. Trench in wood junction A.20 & 7.0	
	Z section	Z.3 keep completed Z.2 keep completed. Intermediate line continued.	
27.5.15.	A. Section	No 11 Sap continued Work on WILLOW LINE continued Work on MAISON ROUGE Intermediate line	
	Z Section		
28.5.15	Section A	No 11 sap continued. Bore hole made to crater Sandbag parapet erected at end Trench road junction A.2.0.&7.0 Parapet widened & trench deepened Sap above Communication trench to HINDENBURG continued	Lieut R. L. Beach H.O. to hospital sick
	Section Z	Continued work on keep Z.2. (improving) Improving MAISON ROUGE LINE for trenches.	

Army Form C. 2118.

WAR DIARY
or
INTELLIGENCE SUMMARY.
(Erase heading not required.)

Instructions regarding War Diaries and Intelligence Summaries are contained in F. S. Regs., Part II. and the Staff Manual respectively. Title pages will be prepared in manuscript.

Hour, Date, Place	Summary of Events and Information	Remarks and references to Appendices
BEUVRY 29.5.15	Junction of Z & A1 Sections 1. Deepening & improving trench on either side of LA BASSÉE R? in front of BRADELL'S Pt. 2. Digging trench in front of the above to connect with South side STAFFORD REDOUBT — on LA BASSÉE R? Z Section. Improvement of keeps & making of O.H. & D Cover. A Section 1. Deepening & improving Trench in front of BRADELL'S Pt. 2. Trench between STAFFORD REDOUBT & Z Section completed 3. Making exit for patrols under parapet S. side embankment in front line Z Section. Improvement — of keeps & making overhead cover	
30.5.15		
31.5.15	A Section 1. Continued deepening & improving trench in front of BRADELL PT. 2. Completed patrol exit. S. side embankment front line 3. M.G. Emplacement S. side LA BASSÉE R.D Started Z Section 1. Improving keeps Z Z O Z X 2. Started sap to new crater 3. Improving communication trenches	

(29 6) W 3332—1107 100,000 10/13 H W V Forms/C. 2118/10.

127/60/5

a/7
DFW

1st Division

23rd Field Coy R.E.

Vol I   1 – 30.6.15

Army Form C. 2118.

WAR DIARY
or
INTELLIGENCE SUMMARY.
(Erase heading not required.)

23rd F'd Co. R.E. 1st Div.

Hour, Date, Place	Summary of Events and Information	Remarks and references to Appendices
BEUVRY 1.6.15.	Started work on Q6½ Slater Posts. Company (less two sections) marched to new billets FONTENELLE FARM (approx 1 mile S.E. of CHOCQUES. Two sections above marched in from CUINCHY — CAMBRIN to BEUVRY	In hands M.W. Salmon R.E. (T'd.) reported.
FONTENELLE F'm 2.6.15	Cleaning up new billets. Two sections joined from BEUVRY	
3.6.15.	Rest: a.m. Route march. p.m. Drill	
4.6.15.	a.m. Route march & musketry. p.m. Drill & musketry	
5.6.15.	a.m. Route march. p.m. Drill & musketry.	
6.6.15	a.m. General parade, route march. p.m. General parade from	
7.6.15.	a.m. General parade. p.m. inspection by G.O.C. 1st Div. Instruction of Infty 1st Bde in bomb throwing.	
8.6.15.	a.m. Route march. Infantry 1st Bde instructed in bomb throwing making entries & exploded company mining entries & officers & N.C.O. of Canadian	
9.6.15	a.m. Route march. p.m. Drill instructed in bomb throwing — p.m. Drill	

Army Form C. 2118.

WAR DIARY
or
INTELLIGENCE SUMMARY.
(Erase heading not required.)

23rd F.Co R.E. 1st Divn

Instructions regarding War Diaries and Intelligence Summaries are contained in F.S. Regs., Part II. and the Staff Manual respectively. Title pages will be prepared in manuscript.

Hour, Date, Place		Summary of Events and Information	Remarks and references to Appendices
FONTENELLE FME			
10.6.15	Rout.	am. Route march. pm. Drill	
11.6.15	"	am. Route march. Instruction in throwing powder intructors pm. Drill. Two officers reconnaissance of water supply	(CAMBRIN, CUINCHY, LABEUVIÈRE)
12.6.15	"	am. Route march. Party 2nd Brigade instruction in bombing pm. Knots & lashings. One officer reconnaissance of water supply	(CAMBRIN)
13.6.15	"	am. Route march. Party 2nd Bde bombing pm. Church. Officer reconnaissance of water supply	(FOUQUIÈRES)
14.6.15	"	Two sections up musing rifle range BETHUNE (all day) am. Route march reconnr. Party 2nd Bde bombing pm. Demolns Schemes &c	
15.6.15	"	Two sections repairing rifle range BETHUNE (all day) am. Remainder (½ sect) explosives lectures & making up pm. charges. pm. bar of stove	
16.6.15	"	am. ½ section finishing rifle range. Remainder instr. in hand Grenades pm. Drill	
17.6.15	"	am. Route march. pm. Drill	
18.6.15	"	am. do	

Army Form C. 2118.

WAR DIARY
or
INTELLIGENCE SUMMARY.
(Erase heading not required.)

23rd F.C. R.E. 1st Divn

Instructions regarding War Diaries and Intelligence Summaries are contained in F. S. Regs., Part II. and the Staff Manual respectively. Title pages will be prepared in manuscript.

Hour, Date, Place		Summary of Events and Information	Remarks and references to Appendices
FONTENELLE F'mes 19.6.15.	a.m.	Two sections packing up preparatory to moving to BEUVRY. Remainder route march & cleaning up billet	
	p.m.	Putting up bivouacs (move cancelled.) Heavy thunderstorm.	
20.6.15.	a.m.	Again packed. Standing by. Fine church parade.	
21.6.15.	a.m.	Standing by. Three sections making typical German trench LABEUVIÈRE all day. Two pontoon wagons BEUVRY for stores.	
22.6.15.	a.m.	3 sections continued work on typical German trench all day.	Birthday Honours
23.6.15.	a.m.	No 4 Section instruction Heavy Pontoon Bridge	Maj. C. Russell Brown — B't Lt. Col.
		" " 3, 2 — do. Explosives	Capt. H.W. Herring } — Mil. Cross
	p.m.	" " 2 do. Heavy Bridge	Lt. J.H. Shepd }
		" " 3 do. Barb'd Spars	2Lt. A.J. Parker }
		" " 4 do. M.G. Emplacements.	C.Q.M.S. Griffin } — D.C.M.
			& Cpl Milne }
24.6.15. RAIMBERT.		Packed up & marched off at 10.30 a.m. to new billets at RAIMBERT. Dismounted men in Schol received in Feb 1/15. Mounted men bivouac. Wagons & horses in the square.	
25.6.15.		Digging out old trenches on side of hill for Bombing practice all day. 2 Infantry working parties	

Army Form C. 2118.

WAR DIARY
or
INTELLIGENCE SUMMARY.
(Erase heading not required.)

23rd F.D. Co. R.E. 1st Divn.

Hour, Date, Place	Summary of Events and Information	Remarks and references to Appendices
RAIMBERT 26.6.15.	Digging out old trenches all day, hole supply being arranged for R.A. in FERFAY area.	
27.6.15.	Wire placed in front of trenches (not in tunnels) hole supply for R.A. Church Parade. p.m. Fatigues.	
LA BOURSE, VERMELLES 28.6.15.	Packed up. p.m. marched through LABUISSIÈRE – NOEUX-LES-MINES to LA BOURSE. In billeting 2 sections on to Advanced Billets in VERMELLES. O.C. + Lt Edwards on ahead to Reconnoitre ground.	
29.6.15.	Y.1. DALY's Keep:– Comn Trenches leading to it deepened. LE RUTOIRE Keep:– Wire strengthened and trench cleaned out. Y.2 HULLOCH Keep:– Connecting Trench improved. Light Ry:– 250ˣ new line laid	
30.6.15.	Y.1. DALY's Keep:– Work continued LE RUTOIRE Keep:– Wire strengthened. Y.2 Light Ry carried to Rly line at HULLOCH Rd.	kept Staff Lt. R.E. for bde. 23rd C. R.E.

1st/5 invasion

12/6410

23rd Field Coy. R.E.

Vol XII

From 1st to 31st July 1915.

Army Form C. 2118

WAR DIARY
~~INTELLIGENCE SUMMARY.~~
(Erase heading not required.)

23rd Fd Co R.E. 1st Div.

[Stamp: 23rd (Field) Company Royal Engineers, AUG 1915]

Hour, Date, Place	Summary of Events and Information	Remarks and references to Appendices
LABOURSE VERMELLES 1.7.15	C.R.E. & O.C. round Y section. Y.1. DALY'S KEEP Dug outs & Com: Trenches improved. LE RUTOIRE KEEP Wire completed & M.G. Emplacement improved. Y.2 Trench Tramway carried on. Tank near LE RUTOIRE covered. Bomb Proof started in Garden City.	
2.7.15.	Y.1 DALY'S KEEP Com: Trenches deepened & widened & Ad:x Firing Steps & M.G. Emplacement improved. Y.2 Splinter proof roof to Tank near Chemin de Cor[n]aille[?]. Dug outs in Garden City continued. Trench Tramway continued.	
3.7.15.	Y.1 DALY'S KEEP Loopholes trenches & splinter proofs completed. Splinter proof roof to tank near Ch. N. de C. Dugouts in GARDEN CITY continued. Digg Communication trench HULLUCH Rd KEEP	

WAR DIARY
or
INTELLIGENCE SUMMARY.
(Erase heading not required.)

Army Form C. 2118

Instructions regarding War Diaries and Intelligence Summaries are contained in F.S. Regs., Part II. and the Staff Manual respectively. Title pages will be prepared in manuscript.

Hour, Date, Place	Summary of Events and Information	Remarks and references to Appendices
LABOURSE VERMELLES 4.7.15	Y₁. DALY'S KEEP. Completed splinter proofs. Y₂. Work in GARDEN CITY continued. Trench Tramway continued (rails within 200' of LE ROUTOIRE). Deepening Trench S. half HULLUCH Rᴅ KEEP.	
5.7.15	Y₁. Two m.g. emplacements near DALY'S KEEP improved, = dugout for detachment commenced. Y₂. HULLUCH Rᴅ KEEP. (continued) deepening S. half. 50' Trench Tramway laid. (many old trenches & dethes 2 fms). GARDEN CITY. Started deepening & widening dugouts.	
6.7.15	Y₂. 200 lengths preliminary trenches to bombproofs dug in G.10.d (support line). HULLUCH Rᴅ KEEP. Continued deepening S. half. Carried on construction of splinterproofs in Ch. Nᴅ de C. 3 Officers 108 O.R. attached for mining work (making bombproofs). Billeted VERMELLES.	

WAR DIARY
or
INTELLIGENCE SUMMARY.
(Erase heading not required.)

Army Form C. 2118

Instructions regarding War Diaries and Intelligence Summaries are contained in F.S. Regs., Part II. and the Staff Manual respectively. Title pages will be prepared in manuscript.

Hour, Date, Place	Summary of Events and Information	Remarks and references to Appendices
LABOURSE. VERMELLES 7.7.15	Y₂ + Bombproofs commenced in support line in CURLEY CRESCENT. Deepening trenches in HULLUCH RD KEEP on S.B. road. Splinter proofs at GARDEN CITY excavated & ready for roofing. Bombproof commenced. 100ˣ Bayan 6 num GARDEN CITY deepened & revetted.	
8.7.15	Two portable magazines & one long to VAUDRICOURT & BETHUNE for timber. Y₂. Specimen splinter proofs in front line commenced. + Bombproof galleries in CURLEY CRESCENT completed. HULLUCH RD KEEP. Trenches deepened & widened in S. loop. GARDEN CITY 1 Splinter proof covered. Bombproof excavation. 100ˣ Bayan 6 revetted & deepened near Ch. ND de Consolation. Y₁. Bromister sg I Brigade RFA. 1 Splinter proof in front line commenced.	
9.7.15	Y₂ " " " dug to depth & plank. tie slip made. + preliminary galleries to bomb proofs in 6'. 2 galleries to bomb proof front line for machine gun detachment commenced. Sanded arm to lift to continue under road to form two bomb proofs behind GARDEN CITY. Duty out - 1 S.P. to from bomb proofs centurion work in typical behind building GARDEN CITY. HULLUCH RD KEEP	

WAR DIARY
or
INTELLIGENCE SUMMARY.
(Erase heading not required.)

Army Form C. 2118

Hour, Date, Place	Summary of Events and Information	Remarks and references to Appendices
LABOURSE / VERMELLES 10.7.15.	Y1. 1 Splinter proof in front line incompleted. 1 Splinter loopholes made in RUTOIRE KEEP to cover communication trenches. Y2. Specimen splinter proofs in front line completed. (18" under parapet). Started two Galleries for bomb proof for M.G. Detachment on HULLUCH RD. Commenced preliminary sapo for bomb proofs at S. end Support line Southern bell HULLUCH RD. KEEP dug to depth. Gallery under road cont. GARDEN CITY – horned roof of completed splinter proof. completed one shaft to bomb proof & commenced chamber. Work on bivouacs for 39th Bde. continued. Two exits through inside started & bomb proof shelter in Support line.	
11.7.15	Y1. Specimen splinter proof in front line completed. DALY'S KEEP. Rest made. Enlargence in front of machine guns to enable them to fire down comb. trenches. Y2. Tunnel through for bomb proofs behind support line. Other 3 tunnels in 1'. in 14. Commenced two new saps for B.P.s & deepened 11 other saps. Digging out the roof to N. bill of HULLUCH RD. KEEP. Making bomb put to N.– of same. Cell gallery under garden 15. shafts tho 4 to do. Batt. H.Q. at GARDEN CITY. Finished roofs of splinterproofs & mess dumont. Digging out bomb proof floors & bags for roof (commut B.P.s) Digging in for chamber from two shafts. (Armed B.P.s)	

WAR DIARY
or
INTELLIGENCE SUMMARY.
(Erase heading not required.)

Army Form C. 2118

Hour, Date, Place	Summary of Events and Information	Remarks and references to Appendices
LABOURSE VERMELLES 12.7.15.	Y1 Stated 10 sapr (for 5th R.W.K.) in support line " 6 sapr (for 5th ") in Dulop Keep Y2 Ten sappers for bomb proofs in support line finished Stated 20 sapr (for 10 R.H.R.) " " Making fire trench between two bells HULLOCH RD KEEP Tunnel under road completed GARDEN CITY - Continued work on 3 bomb proofs CHAPEL ALLEY deepened for 150 X eastwards of HULLOCH RD KEEP	
13.7.15.	Y1 4 Bomb proofs commenced in support line Carried on sap for 3 bomb proofs DALY'S KEEP Y2 4 Bomb proofs commenced in support line Carried on with excavation of chamber of bomb proof GARDEN CITY Excavating splinter proof to make it bomb proof " Y3 Continued work on bomb proofs in support line.	
14.7.15.	Y1 5 bomb proofs in course of excavation between B1 & A2 DALY'S KEEP Work on two bombproofs Y2 5 bomb proofs in course of construction in support line 12 " " " CURLEY CRESCENT complete except for chamber) (CONT'D)	

WAR DIARY
or
INTELLIGENCE SUMMARY.
(Erase heading not required.)

Army Form C. 2118

Instructions regarding War Diaries and Intelligence Summaries are contained in F.S. Regs., Part II. and the Staff Manual respectively. Title pages will be prepared in manuscript.

Hour, Date, Place	Summary of Events and Information	Remarks and references to Appendices
LABOURSE / VERMELLES 14-7-15	Y_2 (cont.?) 1 bomb proof in course of excavation, roof for excavators road dug to depth but not roofed (M.D. de CONSOLATION). Also 1 splinter proof roofed.	
	Y_3. 2 bomb proofs in support line finished, there were under construction.	
15-7-15	Y_1. 5 bomb proofs in support line under construction	
	2 " " " DALY'S KEEP " "	
	Y_2. 5 " " " Support line " "	
	2 " " " GARDEN CITY " "	
	CHAPEL ALLEY deepened for 100' near HULLUCH RD KEEP under construction.	
16.7.15	Y_1. 5 bomb proofs in support line 40% completed	
	2 " " " DALY'S KEEP under construction	
	Y_2. 2 " " " Support line half completed, 6 others under construction	
	2 bomb proofs GARDEN CITY. half completed.	
	Y_3. 3 " " " in support line 90% "	
	1 " " " " " 35% "	
	5 under construction	
	1st CENTRAL KEEP 60% completed, 1 bomb proof under construction.	
	1 " in front line started.	

WAR DIARY
or
INTELLIGENCE SUMMARY.
(Erase heading not required.)

Army Form C. 2118

Hour, Date, Place	Summary of Events and Information	Remarks and references to Appendices
LABOURSE VERMELLES { 17.7.15	Y1. Work on 5 bomb proofs in Support line continued Y2. " " 2 " " " " DALY'S KEEP " " " 8 " " " " Support line " " " 2 " " " " CHAPEL KEEP " Y3. 3 bomb proofs practically finished, 1 nearly half finished, Two others under construction, in support line 3 saps front line started Work on CENTRAL KEEP continued	GARDEN CITY was to be known as CHAPEL KEEP.
18.7.15.	Y1, Y2, Y3. Same as for 17.7.15.	
19.7.15.	Y1. 5 Bomb proofs in support line 50% completed 2 " " " " DALY'S KEEP 25% " 1 " " " " LE RUTOIR " commenced. Y2. 4 " " " " Support line 50% completed 4 " " " " " " under construction 1 " " " " Battⁿ H.Q. CHAPEL ALLEY completed Y3. 4 bomb proofs practically finished (3 on 17ᵗʰ + 1 = 4) 1/4 completed, 2 others under construction. Work on CENTRAL KEEP continued. " " 3 saps in front-line continued.	

WAR DIARY
or
INTELLIGENCE SUMMARY.
(Erase heading not required.)

Army Form C. 2118.

Instructions regarding War Diaries and Intelligence Summaries are contained in F. S. Regs., Part II. and the Staff Manual respectively. Title pages will be prepared in manuscript.

Hour, Date, Place	Summary of Events and Information	Remarks and references to Appendices
LABOURSE VERMELLES 20.7.15	Y1. 3 new bomb proofs in support line 25% complete. 2 " " " DALY'S KEEP nearly 1/2 commenced 1 " " " " " Y2. 5 " " in support line 50% complete 3 " " " " 25% " 2 " " " " under construction Y3. 3 dugouts in front line under construction 4 bomb proofs practically finished, 6 others under construction CENTRAL KEEP, work similar to that on Y1 front.	
21.7.15	Y1, Y2, Y3 work similar to that on 20 inst.	
22.7.15	" " " " " " " "	Lt. Stafford to H.Q. 1st Army as S.O.R.E. to G.H.Q.
23.7.15	Y1 10 bomb proofs in course of construction in support line. 3 " " " " DALY'S KEEP. 3 " " " " LERUTOIR KEEP Y2. 11 " " " in support line bomb proofs for Battalion HQ. finished CHAPEL KEEP Y3. 10 bomb proofs in hand in support-line handed over bomb proofs for Pretorian HQ. in CENTRAL KEEP	2/Lt W.R. Wilson R.E.) reported for duty, vice Lt Stafford

WAR DIARY
or
INTELLIGENCE SUMMARY.

(Erase heading not required.)

Army Form C. 2118

Hour, Date, Place	Summary of Events and Information	Remarks and references to Appendices
VERMELLES – LABOURSE 24.7.15	Y1, Y2, Y3. Work sections to that dam now 28.7.15 – fixed up new trench under tramway near HULLUCH ROAD. Commenced Tunnelling under road.	
25.7.15	Y1 (a)(b) bomb proofs in support line, under construction. (b) 1 " " " DAY'S KEEP finished. (c) 3 " " " LERUTENR KEEP in hand. Y2. all bomb proofs in support line in hand. (b) Improved 1 splinter proof for R.E. Section. (c) Continued work on tunnel under HULLUCH ROAD. Y3. Similar to that on 23.7.15	
26.7.15	Y1.(a) " " " 25.7.15 (b) 2 bomb proofs, DAY'S KEEP completed. Y2 (a) Similar to that on 25.7.15 (b) " " " " (c) Tunnel under road completed. Y3. Work on 5" dugouts continued 2 bomb proofs in support line completed.	

WAR DIARY
or
INTELLIGENCE SUMMARY.
(Erase heading not required.)

Army Form C. 2118

Hour, Date, Place	Summary of Events and Information	Remarks and references to Appendices
LABOURSE. 27.7.15 VERMELLES	Y1. 14 bomb proofs in support line under construction 1 " " " DALY'S KEEP " 3 " " " KERUTOIR " Y2. 11 " " " Support line " 1 Splinter proof " CHAPEL KEEP finished VERMELLES LINE: Cutting through railway embankment to join up. Y3. Work on 5 caps in front line 3 bomb proofs in front support line under construction 1 bomb proof Built & its finished	
26.7.15	Y1. Same as on 27.7.15 Y2. Strengthening communication trench & making loophole hammers CHAPEL KEEP. Cutting thro' vy. completed Y3. Same as on 27.7.15	
29.7.15	Y1. 1 bomb proof support line completed. In hand 13. Remainder same as for 27.7.15 Y2. 2 bomb proof support line completed. In hand 9. 200' wire put up CHAPEL KEEP Y3. 3 bomb proofs in support line completed. In hand 8. Remainder of work same as for 27.7.15	

Army Form C. 2118.

Instructions regarding
War Diaries and Intelligence Summaries
are contained in F.S.Regns, Part II,
and the Staff Manual respectively.
Title pages will be prepared in manuscript.

War Diary
or
INTELLIGENCE SUMMARY

[Stamp: 23rd (FIELD CO...) ROYAL ENGINEERS AUG. 1915]

Hour, date, place	Summary of Events and Information	Remarks and references to Appendices
LABOURSE VERMELLES } 30.7.15	Y1. One bomb proof in support line complete; 13 in hand. Two " " Day's Keep " 1 " Three " " Lerutoir Keep in hand. Y2. Two bomb proofs in support line complete; 9 in hand. Continued work on Chapel Keep. M.G. emplacement under construction near Hulluch Road. Y3 work on 5 saps 5 bomb proofs in support line complete; 6 in hand. Remainder of work same as on 27.7.15.	
31.7.15	Y1 Y2. Work similar to that on 30.7.15. Y3. Work on 5 saps. 7 bomb proofs in support line complete; in hand 7 Two female proof houses under construction in Central Keep. Improved commenced of communication trench at entrance to keep. One bomb proof under construction.	

121/6695

1st Division

23rd Field Coy: R.E.

Vol XII

1 - 31. August. 15

Army Form C. 2118.

Instructions regarding
War Diaries and Intelligence Summaries
are contained in F.S.Regns, Part II,
and the Staff Manual respectively. Title pages will be prepared in manuscript

War Diary
or
INTELLIGENCE SUMMARY

Hour, date, place	Summary of Events and Information	Remarks and references to Appendices
LABOURSE VERMELLES 1.8.15	Y1 Section. Work on bomb posts in Support Line Contained " DAVYS KEEP	
	Y2 " " " " " " " LEKUTOIR "	
	" " " " " Support Line " CHAPEL KEEP	
	Y3 " Continued with 2 coys. Work on bomb posts in Support Line CENTRAL KEEP. Two Pround posts hammer a worked in communication trench. One trench post under construction	
	Y2 " N.C.O employment on roadway	
2.8.15	Y1, Y2, Y3 Work Similar to that on 1.8.15 CHAPEL KEEP burning	
3.8.15	Y1, Y2, Y3 day in Y2 Placing R.S.J. for new cement roof to dugout	New System of numbering adopted

Army Form...

Instructions regarding
War Diaries and Intelligence Summaries
are contained in F.S.Regns,Part II,
and the Staff Manual respectively.
Title pages will be prepared in manuscript.

War Diary
or
INTELLIGENCE SUMMARY.

Hour, date, place	Summary of Events and Information.	Remarks and references to Appendices
LABOURSE VERMELLES 4.8.15	Y Section. Preparing working parties additional for positions. Cannot, must use dugout dug-outs. Communication trench into keep alright? Continued work on same. Commenced laying to new communication trench & started 40' of straight. DALY'S KEEP. CENTRAL KEEP mining continued, around him to put forward? LE RUTOIR " Two bomb posts in hand Continued work on bomb posts in support line.	
5.8.15	Work similar to that on 4.8.15 work started on two incinerators at VERQUIN.	on 6/8/15 2/Lt? Martin to O.C. IX Corps for special duty under said Engineer
6.8.15	" " " " " " Loophole houses in new communication trench to DALY'S KEEP finished.	
7.8.15	work similar to that on 4.8.15 " " " " " CENTRAL KEEP	
8.8.15	" " " " " mining completed. Additional timber put up in entrance to bomb posts DALY'S KEEP	

Instructions regarding
War Diaries and Intelligence Summaries
are contained in F.S.Regns, Part II,
and the Staff Manual respectively.
Title pages will be prepared in manuscript.

War Diary
or
INTELLIGENCE SUMMARY

Hour, date, place	Summary of Events and Information.	Remarks and references to Appendices
LABOURSE / VERMELLES 9.8.15	Bomb proofs in Support line. 13 complete, 35 in hand. CHAPEL KEEP. Improving fire positions, concrete roof to dug out. Wiring frontage 8/14 finished. Work on 5' saps continued. CENTRAL KEEP. Revetting parapets. One bomb proof complete, one in hand.	
10.8.15	Bomb proofs in support line. 17 complete, 34 in hand. Continued work on CHAPEL KEEP and on 5' sap. CENTRAL KEEP. Revetting parapets continued, one bomb proof in hand. Patially dug splinter proofs continued. Two bomb proofs in LE RUTOIR KEEP completed.	
11.8.15	20 Bomb proofs in support line complete. 36 in hand. CHAPEL KEEP. Cements roof to dugout completed to 12". Wire frontage covered with earth. Thickened rear. 5' saps in hand. JUNCTION KEEP trav... CENTRAL KEEP. Covered in splinter proof & continued work on an bomb proof & revetting parapets	

Instructions regarding
War Diaries and Intelligence Summaries
are contained in F.S.Regns, Part II,
and the Staff Manual respectively.
Title pages will be prepared in manuscript.

War Diary
or
INTELLIGENCE SUMMARY

Hour, date, place	Summary of Events and Information.	Remarks and references to Appendices.
LABOURSE VERMELLES	12.9.15	20 Bomb proofs in support line complete, 36 in hand. Worked on CHAPEL KEEP & 5 sap: Started putting up splinter proof cover round water supply in LE RUTOIR. Continued work on bomb proof & new splinter proof in CENTRAL KEEP.
13.8.15	Work same as on 12th. Two new sap-posts started. Wiring round CHAPEL KEEP complete.	
14.8.15	20 bomb proofs support line complete. 35 in hand. Worked on 7 saps. LE RUTOIR KEEP, one will put in working order, spillway to another erected & fitted. Splinter proof cover erected on CENTRAL KEEP. One bomb proof, one splinter proof complete. One & each one in hand.	
15.8.15	Two new bomb proofs in support line started. Sentry posts in front line commenced. Remainder of work same as on 14.8.15	
16.8.15	Work similar to that on 15.8.15.	

Army Form C.2118

Instructions regarding
War Diaries and Intelligence Summaries are contained in F.S.Regns, Part II, and the Staff Manual respectively. Title pages will be prepared in manuscript.

War Diary or Intelligence Summary

Hour, date, place	Summary of Events and Information.	Remarks and references to Appendices
LABOURSE / VERMELLES 17.8.15	24 bomb proofs in support line completed. 35 " " " " " in hand. CHAPEL KEEP. New metal hut-on iron dugouts. Roof of another dugout in place secured. 7 Saps in hand. On CHAPEL KEEP & H.Q. LE RUTOIR work continued.	under construction
18.8.15	28 bomb proofs in support line completed. 34 " " " " " " Remainder of work similar to that on 17.8.15"	
19.8.15	Similar to that on 18.8.15"	
20.8.15	30 bomb proofs in support line completed. 34 " " " " " in hand. CHAPEL KEEP. Work on dugout continued. Seven saps in hand. LE RUTOIR FARM. Continued work in splinter proofs round wells. Splinter proof CENTRAL KEEP completed.	
21.8.15	Work similar to that on 20.8.15	

Army Form C.2118

Instructions regarding
War Diaries and Intelligence Summaries
are contained in F.S.Regns, Part II,
and the Staff Manual respectively.
Title pages will be prepared in manuscript.

War Diary
or
INTELLIGENCE SUMMARY

Hour, date, place	Summary of Events and Information.	Remarks and references to Appendices
LABOURSE VERMELLES { 22.8.15	31 Bomb proofs in support line complete. 33 in hand. Work on dugout in CHAPEL KEEP continued. Seven saps in front line (opposite HOHENZOLLERN). Splinter proofs to wells in LE RUTOIR FARM completed. Shell proof in BREWERY VERMELLES half completed.	
23.8.15	Work similar to that on 22.8.15	
24.8.15	do do do	
25.8.15	do do do	
26.8.15	Work on bomb proofs continued. (Number moved from Y1 to Y2 & work on bomb proofs in Y1 stopped). Saps continued. Communication trench JUNCTION KEEP — M/G Emplacement CENTRAL KEEP marked out & digging of this trench & construction of JUNCTION KEEP commenced.	
27.8.15	33 bomb proofs in support line finished; 35 in hand. Work on splinter proof in CHAPEL KEEP & on 7 saps in front. HOHENZOLLERN continued. Shell proof BREWERY VERMELLES finished.	

Army Form C.2118.

Instructions regarding
War Diaries and Intelligence Summaries
are contained in F.S.Regns,Part II,
and the Staff Manual respectively.
Title pages will be prepared in manuscript.

War Diary
or
INTELLIGENCE SUMMARY

Hour, date, place	Summary of Events and Information.	Remarks and references to Appendices
LABOURSE / VERMELLES 28.8.15	Work on bomb proofs continued. Splinter proof in hand. Eight caps in hand. Communication trench Siding 2 HULLUCH ALLEY – F5 – CURLY CRESCENT & CENTRAL KEEP – JUNCTION KEEP – Trench JUNCTION KEEP – CHAPEL ALLEY dug to 2' depth.	
29.8.15	Work on bomb proofs & caps continued. Three bomb proofs JUNCTION KEEP started. Started digging trench Siding No 2 HULLUCH ALLEY – F5 CURLY CRESCENT.	
30.8.15	Work on as on 29.8.15.	
31.8.15	Work as on 25.8.15. Only one bomb proof in JUNCTION KEEP worked on. Making a new R E Store in MARSDENS KEEP.	

for Capt RE OC 2/3rd D? Eng?s

13/7470

1st Division

23rd F. Co. R.E.

Sep - Dec '15

Vol XIII

Army Form C.2118

Instructions regarding
War Diaries and Intelligence Summaries
are contained in F.S. Regns, Part II,
and the Staff Manual respectively.
Title pages will be prepared in manuscript.

WAR DIARY
or
INTELLIGENCE SUMMARY

23rd Field Coy. R.E.
Sept. 1915

Hour, date, place	Summary of Events and Information	Remarks and references to Appendices
LABOURSE VERMELLES 1.9.15	Yl Section. Continued work on unfinished bomb proofs in old support line & worked parties for new bomb proofs. 60 bomb proofs numbered & handed over in MILL KEEP strong pt.	1 Officer 74 I.R. Infantry attached for special work
2.9.15	Yl Section. Sixth bomb proofs at T.1 made, two support lines near sap D-E. Two new bomb proofs started in old support line & four pit were retimbered. Supports, stores, erecting pit props & building accommodation at MILL KEEP. Establishing a store at LE RUTOIRE FARM.	1 Officer 74 I.R. as above remained from LABOURSE to billets in PHILOSOPHE
3.9.15	Making throwing-in traps & cutting across to front line. Two bomb proofs started in DAY'S PASSAGE. Bomb proofs started on N-S sides of sap C.D.E. old support line — two new bomb proofs in hand & a new communication trench to complete trench. MARSDENS KEEP — LE RUTOIR dug to depth of 3'. Two ready in hand	3 Officers 125 I.R. Infantry attached 23rd Coy., moved from VERMELLE to new billets in PHILOSOPHE

Instructions regarding
War Diaries and Intelligence Summaries
are contained in F.S. Regns, Part II,
and the Staff Manual respectively.
Title pages will be prepared in manuscript.

Army Form C. 2118.

War Diary

23rd Field Co. R.E.

Sep. 1915

INTELLIGENCE SUMMARY

Hour, date, place	Summary of Events and Information	Remarks and references to Appendices
LABOURSE VERMELLES 4.9.15	Y1 Section: Stores on special service to front line – widening a widening trench for same. 2 bomb posts in DAVY'S PASSAGE & 12 bomb posts in new support line in hand. 2 bomb posts old support line in hand. 150" communication trench CORONS DE RUTOIRE – RUTOIRE with communication trench CORONS DE RUTOIRE – RUTOIRE work started on	Annex to improve work then sections started work at 9 from a trench representing 11 am. The work required Wagon & horse lines moved to DROUVIN.
5.9.15	A further number of recesses repaired – work started on Y2 & Y3 Section to MARSDEN'S KEEP & Old Bosch Tract. Remainder to DROUVIN.	
DROUVIN LABOURSE VERMELLES 6.9.15	One third the required number of recesses completed. Remainder of work same as on 5.9.15. FRENCH ALLEY improved & a new trench (200') dug connecting FRENCH ALLEY with LE RUTOIRE KEEP	
7.9.15	Recesses front-line completed a numbered & a running made showing position of these & bomb posts. Improving & continuing FRENCH ALLEY to FRONT LINE	
8.9.15	Deepening & widening FRENCH ALLEY – A further 250" Moved up towards BOYAU 16 Work the trench; one 10 bomb posts in wire supporting

Army Form C. 2118.

Instructions regarding
War Diaries and Intelligence Summaries
are contained in F.S. Regns, Part II,
and the Staff Manual respectively. Title pages will be prepared in manuscript.

War Diary
or
INTELLIGENCE SUMMARY

23rd Field Coy R.E.
Sept 1915

Hour, date, place	Summary of Events and Information	Remarks and references to Appendices
DROUVIN LABOURSE VERMELLES 9.9.15	Deepening & widening FRENCH ALLEY continued. Work on bomb proofs in old & new Support lines continued.	
10.9.15	Same as to 9.9.15	
11.9.15	Improving FRENCH ALLEY — Slopes cut giving access to trench from road near LE RUTOIRE — Trench deepened & in position with LE RUTOIRE ALLEY — Placing notice boards. Where LE RUTOIRE strengthened & brick rubble culvert. Work on opening up old trenches running S.W from FRENCH ALLEY continued. Work on bomb proofs continued — those completed.	
12.9.15	Continued deepening & widening FRENCH ALLEY. Bdl Hd. LE RUTOIRE — cellar strengthened & 9" brick rubble put down. Work on bomb proofs continued.	
13.9.15	Same as on 12.9.15 & in addition making bridges for R.A.M.C. Ramp cut into FOSSE WAY just N. of LE RUTOIRE	
14.9.15	Deepening & widening FRENCH ALLEY. Strengthening Bde. H.Q. LE RUTOIRE making bridges for R.A.M.C. Repairing special version by in front line damaged by shell fire. Work on bomb proofs continued.	

Army Form C. 2118.

Instructions regarding
War Diaries and Intelligence Summaries
are contained in F.S.Regns, Part II,
and the Staff Manual respectively.
Title pages will be prepared in manuscript

23rd Field Coy RE
Sept 1915

War Diary
or
INTELLIGENCE SUMMARY

Hour, date, place	Summary of Events and Information	Remarks and references to Appendices
DROUVIN LABOURSE VERMELLES 15.9.15	Continued work strengthening Bde HQ LE RUTOIRE FM. Repairing special recesses in front line (damaged by shell fire). Bomb-proofs in Old Support line – 2 nos being made. Communications to new Support line 12 under construction & 2 completed. Bde HQ DALY'S Passage practically completed	
16.9.15	Same as for 15.9.15. Also 2 ramps started (from east of FOSSE WAY), return and of WELL LANE) Timbering special recesses in front line.	
17.9.15	Bde HQ LE RUTOIRE completed. Two ramps dug a track splitched WELL LANE to FOSSE WAY. Bomb proofs under construction	
18.9.15	Increasing accommodation in Dugouts MARSDENS KEEP. Trench dug between Bde HQ DALY'S PASSAGE & WELL LANE Special recess front line timbered Bomb proofs continued	

Army Form C. 2118.

Instructions regarding
War Diaries and Intelligence Summaries
are contained in F.S. Regns, Part II,
and the Staff Manual respectively. Title pages will be prepared in manuscript.

23rd Field Cy RE
Sept. 1915

War Diary / INTELLIGENCE SUMMARY

Hour, date, place	Summary of Events and Information	Remarks and references to Appendices
DROUVIN / LABOURSE / VERMELLES 19.9.15	Improving accommodation MARSDEN'S KEEP, bomb and trench proofs continued	
20.9.15	hauling road materials MARSDEN'S KEEP Remainder of work similar to that on 19.9.15	Nos 1,3 & 4 Sections in BREWERY VERMELLES. No 2 " " MARSDEN'S KEEP
21.9.15	Work similar to that on 19.9.15	Lt Col Rennell Brown moved to MARSDENSKEEP
22.9.15	do do do	
23.9.15	Finishing up work, inspection & issue of various stores etc.	
24.9.15	H.Q. moved to MARSDEN'S KEEP. Sections to battle positions (2 to front line; 2 to DALY'S PASSAGE) Attached Memo on philosophe.	
25.9.15	Coy forward at allotted time. Memo from PHILOSOPHE – DALY'S PASSAGE 9.30 a.m. Then forward to 1 ½ 2 Section to front line " " Working in Keeps 33. 29. Trench Cemetery.	Lt Mullins wounded. 2 Lt Edwards gassed.
26.9.15	Continuation of work in Keeps 33. 29 Trench Cemetery. In evening moved to K 32.	See Special Report.
27.9.15	Coy. Withdrawn 3.30 a.m. Memo withdrawn to old German front line	

Army Form C. 2118.

Instructions regarding War Diaries and Intelligence Summaries are contained in F.S.Regns, Part II, and the Staff Manual respectively. Title pages will be prepared in manuscript.

War Diary or Intelligence Summary

23rd Field Coy RE
Sept - Oct 1915

Hour, date, place	Summary of Events and Information	Remarks and references to Appendices
MAZINGARBE LES BREBIS 28.9.15 NOEUX LES MINES MAZINGARBE		
29.9.15	Wagon lines shifted Drouvin to Mazingarbe in afternoon. Delayed on way, did not reach bivouac till after dark. Mines kitchen from German Fnd line to PHILOSOPHE in afternoon.	
30.9.15	No 2 Lt. + O.C. + Capt. from "Meudon Ref" to LES BREBIS Wagon lines from SAULCHOY FARM to " Remainder 1 Coy from Brewery. VERMELLES to LES BREBIS	Nikhorow ME 2nd Lt. Cohen joins
1.10.15	Coy. from LES BREBIS to NOEUX LES MINES	Lt Mullins leaves to hospital
2.10.15	Refitting men, lost cardigans	2nd Lt. Vanstone joins
3.10.15	As above	Lt. Col Revel Brown leaves Coy as C.R.E. 1.Div.
4.10.15	Standing by all day expecting orders to move	
5.10.15	Coy. Leaves for MAZINGARBE (SAULCHOY FARM) Let 1-3 to QUALITY ST	
6.10.15	Wiring Front line	
7.10.15	Working on 1st Bde HQr. Splendid Bivouac	
8.10.15	Fencing Sitting line trenches	2nd Lt N.H Pottinger joins 10/17/15

Army Form C. 2118.

Instructions regarding
War Diaries and Intelligence Summaries
are contained in F.S.Regns,Part II,
and the Staff Manual respectively.
Title pages will be prepared in manuscript.

23rd Field Coy RE
Oct 1915

War Diary / Intelligence Summary

Hour, date, place	Summary of Events and Information	Remarks and references to Appendices
MAZINGARBE 9.10.15	Sect. 1 relieved by Sect 2 at QUALITY ST.	
10.10.15	Work on front line T. heads &c.	
11.10.15	Sect. 4 in Batt'n. ST'n + Trench	2nd Lt Salmon slightly wounded (L.D.)
12.10.15	Work on front line T. heads.	
13.10.15	2 a.m. Sect. 1 joins Sect 4 in Batt'n ST'n	see special reports.
LOZINGHEM 14-10-15	Coy. leaves for LOZINGHEM. Dismounted sections by train. Pars for as LILLERS. Remainder via BETHUNE, CHOCQUES. Settled in billets & cleaned up.	
15-10-15	Rest.	
16-10-15	A.M. Baths, clean arms inspection. P.M. Church Parade.	
17-10-15	Bicycle road making at HESDIGNEUL. Half section with pioneer instruction. Remainder. A.M. Route march P.M. Drill	Units formed for pioneer instruction Black Watch 2 N.C.O. 12 O.R. Cam'n Highr 2 " 12 " 10th Gloucesters 2 " 12 " Royal Warks 2 " 13 " 8th Berks 2 " 12 " 17-10-15. Lt. Wilson goes on leave.
18-10-15	Same as for 18.10.15. Bathing.	
19.10.15	Officer 5 O.R. to 1 Bde H.Q. LILLERS to instruct Bde. wiring party. 10 O.R. to FERFAY to report O.C. M.M.G.	

Army Form C. 2118.

War Diary 23rd Field Coy R.E.
Instructions regarding War Diaries and Intelligence Summaries are contained in F.S. Regns, Part II, and the Staff Manual respectively. Title pages will be prepared in manuscript.

INTELLIGENCE SUMMARY Oct. 1915.

Hour, date, place		Summary of Events and Information	Remarks and references to Appendices
LOZINGHEM.	20-10-15	1 Section road making at HESDIGNEUL. 1 Section engaged with instruction of pioneers 9 Bolweiring party. 10 O.R. at FERFAY. Remainder of Coy. A.M. Route march. P.M. Drill & lecture on use of Explosives.	
	21-10-15	Details: same as 20-10-15. Remainder of Coy. A.M. Route march. P.M. Knots & lashings, use of spars.	
	22-10-15	Details same as 21-10-15. Remainder of Coy. A.M. Route march. P.M. Marching order kit inspection.	
	23-10-15	Inspection of three Field Coys. 1st Divn. by C.R.E.	1 Officer & 5 O.R. returned from 1st Bde. Pioneer instruction, LILLERS. Capt. Dawson on leave. Lt Wilson rejoined Coy from leave.
	24-10-15	Church parades.	
	25-10-15	1 Section road making at HESDIGNEUL. 1 " engaged with instruction of pioneers. 10 O.R. at FERFAY. Remainder of Coy. oral instruction & weather.	
	26-10-15	Details: same as 25-10-15. Remainder of Coy. A.M. Instruction in marry. P.M. Route march. Lecture to hospital section by A.D.V.S.	
	27-10-15	Details same as 25-10-15. A.M. 4 men building huts at LABUISSIÈRE. Remainder of Coy. instruction & drill. Lecture by C.R.E.	Draft of 18 sappers & 2 drivers joined.

Army Form C. 2118.

Instructions regarding
War Diaries and Intelligence Summaries
are contained in F.S.Regns, Part II,
and the Staff Manual respectively.
Title pages will be prepared in manuscript.

23rd Field Cy R.E.
Oct. 1915.

War Diary
of
INTELLIGENCE SUMMARY

Hour, date, place	Summary of Events and Information	Remarks and references to Appendices
LOZINGHEM 28-10-15	Work at HESDIGNEUL, LABUISSIÈRE, & FERFAY continued. 1 Officer & 20 O.R. attended King's parade near HESDIGNEUL. Remainder of Coy. on motorbus p.m. drill. Instruction of pioneers continued.	
29-10-15	Special work as on 28-10-15. Remainder of coy: Drawing & improving waggon lines & horse shelters.	Pioneers returned to their Battalions.
30-10-15	Same as 29-10-15. Completion of pioneers course.	
31-10-15	Same as on 30-10-15. Reinsundre church parade.	

M.H. Green? Lt. RE
23rd Field Cy RE

"A" Form. Army Form C. 2121.

MESSAGES AND SIGNALS.

No. of Message

Prefix .... Code .... m. | Words | Charge | This message is on a/c of .... Service. | Recd. at .... m.

Office of Origin and Service Instructions.

Sent — At .... m. To .... By ....

(Signature of "Franking Officer.")

Date .... From .... By ....

TO

Sender's Number.	Day of Month	In reply to Number	AAA
*			

From

Place

Time

The above may be forwarded as now corrected.

Censor.

(Z)

Signature of Addressor or person authorised to telegraph in his name.

* This line should be erased if not required.

was utilised for the trench connecting "Keep 89" with Keep at G 18 C 8.2. Infantry Working Parties working on the trench & Sappers on the Keep throughout the night of Sept 26th - 27th.

Sept 27"
2.30 a.m.
Lt. Col. Russel Brown arrived about 2.30 a.m. with rations, & about 4 a.m. the Sappers working at G 18 C 8.2 handed over their picks & shovels to the Coldstream Guards who had then arrived at this point.
This Keep had been dug to an average depth of over 3' by 4 a.m. the Connecting trench from "Keep 89", to an average of 2'6" for half the distance the remaining half being "spit trked".

6. a.m.
A few of the R.E. returned to VERMELLES being relieved by those who had recovered from "gassing", under Lt. Edwards R.E.
They made their Head Quarters in DALYS PASSAGE & were kept at the disposal of 1st Bde. till conclusion of operations. The Infantry miners attached to R.E, with their officers, remained in the German lines near "the HAIE" till relieved on the afternoon of 28th September.

W Watson
Lt R.E.
23rd Field Co. R.E.

(5)

"A" Form.

Army Form C. 2121.

MESSAGES AND SIGNALS.

No. of Message

Prefix .... Code .... m.	Words	Charge	This message is on a/c of	Recd. at .... m.
Office of Origin and Service Instructions.	Sent		.... Service.	Date
	At .... m.			From
	To			By
	By		(Signature of "Franking Officer.")	

TO

Sender's Number.	Day of Month	In reply to Number	AAA

From

Place

Time

The above may be forwarded as now corrected. (Z)

Censor. Signature of Addressor or person authorised to telegraph in his name.

* This line should be erased if not required.

Sept 25th Heavy firing was heard on left flank
8 p.m.   about 8pm.; evidently from a point
          some little distance North of G.18 B.35.
          The Wiring Party which had put a thin
          line of wire round "Keep 35" early in
          the afternoon, placed some wire round
          "Keep 89" in the evening.
8.30 p.m. Lt.Col. Russel Brown arrived & arranged
          for garrison & Commands of Keeps & Trench.
Sept 26th Digging continued throughout the night of
4 a.m.   Sept 25th–26th & all the men in trench
          & Keeps "stood to arms" from 4 a.m till
          dawn, after which digging was resumed
          till heavy shelling made work impossible.
11. a.m. Capt. Campbell, Black Watch who had been in
          charge of Garrison of "Keep 89" was called to
          his Bttn H.Q. & on his return at 11 a.m.
          immediately led his platoons out towards
          Hulloch. Shortly afterwards, owing to
          orders received, the majority of the Sappers
          with Working Parties of Infantry, withdrew
          from the Connecting trench between Keeps
          "35" & "89" to Main German Communica-
          tion trench, afterwards returning in time
          to start work on a third Keep & its
          Connecting trench.
6 p.m.   This third Keep was commenced at dusk
          about G.18 C.63 but after interviewing
          Brig. Gen. Ready, the position of Keep was
          altered to G.18 C.82 which is the point
          referred to as "Keep 52".
          Part of G.18 C.63 Keep ("False Keep") was

"A" Form. Army Form C. 2121.
MESSAGES AND SIGNALS.

11 am. The Second Working party, consisting of 2 Sections R.E. with a number of attached Infantry men (S.W.B. & Black Watch), advanced from British firing trench near Sap D, crossing the open in extended order with a few of 1st Bde. Wiring party as scouts.

Keeping to the South of "the HAIE" they crossed German front & support trenches & came under fire from Right flank, being forced to lie down, having lost a number of men.

11.30 am. The rest of the distance to G.18 B.35 was made in the German Main Communication trench leading to Hulloch, without further incident & the party set to work on the Keep & on fire stepping existing trenches in conjunction with the Northern Group of 1st Working Party already at this point.

The remainder of Attached Infantry miners who had all moved from PHILOSOPHE in the morning, joined hands at G.18 B.35

12. am by 12 noon.

From information received in the neighbourhood of Hulloch, it appeared that HULLOCH had not been captured, so parties were all retained at & near "Keep 35" (G.18 B 35) till touch was made with Southern Group of 1st Working Party at G.18 C 89 (Keep 89)

4 pm. at 4 p.m. Sappers then set to work on a trench connecting these Keeps "35" & "89" work being continued on both Keeps and connecting trench all night.

(3)

"A" Form. Army Form C. 2121.

MESSAGES AND SIGNALS.

No. of Message

Prefix ... Code ... m.	Words	Charge	This message is on a/c of ... Service.	Recd. at ... m.
Office of Origin and Service Instructions.				Date
	Sent			From
	At ... m.			
	To			
	By		(Signature of "Franking Officer.")	By

TO

Sender's Number.	Day of Month	In reply to Number	AAA

From

Place

Time

The above may be forwarded as now corrected. (Z)

Censor. Signature of Addressor or person authorised to telegraph in his name.

* This line should be erased if not required.

(688-9) —McC. & Co. Ltd., London.— W 14142/641. 225,000. 4/15. Forms C 2121/10.

towards BOIS CARRÉE, losing a few men on the way. They were forced to lie down in front of the wire at T head South of the BOIS owing to heavy front & flank fire, which caused considerable losses to R.E & Black Watch.

Eventually the enemy's wire was cut & the party crawled into the shallow dummy T head trench at G.17.A.9.4.

7.40. a.m. The Northern half of 1st Working Party continued their advance towards the German Main Communication Trench leading to "Hulloch" & were joined by their Black Watch working party. All proceeded by this trench to their objective G.18.B.35 where work was immediately started on a Keep under rifle fire from the Left Flank & Rear. Some of the fire from rear was probably our own fire against Germans still holding out South of BOIS. CARRÉE.

9.30. a.m. The Section at BOIS CARRÉE G.17.A.9.4 was heavily shelled with H.E. for about half an hour & no progress could be made till 1.30 p.m. when a red flag was noticed East of BOIS CARRÉE.

Those remaining of No 3 Section R.E. with the Black Watch working party then advanced & ultimately reached the point G.18.C.8.9 where work on a Keep was started under a fairly brisk fire, the Officer in charge, Lt Mallins R.E., being wounded.

"A" Form.

Army Form C. 2121.

MESSAGES AND SIGNALS.

No. of Message

Prefix .... Code .... m.	Words	Charge	This message is on a/c of:	Recd. at .... m.
Office of Origin and Service Instructions.	Sent		.... Service.	Date
	At .... m.			From
	To			
	By		(Signature of "Franking Officer.")	By

TO

Sender's Number.	Day of Month	In reply to Number	AAA
*			

From	
Place	
Time	

The above may be forwarded as now corrected.	(Z)
.... Censor.	.... Signature of Addressor or person authorised to telegraph in his name.

* This line should be erased if not required.

(688-9) —McC. & Co. Ltd., London.— W 14142/641. 225,000. 4/15. Forms C 2121/10.

They succeeded in joining up with Nos 1 & 4 Sections R.E. in our front trenches & followed up the attack.

Sept 25th } From 5.50 a.m to 6.30 a.m Nos 1 & 4 Sections
5.50 a.m } R.E. in front trenches were fully occupied in assisting 187th Co. R.E. in operating gas cylinders. In some cases the 23rd Co. Sappers had to take complete control owing to casualties in 187th Co. R.E. Several of the men were put out of action by the gas but most of them succeeded in finishing the work & then collected in & near a bomb-proof in Sap II as arranged.

7.20. a.m. The R.E. and Infantry forming the Northern & Southern groups of 1st Working Party under the late Capt. R.C. Anderson, Black Watch, advanced from their positions in DALY'S PASSAGE at 7.20 a.m.

The R.E. of the Northern group who were led by Lt Salmon R.E., on approaching "the HAIE" at G 17 A 92 met about a Company of Infantry in some disorder without officers who were going in the wrong direction. This officer rallied them & took them along with him into the German trenches.

No 2. Section R.E. then lay down to wait for their working party of Black Watch & to let the Supporting Infantry get ahead as originally arranged.

The Southern half of 1st Working Party under Lt Mallins R.E moved on towards Bois Carrée,

"A" Form. Army Form C. 2121.
MESSAGES AND SIGNALS.

Narrative of Operations from 24th to 28th Sept. 1915
re work of 23rd Field Co. R.E. + two attached Infantry
Working Parties.

Sept. 24th   The 23rd Fld. Co. R.E. was split up into its
8.30 p.m.   normal 4 Sections, each having about half
           a Coy of Infantry attached as working party.
Nos 2 + 3 Sections R.E. each had half a Co. of the
Black Watch attached with about a dozen men of
1st Bde. working party.
The work of these two parties (called Northern +
Southern group of 1st Working party) was co-ordinated
by the late Capt. Anderson of the Black Watch who had
previously arranged all details with O.C. 23rd Fld. Co. R.E.,
to whom he reported that all was ready + officers + men
in position in DALY'S PASSAGE by 8.30 p.m. on Sept 24th.

Nos 1 + 4 Sections of 23rd Fld. Co. reported themselves
in position in the front line trenches by 8.30 p.m. on
24th Sept.
These two Sections of R.E. assisted the 187th Co. R.E.
during the night of 24th–25th Sept in arranging
details to make the gas cylinders more secure
+ in making arrangements to operate these
cylinders in the morning.
These sections also had about half a Co. of Infantry
miners attached to them called the Northern +
Southern groups of 2nd Working Party, but as
there was not room in the front trenches for
these miners, they remained in PHILOSOPHE
and were wired for about 9.0. a.m on 25th Sept.
, after the assault had been launched.

1 / B. mann

23ᵗᵉ J̊. Cav Rt.
No. 1
vol. XIV

9447/21

450
472
474
480

Army Form C. 2118.

Instructions regarding
War Diaries and Intelligence Summaries
are contained in F.S. Regs., Part II,
and the Staff Manual respectively.
Title pages will be prepared in manuscript.

War Diary 23rd Fd. Co. R.E.
or
INTELLIGENCE SUMMARY. November 1915

Hour, date, place	Summary of Events and Information	Remarks and references to Appendices
LOZINGHEM Nov. 1st 1915 Monday	Work on Hutments Roads at HESDIGNEUIL continued " " Bomb School FERFAY " " Horse Shelters Standings LOZINGHEM started	Capt Duncan returns from leave
2/11	Same as above	2/Lt Pettitin relieves 2/Lt Venestrout i/c works at HESDIGNEUIL
3/11	As above 2/Lt Wharrie + 3 Sgts from 1st Bde report for Instruction in Pioneer work.	2nd/Lt Munro (8th Bde) reports for Instruction as Brigade Pioneer
4/11	Works as above. Pioneer Class of 10 Sappers from 23rd Fd Co started Instructional Course – Lt Munro + 3 Bde Sgts attending	
5/11	Works as above continued Material for Farm Hutments arrive LILLERS station Pioneer Instruction continued	2/Lt Cohen a/g Adjt + O.R.E.
6/11	Works at HESDIGNEUIL FERFAY LOZINGHEM } continued LILLERS Pioneer Instruction continued Baths at REIMBERT	

Army Form C. 2118c

Instructions regarding
War Diaries and Intelligence Summaries
are contained in F.S. Regns, Part II,
and the Staff Manual respectively.
Title pages will be prepared in manuscript

War Diary
INTELLIGENCE SUMMARY 23rd Fld Co RE
November 1915

Hour, date, place	Summary of Events and Information	Remarks and references to Appendices
LOZINGHEM. Sunday Nov 7th 1915.	Works carried on under:— Hutments & Roads HESDIGNEUL FERFAY LOZINGHEM LILLERS. Standings Hutments Instructional Class for hutments of 1st Bde Rnes G.k.	
8/11	Works as above. Baths Reimbert.	" Lt Edwards returning from leave
9/11	Works as above.	
10/11	do.	C.R.E. 47th Div. inspects Hutments at HESDIGNEUL ~. (1st Div. Officers Course at Lillers)
11/11	do.	
12/11	Lecture 2–3 march to PHILOSOPHE by 2.30 pm " Lt Patterson with Cyclists hut left thro' k billets command under " Lt. Salmon occupy Advanced Billets to FORT GLATZ	" Lt. Salmon to Fort Glatz " Lt. Patterson to Fort Glatz
Saturday 13/11	Lecture 1 — A with H.Q., marched to march from LOZINGHEM at 9 am arriving at PHILOSOPHE 3 pm RIAZINGARBE Horse lines to " SAULCHOY FARM — PHILOSOPHE H.Q. Lecture 1–A to Billets Advanced Lecture cleaning out trenches at Fort Glatz	

Army Form C. 2118.

Instructions regarding
War Diaries and Intelligence Summaries
are contained in F.S. Regns. Part II,
and the Staff Manual respectively.
Title pages will be prepared in manuscript.

War Diary
or
INTELLIGENCE SUMMARY

23rd Fld Co. R.E.
November 1915

Hour, date, place	Summary of Events and Information	Remarks and references to Appendices
MAZINGARBE. PHILOSOPHE		
Sunday Nov. 14 1915	Cleaning out billets at PHILOSOPHE, firing baths & drying rooms. Also Lectures clearing up Stores etc. Spring Kindes.	
15/11	Also cuts knowing new Support Trench. G.24 d.63 – G.30 d.6F Ren. L.I.R. in Snell Road, making Rifle Cocks. Road Runners etc.	
16/11	Repairing LOOS ALLEY G.30 C.41 – G.29 D.5F Harrieston Post. made at 65 metre point Lens Road & Snell Road repaired. Repairing & laying narrow gauge track Quality St – Fort Glatz.	
17/11	LOOS ALLEY repairs continued. Work on Roads Rly. continued	
18/11	Above works continued 3 Bridges made in Granay Bourbonteria Rd { G.29 d.5F 30 a.27 24 c.71 } Double Sentry Post with 3 loopholes made in Fosse Trench about H.19 c.P2. Work on Rifle Racks Continued (converting K. toll fixed bayonets) Making 10 intermediate L.P.s & framed Periscope	
19/11	Sictions 1 & 4 return Billets 2 & 3 at Fort Glatz Loos Alley Repairs Continued A Grend Double Sentry Post made + Fire Trench at H.19 c.8.5. Slat made with Home Butter at Sandbag Farm Work on Periscope Bomb Store etc. continued	ii Lt Edwards iii Lt Vansittart & Fort Glatz

Army Form C. 2118.

Instructions regarding
War Diaries and Intelligence Summaries
are contained in F.S.Regns,Part II,
and the Staff Manual respectively.
Title pages will be prepared in manuscript

War Diary
or
INTELLIGENCE SUMMARY

Hour, date, place	Summary of Events and Information	Remarks and references to Appendices
MAZINGARBE – PHILOSOPHE – FORT GLATZ.		
Nov 20th 1915	Loos Alley Repairs continued - other work as above + Repairs to Snell Road. including 8 Infantry Bridges Inspection of "Keeps" + "Defended Localities"	
Sunday Nov 21st	Loos Alley Repairs - Tosh Alley Repairs Fraud. Ft. Glatz & Tosh Alley started Periscope Bout Proof started at G.30 d 53. Tramway Completed from Charing Cross (Quality St) to Victoria St. Horse Shelters continued Fort & Rifle Rock, Bout Bros etc.	
22/11	Work as above. Meeting experimental Revettment of Wire Canvas.	" Lt Cohen goes on leave (from 1st D.E.)
23/11	Bout Proof Periscope St G.30 d 55 in hand Extension of Tramway from Fort Glatz to Posen Alley started Chalk Pit Well H 25 a 95 being cleared St. Horse Shelters, Bout Bros etc continued	
24/11	Bout Proof Work as Well continued Repairs to Lens Rd in hand, Dug out at Victoria St started Horse Shelters etc cont.	
25/11	Bout Proof contd. Well carried, branching trench made. Tunnel started Lens Rd. repairs Victoria St dug out Horse shelters contd.	
26/11	Tramway Fort Glatz - Posen St. &c started Bout Proof - Well contd - Horse Shelters Victoria St dug out cont.	26/11 Lottrie Ruleys " Lt Salmon , " Lt Patterson return " Lt Edmonds , " Lt Tanstone

Army Form C. 2118.

Instructions regarding
War Diaries and Intelligence Summaries
are contained in F.S. Regns, Part II,
and the Staff Manual respectively.
Title pages will be prepared in manuscript.

War Diary
or
INTELLIGENCE SUMMARY   23rd Fld Co. RE
November 1915

Hour, date, place	Summary of Events and Information	Remarks and references to Appendices
MAZINGARBE - PHILOSOPHE FORT GLATZ		
Saturday 27/11/15	Work continued on Fort Glatz - Posen Alley Tramway extension. Periscope Bomb Proof at G.30.d.55 complete with exception of periscope holes. Continued work for Chalk Pit Well. Improving below St-Chaing Camp Tramway. Repairing Lens Road. Making Rifle Racks, Trench Bomb Boxes etc. Horse Shelter, Sandchry Farm	
28/11/15	Work as above. Improving Fire trench at H.25.a.52. Stay mill & work "Sample Shelter" in Old German Front Line (10th Avenue) near Posen Station	
29/11	Periscope Bomb Proof Completed. Work on Tramways continued. " " Chalk Pit Well " Sample Shelter, Horse Shelter etc continued. Improving Support Line G.20 d FP	
30/Nov	Tramways, trenches & shelters as above continued. Machine Gun emplacement H.19 c 77 started. Tracing Redoubt Lens Road & 85 Metre Point. 3rd Bde Nuno tramway under W.V Patterton Asst 120 yards H.19 c SF (Bde Nuny Officer Wounded) Horse Shelter finished	

23rd Pioneers Coy. R.E.

Dec / Vol. XV

Army Form C. 2118.

Instructions regarding
War Dairies and Intelligence Summaries
are contained in F.S.Regns,Part II,
and the Staff Manual respectively.
Title pages will be prepared in manuscript.

War Diary
or
INTELLIGENCE SUMMARY 23rd Field Co RE
December 1915

Hour, date, place	Summary of Events and Information	Remarks and references to Appendices
MAZINGARBE, PHILOSOPHE FORT GLATZ		
Wed. Dec 1st 1915	Work on Reps. Continued. Improving Front line Trench at H.25.C.15. 3rd Bde Wires working with ii Lt Patterson at H.19.C.58. 10th Avenue Shelter in progress. Repairs made to Lens Road.	ii Lt Cohen returns from leave
2/12/15	Fort Glatz - Posen Alley Ry. work continued. Working on Fire Trench - 10th Avenue, Sample Shelter. Alterations made to 65 Metre Point Observation Stn.	ii Lt Cohen returns ii Lt Salmon at Fort Glatz
3/12/15	Front line Trench - 10" Av. Shelter continued. New Reserve Trench bow" from G.30.B.22 - G.24.d.34 - Road Sap. Fort Jostlin 200'A' length -15" "front". Making M.G. emplacement between Chalk Pit Pond to Repairs to Lens Road. Making Canvas now revetting for number plates H.25-1 etc.	ii Lt Salmon goes on leave
4/12	2 Lectures with Infantry on Front line Trench South of Strand Alley "Sample Shelter" in 10" Avenue (old German Front line) near Posen Stn. found interfered by Infantry. Repairing Lens Rd. Making Revetment, number plates etc.	
5/12	Repairing Front line Trench as above. Making M.G. emplacements H.31.A.2.8 Siting Northern Sap Redoubt. Making Revetment etc.	

Army Form C. 2118.

Instructions regarding
War Diaries and Intelligence Summaries
are contained in F.S. Regns, Part II,
and the Staff Manual respectively.
Title pages will be prepared in manuscript.

War Diary
INTELLIGENCE SUMMARY

23rd Field Co. R.E.
December 1915

Summary of Events and Information

Hour, date, place		Remarks and references to Appendices
MAZINGARBE, PHILOSOPHE		
6/12	No Section on Lens Road Repairs: making Road Crossing for Chaurg. Bars. Fr. G.14 d 5.7 by our Shaft Road I/G 28 d 7.0.	Lecture on Fort Gliely (W/Lts Colvin & Pitcairn) return to PHILOSOPHE relieved by 2nd N'land R.E. evening of 6-7th. 23rd F.H. Eng. to Reserve
7/12	Work Carrying on above at G.28 d 90 Continued. Repairing Lens Road G.13 d O.5 to G.34 B.41. Carting & breaking road metal for Road Repairs. Building experimental M.G. emplacement, tried out best making Wire canvas overhead, repairing roofs & billets etc.	
8/12	Started Divl. Observation Post G.23 d 27. Preparing & carting material M.G. emplacement started at Fosse No. 7 G.27 c 63. Maintaining Lens Road. Making wire Bands Th. "Braids" for Trenches etc. Carting & breaking road metal	
9/12	Divl. Observation Post Continued G.23 d 27. M.G. emplacement G.27 c 63 – Carting material Preparing new Station of Chaurg. Cars in houses maintenance of Lens Road Continued. Wire Bands etc as above.	
10/12	Divl. Observation Post G.23 d 27 finished M.G. emplacement G.27 c 63 Continued Other work as above.	
11/12	Preparing material for Fosse No. 7 defences Repairing Shell damage to Lens Road Breaking road metal making Wire Bands etc.	

Army Form C. 2118.

Instructions regarding
War Diaries and Intelligence Summaries
are contained in F.S.Regns, Part II,
and the Staff Manual respectively.
Title pages will be prepared in manuscript

War Diary
or
INTELLIGENCE SUMMARY

23rd Fld. Co. R.E.

December 1915

Hour, date, place	Summary of Events and Information	Remarks and references to Appendices
MAZINGARBE. PHILOSOPHE.		
Sunday 12/12	Defence Scheme Focus No. 7. Making Covered Ways & M.G. emplacements. Repairing Lens Road - Cartey & breaking Road metal. Chaney Cross Station. Nitlet Bends etc.	(i) Lt Salmon returns from leave. Sgt Lawson (London Scottish) reports to L.S. H.Q. on attaining Commission in R.E.
13/12	do	
14/12	do	
15/12	do - making Experimental Revetment of Expanded metal	
16/12	do - inspecting traps	
17/12	do. above. Two Lectures returns to Lectures of 26th Field Co. R.E. at 58 Metre Point in afternoon of 18th to times for every hour.	Lt Edwards } F 58 Metre Point. (ii) Lt Pallastre
18/12	Altering two M.G. emplacements No. 6. 7. between WINGS WAY & HAY ALLEY Finished Loth out Post about 50' South of Junction of Front Line & WINGS WAY. Assisting R.A.M.C. hut construction of Dressing Station. Collecting Scattered Stores carrying same to Quarry Dump G.17 d 35 Extinguishing Fire - Dug out - Repairing Dug out - improving Trenches at 58 Metre Point. Focus No. 7 Defences continued	
19/12	Finished work on Nos. 6. 7. M.G. Emplacements Altering Nos. 5. M.G. Continued Dressing Station VENDIN ALLEY, near Quarry Dump. Improving trenches &c at 58 Metre Point - 30 french troops to hand Focus No. 7 defences contd. - Shaft Sinking & hand for M.G.E's Making min. frames for above. Two humbler Flats & hand. Sawing timber for revetting	

Army Form C. 2118.

Instructions regarding War Diary 23rd Field Coy. R.E.
War Diaries and Intelligence Summaries
are contained in F.S. Regns, Part II, INTELLIGENCE or SUMMARY.
and the Staff Manual respectively. December 1915
Title pages will be prepared in manuscript

Hour, date, place	Summary of Events and Information	Remarks and references to Appendices
MAZINGARBE, PHILOSOPHE 58 Metre Point 20/12	No 5. M.G. Emplacement improved. Look out Post made near H.Q. M.G.E. R.A.M.C. Dressing Stn. continued. Improving trenches & dug outs at 58 Metre Point. Defence Scheme Fosse No 7 continued. Cement Cases made for same. Preparing material for Revetments.	(ii) Lt. Vanston proceeds on Leave. (iii) Lt. Harmon 3rd Welsh (att. 2nd Welsh) reports from 1st Div Officers School.
21/12	Improving & rebuilding M.G. Emplacements to Front Line. Revetting Front Line Parapet near Northern Sap. Fosse No 7 Defence Scheme. Sawing & cutting timber for Revetting.	(iii) Lt. Salmon goes sick.
22/12	M.G. emplacements contd. Front Line Revetting " R.A.M.C. Dressing Station contd. Repairing & maintaining Lens Road. Making Look-out-Post Plates.	
23/12	Continued work on M.G. Emplacements. do Front Line Revetting South of NORTHERN SAP. do R.A.M.C. Dressing Stn. do Lens Road. Look out Post Plates	
24/12	do above.	(viii) Lt. Cohen relieves Lt. Edwards at 58 Metre Point. Sections 2 & 3 relieve Sects. 1 & 4 do

JAN 1916
23rd (FIELD) COMPANY
ROYAL ENGINEERS

Army Form C. 2118.

Instructions regarding
War Diaries and Intelligence Summaries
are contained in F.S.Regns,Part II,
and the Staff Manual respectively.
Title pages will be prepared in manuscript.

War Diary
or
INTELLIGENCE SUMMARY 23rd Field Coy.
December 1915

Hour, date, place		Summary of Events and Information	Remarks and references to Appendices
MAZINGARBE – PHILOSOPHE			
58 Metre Point	23/12	Work continued on M.G. Emplacements ~ Front Line Revetting. Revetting trenches at 58 Metre Point. Collecting German loop hole plates for Loch out Posts. Repairing Lens Road at Victoria St. Making Frames for mine Shaft, Ladders & Look out Post Plates	(i) Lt. W.G. Smith joins Coy. (ii) Lt. Haxman (att 3rd Hills) leaves. Lt. Fenner 8th Berks report from 1st Div. Lt. Delabere 10th G.H.s. } Officers School
	24/12	M.G. Emplacements cont'd Front Line Revetting cont'd between HAY ALLEY & NORTHERN SAP. Work cont'd on Dressing Station. Shaft-Sinking at Forge No.7 resumed. Lens Road Repairs cont'd Look out Plates, ladders, mine cases et hung nids	" Lt Salmon report from Hospital
	27/12	M.G. emplacement etc rather work as above	Lt. Edwards to 1st Div. Officers School - Mazingarbe
	28/12	As above	" Lt. Vanstone returns from leave
	29/12	M.G emplacement rather work as above but exception of Front Line Revetting. Material carried & Indenting of Mines for Revetting RESERVE TRENCH about G.18 a 7.6	Lt. Fenner 8th Berks) from 1st Div Officers School "Lt. Delabere 10th Glos) Complete period with Coy. " Lt Vanstone returns " Lt Pittatore at 58 Metre Point 1:4 Letters Adven. Salon ? at " " (iii) Lt. Ellis (London Scottish) from 1st Div. Officer School
	30/12	M.G emplacements cont'd ~ Reserve Trench Revetting Cont'd.	to 23rd Fld Co. for instruction
	31/12	M.G emplacement cont'd (Nos 2 & 3) trucked out ~ Spitlocked 16 Traverse of DEVON LANE for Handing over Lens Rd, Repairs Cont'd Forge No.7 Defence Scheme Cont'd Summary Point Boards made etc	" Lt. Salmon returns " Lt. Cohen O/C delivers lecture at 1st Div Officers School

1ST DIVISION
DIVL. ENGINEERS

23RD FIELD COMPANY R.E.

JAN - DEC 1916.

1ST DIVISION
DIVL. ENGINEERS

1st Divisional Engineers

23rd FIELD COMPANY R. E.

JANUARY 1916.

Army Form C. 2118.

Instructions regarding
War Diaries and Intelligence Summaries
are contained in F.S.Regns, Part II,
and the Staff Manual respectively.
Title pages will be prepared in manuscript.

23rd Field Coy.

WAR DIARY
or
INTELLIGENCE SUMMARY

January 1916

Hour, date, place	Summary of Events and Information	Remarks and references to Appendices
PHILOSOPHE. MAZINGARBE. 58 Metre Point 1/1/16	Machine Gun Emplacement N°9. 10. T heads off Devon Lane. 16 bays 2'6" deep. 8 men sheltered. Fosse N°7 Defence Guild. Maintenance of Lens Road.	
2/1	M.G.E. Guild. 8 additional T heads faced to DEVON LANE. Fosse N°7 Defence. Lens Rd. Reserve Guild. Working on CHARING CROSS – FORT GLATZ RX. Assistance given on LONE TREE & NORTHERN SAP REDOUBTS	
3/1	On M.G.E.s N°10 to 12. Straightening N° Sap 45. Repairing floors in Dug-outs (N°10 & 6/6 H.Q.) assistance given on Redoubts as above. On Fosse N°7, Charing Cross by wire obstacles, Lens Road. Cutting timber for RESERVE TRENCH Revetment.	ii Lt Ellis (Lieut. Scots) from 1st Div. Officers' School from 23rd Fld Cy. R.E. to Div. H.Q.
4/1	On M.G.E. N°12. Revetting T heads of DEVON LANE. On N°10, 6/6 H.Q. Dug-out. Working on Fosse N°7 & Lens Road. Started Sample M.G.E. at Mazingarbe.	ii Lt Vaudin — ii Lt Salmon both returns 1st returned by 2 Lectures 1st Lowland R.E.
5/1	On Fosse N°7 & Lens Road. Making Box for Signallers. Sample M.G.E.	

Army Form C. 2118.

Instructions regarding
War Dairies and Intelligence Summaries
are contained in F.S.Regus,Part II,
and the Staff Manual respectively.
Title pages will be prepared in manuscript

War Diary
or
INTELLIGENCE SUMMARY

23rd Field Co. R.E.

January 1916

Hour, date, place	Summary of Events and Information	Remarks and references to Appendices
PHILOSOPHE MAZINGARBE		
6/1	Working on Fosse No 7 & Lens Road. Sample M.G.E. Making notice Boards	
7/1	On Fosse No 7 & Lens Road. Making Bridges. Improving Road for Heavy Gun. - Quality St. Shelters. Framing Timber for Heavy Gun Emplacement cover. Sample M.G. Emplacement. a Dug out } at Mazingarbe " Snipers Post Making & Painting Notice Boards.	
8/1	Working on Fosse No 7 - Lens Road. Making Frame Covers for Heavy Gun Emplacement. Carting Steel Rails. Playing same in place of wooden Rails on CHARING CROSS. FORT GLATZ RY.	Capt P.J. Mackay R.E. from Asst-SVDE to Command 23rd Field Co R.E. - Acting as C.R.E.
9/1	M.G.E. & Sample Snipers Post built at MAZINGARBE. Contd. making notice Boards.	
10/1	Still work on Fosse No 7 & Lens Road. Loading & Carting shale for Lens Road. Relaying CHARING CROSS - FORT GLATZ RY. Other work as above Contd.	# Lt Lefroy (73rd F.A.R.E.) to our work on loan " Lt Cohen to 73rd FM G.R.E. 2 others 11/1/16 - Taken over trench Stores
11/1	Work as above Contd.	
12/1	As above. About 600 yds. Steel Rails laid to date	Capt E.F.S. Danson leave Exp. Proceeds to Chateau on duty

Army Form C. 2118.

Instructions regarding
War Dairies and Intelligence Summaries
are contained in F.S.Regns,Part II,
and the Staff Manual respectively.
Title pages will be prepared in manuscript

War Diary 23rd Field Co. R.E.
INTELLIGENCE SUMMARY
or
               January 1916.

Hour, date, place	Summary of Events and Information	Remarks and references to Appendices
PHILOSOPHE, MAZINGARBE		
13/1	Fosse No 7 Defences Contd. Lens Road Repairs Contd.	2nd Lt Curbey (174th Fd. Co. R.E.) arrived to take over billets. Lt. Edwards (23rd Fd.G.Q.E) actg. Adjt. 1st D.E.
LILLERS 14/1	Dismounted men by road to Noeux-le-Mines. Thence by train to LILLERS. Transport to NOEUX - 10.30 a.m. entrain NOEUX 12.15 p.m. arrive 1p.m. Transport by Road to LILLERS. Afternoon spent cleaning billets	Lt. Johnson (73rd Fd Co R.E.) took over to hand 13/1/16
15/1	Cleaning billets & stables. Started erection of additional staff shelters. Men put on preparing Roads (Head Riding CCS) Stalls made in Huts etc to Head Riding CCS.	
LILLERS ALLOUAGNE 16/1	Sundry small repairs effected on Private property & settlement for claims for damages against XV Div. Huts & Roads at H.Q. CCS Contd. Work on Stables Contd.	2nd Lt Cohen took section No 3 to Allouagne & Frame Repr of 1st Bde to Pioneer work.
17/1	Contd small repairs as above Sundry small works executed for 1st Div. 1st DE. RADOS etc etc Huts & Road H.Q. Casualty Clearing Stn. Contd. Work on Stables Allotts Contd. Pioneer class of 1st Bde under Lt. Cohen No 3 Sech started at ALLOUAGNE	Capt. E.F.S. Dawson leaves by permission to Chatham

Army Form C. 2118.

War Diary 23rd Field Co. R.E.
INTELLIGENCE SUMMARY
January 1916

Instructions regarding War Diaries and Intelligence Summaries are contained in F.S. Regns, Part II, and the Staff Manual respectively. Title pages will be prepared in manuscript.

Hour, date, place	Summary of Events and Information	Remarks and references to Appendices
LILLERS		
ALLOUAGNE		
18/1/16	Section drill 8.30 - 9 a.m. Work on Huts. Roads. W. Riding. O.C.S. Repairs to Billets. Clearing up stables etc. Drill in afternoon 1.45 p - 2.30 troops only	
19/1/16	Drill 8.30. 9 a.m. - 3 Sections horses 9.15 - 12.30. Practice Parade of 23rd Fd Co R.E. with 2nd Inf Bde - 4 Sections with 4 Tool Carts paraded at 2.30 p - march to Inspection ground near PHILOMEL CHATEAU	# Lt Cohen marches in from ALLOUAGNE with L.J. No 3 in afternoon
20/1/16	Drill 8.30. 9 a.m. - 4 Sections 9.15 - 11.30 a.m. horses 12.25 p.m. Parade 1.50 p.m. 4 Sections Section Tool Carts march to Inspection Ground PHILOMEL CHATEAU - for Inspection with 2nd Inf Bde by Allied C-in-C General Joffre. Return to billets by 5.20 p.m.	# Lt Cohen. Section No 3 march back to ALLOUAGNE 6.30 p.m
21/1	Huts. Roads. Stables etc. Repairing billets. Sunday Bde Div Ints Painting Tool carts etc	
22/1	7.10 - 7.30 a.m. Running Exercises for entire Coy. 8.30 - 9 a.m. Drill. Huts. Roads etc as above Contd.	" Lt Cohen w. S.C. 3 relieved by " Lt Pettitts " Section No 1 at ALLOUAGNE. Promoted Pioneers of 1st Bde. Lt Edwards reports for duty from 1st DE

Army Form C. 2118.

Instructions regarding War Diaries and Intelligence Summaries are contained in F.S.Regns, Part II, and the Staff Manual respectively. Title pages will be prepared in manuscript

War Diary 23rd Field Co. R.E.
INTELLIGENCE SUMMARY or
January 1916

Hour, date, place		Summary of Events and Information	Remarks and references to Appendices
LILLERS - ALLOUAGNE			
	23/1	7.10 – 7.30 a.m. Running Exercise. 6.30 – 9 a.m. Drill. Work on Huts. Roads Anti?	
	24/1	As above	
	25/1	As above	
	26/1	As above. Guard ditches to Canal at P.20 & huts 35.a to take over Positions at from XIII Div. Wd returned in from XV Div found under orders to remain.	
	27/1	Lectures 2 + 3 paraded 8.15 a.m. marched to Canal P.20 for Pontoon Instruction returning in afternoon by motor lorries. L.Cpl. 4. hit posted posted 1 on Huts Road West Riding C.C.S. Lillers	
	28/1	As on 27th inst. Officers from 1st Divl. School inspected P.E. Pool and equipment etc (also Pontooning on Canal.	11 Lt Salmon with 20 men & Cpl 2 march to Allouagne in evening to relieve 11 Protective Cpl No 1 with Proven Convoy
	29/1	Sects. 1 + 4 march to Canal for Pontoon drill, return in afternoon by bus Cpl 3 Sections & Cpl 2 in Huts, roads begin painting etc	
	30/1	As above	

Army Form C. 2118.

Instructions regarding
War Diaries and Intelligence Summaries
are contained in F.S.Regns, Part II,
and the Staff Manual respectively.
Title pages will be prepared in manuscript

23rd Field Coy RE

War Diary
or
INTELLIGENCE SUMMARY

January, 1916

Hour, date, place	Summary of Events and Information	Remarks and references to Appendices
LILLERS 31/1/16	Sect No 1 parade 8 am & marched to BURSURE for rifle Practice on Range. Sect No 4 on Hutts, Roads etc. Sect No 3. bridging in N.R.C.C.S. pond, hut held on trestle etc.	2 Lt Salmon proceeds Power Instruction Class at ALLOUAGNE & returns. 2 Lt LILLERS in afternoon

Moordonagh Capt RE
O.C. 23rd (W) Coy RE
2/2/16

1st Divisional Engineers

—————

23rd FIELD COMPANY R. E. :: FEBRUARY 1916

D.A.G.
 G.H.Q.

   War Diary of 23rd (Field) Coy. R.E.,
for February, 1916, forwarded for retention.

                                    [signature]
                                  Captain R.E.
           Commanding 23rd (Fld.) Coy. R.E.

H 3/16

Army Form C. 2118.

War Diary
or
INTELLIGENCE SUMMARY

23rd Field Coy. RE
February 1916

Hour, date, place	Summary of Events and Information	Remarks and references to Appendices
LILLERS		
1/2	Sct No 2 paraded 9 am marched to BURBURE to taped practice No 1 on Wilding trestle. Bridging experiments on W.R.C.C.S. pond No 3 on huts etc No 4 Road etc.	
2/2	Sct No 3 on Range & Trestling Carpenters of other Scts on Huts Balance Road etc.	
3/2	Sct No 4 Musketry 2 Trestling Other Sections on Huts Road	
4/2	Huts Road etc	
5/2	Inspection of 3 Field Coys by G.O.C. 1st Dn	
6/2	Church Service + morning Works in afternoon	
7/2	Divisional march for whole Coy. less details	
8/2	Works	Lt Cohen + 2 men for Lebrun to Les Brebis
9/2	Sct 1. Route march 2 Squad entrenched under shell + bullets + Gas attack Works	

Army Form C. 2118.

Instructions regarding
War Diaries and Intelligence Summaries
are contained in F.S.Regns,Part II,
and the Staff Manual respectively.
Title pages will be prepared in manuscript.

WAR DIARY or INTELLIGENCE SUMMARY

23rd Field Coy R.E.
February 1916

Hour, date, place		Summary of Events and Information	Remarks and references to Appendices
LILLERS	10/2	No 2 Sect. Route March. 1 Drill. Lecture Works - Baths	2nd Lt Cohen returned to LILLERS
	11/2	No 3 Sect. Route March Road	
	12/2	Pontoons taken to NOEUX LES MINES & left there under guard 2nd Lt Patterson & 1 L.Cpl 1 K LES BREBIS wagons returning to LILLERS same night. No 1 Section under Lt. Pilkington to LES BREBIS by bus	
	13/2	Road etc	2nd Lt T.A. Street (10"Glos) attached from 1st Do Officers School
	14/2	do	2nd Lt. H. Orr 10"Glos } attached with numerous 2nd Lt. Morris 8" Berks
LES BREBIS	15/2	"Demonstrated" by train to NOEUX LES MINES 8.10 a.m thence march to Billet in LES BREBIS h/d Section etc. by road to LES BREBIS 8.30 a.m. - 2 p.m.	2nd Lt Salmon with L.cpl No 2 & LOOS with 2 lt 2nd Lt Pilkington. L.J. No 4
LOOS	16/2	2 Sections on Defences of LOOS under Commandant of LOOS One Section on Fosse No 2 Road Billet Repairs platho etc	
	17/2	LOOS Defences cont'd Fosse No 2 Road Cont'd Repairs to Billet stables etc to lead... — Wired party to Tenth Inspector ?..	2nd Lt Street detached from 23rd Fd Co R.E. 2nd Lt. Orr (10" Glos) to LOOS with 2nd Division

Army Form C. 2118.

Instructions regarding
War Diaries and Intelligence Summaries
are contained in F.S. Regs, Part II,
and the Staff Manual respectively.
Title pages will be prepared in manuscript.

War Diary
or
INTELLIGENCE SUMMARY

23rd Field Coy R.E.

February 1916

Summary of Events and Information

Hour, date, place		Remarks and references to Appendices
LES BREBIS LOOS		
18/2	Loos Defences Cont'd. Lt No 3 Strengthening & improving Front Line Wire from CARFAX RD to HAYMARKET, North of DOUBLE CRASSIER. Forming No 2 Road Cont'd. Wind gauges etc.	Capt. Gentry Buck (8th Bucks) attached from 1st Div. School.
19/2	Loos Defences Cont'd. Shots of Wire pickets etc made at forward line near Carfax Rd. & Connection with Front Line Wiring. Wind Gauges etc.	" 2nd Horne Wilkinson with #3 attached Gds. Bdes. Mining to 173rd R.E.
20/2	Loos Defences Cont'd. Front Line Wiring Cont'd near Carfax Rd. Wiring on Forming No 2 Road. Revetment last from Rly Siding to road. Front gauges etc. Ammo metallic - Mine Building. Repairs to Billets etc etc.	
21/2	Loos Defences Cont'd. Forming No 2 Road. Trucks of Stone fired metal unloaded from Rly. Siding during night. Cleaning up Billet Roads etc. Making Tin Trench hole to Maloo - Surface Frames etc	Capt. McKerley R.E. slightly wounded by shell (at duty)
22/2	Loos Defences Cont'd. W Let Wiring front line Haymarket to Regent St. Western from No 2 Road with No Infantry - Contg. etc etc	" Smith & Latham with Let No 3 - after having - to billets in Loos.

Army Form C. 2118.

Instructions regarding War Diaries and Intelligence Summaries are contained in F.S.Regns, Part II, and the Staff Manual respectively. Title pages will be prepared in manuscript

War Diary or Intelligence Summary

23rd Field Coy RE
February 1916

Hour, date, place	Summary of Events and Information	Remarks and references to Appendices
LES BREBIS		
23/2	Loos Defences Contd. Fosse No 2 Road - Stone from trucks + by rail taken by tram line to road. Making Sniping Loop hole Fence. Iron number plates et.	(i) Lt Pottinger Sect 1 to Les Brebs from Loos. (ii) Lt Smith Sect 3 to Loos. Capt Gentry Birch (8" Berks) to 1st Divn.
24/2	Loos Defences Contd. 100 Inf hockey in Fosse No 2 Road Carting Stone & not drawing, making up holes etc. Horses Brands Shifting loop holes as cont. Repairing Stables, billets etc	1st Lt to Loos
25/2	Loos Defences Contd. Billets changed to Loos. Repairs to Stables at Sunday jobs done at Divl Amm.	(i) Lt Vandin, Sect 4 to Loos relieving (ii) Lt Salmon Sect No 2.
26/2	Loos Defences Contd. Working on Fosse No 2 Road Reconnaissance made of London Road Keep. Further alterations to Fosse No 2 Road except. Repair alterations to Div Clo being made. Carting bricks for General repairs et. Sniping Post loop hole has been made.	Lt Edwards (Sct 1 DE) leaves Coy Sick.
27/2	Loos Defences Contd. Number Plates with boards made North on Fosse No 2 Road etc Trench Number Plates made to road et Clearing up + maintaining roads in Les Brebis	

Army Form C. 2118.

Instructions regarding
War Dairies and Intelligence Summaries
are contained in F.S.Regns, Part II,
and the Staff Manual respectively.
Title pages will be prepared in manuscript.

War Diary
or
INTELLIGENCE SUMMARY

23rd Field Coy R.E.
February 1916

Hour, date, place	Summary of Events and Information	Remarks and references to Appendices
LES BREBIS 28/2	Loos Defences Cont'd. Repairing trolly rail-at Div. Batts. Alterations & repairs Cont'd at Div. Club. Making Dugouts top hot tries french plates &c	Lt. Forman (I.R.H) from Div. Off'rs School attached 1 25 Feb to Coy R.E
29/2	Loos Defences Cont'd. Repairing trolley rails at Div. Batts. alterations & repairs at Div. Club. Making Trench plates for Front Line. Cutting bricks for Incinerators. Cleaning maintaining roads in Les Brebis. Assembling Dome Aerator Shed troughing & casting to trial.	

Munsbury
Captain R.E.
Commanding 23rd (Fld.) Coy. R.E.

1st Divisional Engineers

23rd FIELD COMPANY R.E. :: MARCH 1916.

D.A.A.

G.H.Q. 3rd Echelon.

War Diary 23rd (Field)
Co. R.E., for March 1916 forwarded herewith.

Vol XVIII

2.4.16.

for Commanding 23rd (Field) Co. R.E.

Army Form C. 2118.

Instructions regarding
War Dairies and Intelligence Summaries
are contained in F.S.Regns,Part II,
and the Staff Manual respectively.
Title pages will be prepared in manuscript

23rd Field Coy. R.E.
War Diary or Intelligence SUMMARY
March 1916

Hour, date, place		Summary of Events and Information	Remarks and reference to Appendices
Les Brebis Loos	1/3	Loos Defences contd. Other work as before. Constructing experimental "Bangalore" Torpedo.	
	2/3	Working on Harrison's "Harts" Craters. Les Brebis work as above. Work on Russian Sap & forward line contd.	Sections in Loos lately now left sector and hut from 23rd Field Coy. Capt Holden R.M.F. & Mmers formerly hut 26th Fd Co. transferred to 23-Fd Co. R.E. for work on Russian Sap.
	3/3	Work on Harrison's "Harts" Craters contd. Russian Sap contd. Les Brebis work as before.	Lt Forman (1" R.H.) finishes his period of attachment to 23rd Fd Co. R.E. & Lt. Orr. to Les Brebis.
	4/3	Work on Harrison's "Harts" Craters contd. Russian Sap. Direction checked & corrected. Total length 129'. Other work as above.	" Lt Ware (L.N.L) from IV.School attached to 23rd Fd Co R.E. " Lt Pollection Lt No1 relieves " Lt Smart Let No 3 in Loos.
	5/3	Contd work on Harrison's "Harts" Craters & Russian Sap. Other work as above.	
	6/3	As above	" Lt Salmon Let 2 relieves Lt Hamilton Let 4 in Loos

Army Form C. 2118.

War Diary

23rd Field Co. RE
March 1916

INTELLIGENCE SUMMARY

Instructions regarding War Diaries and Intelligence Summaries are contained in F.S. Regns, Part II, and the Staff Manual respectively. Title pages will be prepared in manuscript.

Summary of Events and Information

Hour, date, place		Summary of Events and Information	Remarks and references to Appendices
LES BREBIS LOOS	7/3	Harrisons Crater. Preparing for sinking shafts. Dissemination flying Fixed wire in front. Harts Crater. Heavy Shells f. R.S. Street in timber framing completed. Deepening Saps etc. Russian Sap Contd. Les Brebis - Stores, Roads, etc -- Strong Wire Entanglement made f. German mill, Kt tests with B. torpedo. Recons. made for alternative London Road tree - Maroc.	
	8/3	Contd. work in Craters, Russian Sap. Shells + Hts to crater tree "removed" by direct Minenwerfer (W) hit. Specially erected entanglement Charge 18" B. torpedo fired + heavy electric - had 2 feet did not explode - entry use almost being used. Other track line work as usual.	1st Lt Nare (L.N.L.) transfer to Record of attachment to 23rd Fld Co RE. Capt Whitley (R.W.F.) Fld Coy fr 175 tr Bgde Brebis.
	9/3	Work stopped in Russian Sap. Harrisons Craters. Strong shells f. R.S. Street newly completed. Harts Crater Shells half rebuilt Other work as before.	2nd Lt Ott (10"Glo.) tr Loos in charge of Russian Sap.
	10/3	Work in Harrisons + Harts Craters Contd. Deep Dug out started in Regent St. by Miners. Back work as above. Finishing hut sockets for attached miners	2nd Lt Morris (8" Border) trd Miners from 173rd Co RE tr 23rd Fld Co RE
	11/3	Work in Craters, D.D. out Contd. Back work as before.	2nd Lt Harmer (2nd Welsh) att. 23rd Fld Co RE fr work with Miners. At Miners t Loos (tr relieve those formerly in Russian Sap)

Army Form C. 2118.

Instructions regarding
War Diaries and Intelligence Summaries
are contained in F.S. Regns, Part II,
and the Staff Manual respectively.
Title pages will be prepared in manuscript

War Diary
or
INTELLIGENCE SUMMARY

23rd Field C. RE
March 1916

Hour, date, place	Summary of Events and Information	Remarks and references to Appendices
LES BREBIS – LOOS		
12/3	Work on Craters – D. Day not contd. Other work as before.	Capt Holden (R.W.F.) from att. 23rd Fd C.R.E. to "Hants Army Troops Co."
13/3	Work on Craters – D. Day as contd. Les Brebis work as above. On Harts Crater during the period to which the Coy. was working two strong Bomber Shelters & long further framing with double roof of R.S. Joists. Were made in addition to the work of maintaining bombers trench approach sap & the construction of long traverses. On Harrisons Crater a Bombers shelter & strong constructed. On Jas & Third + Harts Crater was established, heavy traverses made, etc. in addition to ordinary trench clearing.	Average 1/120 attached miners + "Carriers" working on Deep Dug out under "attached" officer. Vide Appendix A
14/3	Loos Defences — working on the various keeps. Rgenl St. D Day and M.G. 29½ contd. (R. shaft damaged by minenwerfer) Les Brebis work as before.	23rd Fd C. relieve 26th Fd C. on Loos Defences – Iron loophole & Craters being returned by 2 Sections of 26th Fd C.R.E. Lt. Adam–Eaton No 3 relieve Lt. Patterson Fd. No 1, in Loos.

– 1 –

Army Form C. 2118.

War Diary 23rd Field Co. R.E.
INTELLIGENCE SUMMARY March 1916

Hour, date, place	Summary of Events and Information	Remarks and references to Appendices
Les Brebis - Loos		
15/3	Loos Defences Contd. Report D. Dug outs contd. Les Brebis Digging trench for Pipe line for Auxiliary water Supply. from L.35.B.18 Towards Power Station L.29.B.23. About 300 yards dug. (Sappers from 3 Fld Co. Pioneers digging) Other work as before.	
16/3	Loos Defences Contd. Deep Dug outs M 6 C 29½ Contd. do M 6 B 59½ started. Pipe line Contd. - about 250 x dug. Other work as before.	
17/3	Loos Defences Contd. D Dug outs at M 6 29½. ~ M 6 B 59½ Contd. Pipe line trench completed - about 600 x in all. Other work as before.	"W" stores (1", 6 lbs.) attached to 23rd Field Co.RE. for work into mines. Lt. Vanstone Sect N° 4 to relieve Lt. Salmon Sect N° 2. in Loos. One Sapper wounded in Loos.
18/3	Loos Defences Contd. Dug outs Contd. Other work as before	

Army Form C. 2118.

Instructions regarding
War Diaries and Intelligence Summaries
are contained in F.S.Regns,Part II.
and the Staff Manual respectively.
Title pages will be prepared in manuscript.

War Diary
INTELLIGENCE SUMMARY

23rd Field. Coy. R.E.
March 1916

Hour, date, place	Summary of Events and Information	Remarks and references to Appendices
Les Brebis –		
19/3	Loos Defences Contd. Dug outs M 6 C.29½, M 6 B 59½ Cont^d On "Village Line" Completed two M.G.Es N°s 11, 12. Maintenance & Harrow Road Cont^d Making Bomb Boxes Road number frame Platio	
20/3	Loos Defences Contd Dug outs Cont^d Road maintenance at Cont^d	
21/3	Loos Defences Cont^d Dug outs " Les Brebis work as before	2/Lt ――― returned from Loos
22/3	As above – A few Sappers instructing Infantry in wiring Recom. made of Quality of Defences & Village Line.	
23/4	Loos Defences Dug outs Cont^d Section working on Village Line. M.G.E's N°s 10A & 11A. Road maintenance et as before.	2/Lt Pilkerton & Lt N°1 relieve Lt Cockram. Lt N°3 + Loos.

Army Form C. 2118.

War Diary
or
INTELLIGENCE SUMMARY

23rd Field Coy R.E.
March 1916

Instructions regarding War Diaries and Intelligence Summaries are contained in F.S. Regns, Part II, and the Staff Manual respectively. Title pages will be prepared in manuscript.

Hour, date, place	Summary of Events and Information	Remarks and references to Appendices
Les Brebis – Loos		
24/3	Loos Defences – Dug. outs cont'd. Sapheads in H.W.E. "Village Line" Maroc. Road maintenance cont'd	Lt Cohen accompanied G.O.C. 170o on inspection of H.W.E.
25/3	Loos Defences – Dug. out cont'd. H.W.E. "Village Line". Maroc. Cont'd. Road maintenance cont'd. Making manure incinerators	" Lt Smith v Cpl No 2 relieve Lt Vanstone Lt No 4 in Loos. " Lt Murro returns to Les Brebis from Loos temporarily relieved by Lt Bisby 8th Berks. (S.Sgt Mortimer - 3 horses killed, 3 wounded, 5 horses) to Les Brebis estab.
26/3	Loos Defences Cont'd. Regent St Dug. out M 6 c 29½ finished Seaforth Alley " M 6 B 59½ cont'd. Road maintenance cont'd.	" Lt Murro (2nd Berks) proceeds on leave
27/3	Loos Defences Cont'd. Seaforth Alley Dug out cont'd M 6 B 59½ South Cp. " " M 5 B 48. Road maintenance cont'd. Fitting footways on mine Bridging & road incinerators.	
28/3	Loos Defences cont'd. Dug. outs cont'd M 6 B 59½ + M 5 B 46. Road maintenance cont'd. Making manure incinerators	" Lt Smith on leave (later than 30 up 6) " Lt Orr to Loos relieving " Lt Wale. Lt Vanstone r Loos relieving " Lt Smith

Army Form C. 2118.

Instructions regarding
War Dairies and Intelligence Summaries
are contained in F.S.Regns, Part II,
and the Staff Manual respectively.
Title pages will be prepared in manuscript

War Diary
or
INTELLIGENCE SUMMARY

23rd Field Coy R.E.
March 1916

Hour, date, place	Summary of Events and Information	Remarks and references to Appendices
Les Brebis - Loos 29/3	Loos Defences Contd. Deep Dug outs Contd. Road maintenance &c - Contd.	
30/3	Loos Defences Contd. Deep Dug outs Contd. Clearing out & trying timing cellars in North Maroc for use by Rennie Coton. Revetments Lovant. Road maintenance Contd.	
31/3	Loos Defences Contd. Dug outs Contd. M 6 B 59½ and M 5 B ≠ 8. Reconnaissance made for Baterloos Ry from Artillery Row Maroc into Loos. Road maintenance &c Contd.	2/Lt Statt relieves 2/Lt Binsley in Loos.

R Rumcher (Captain) R.E.
O.C. 23rd (Field) Coy R.E.
2.4.1916

Appendix A

To C.R.E.
1st Division

I have noted with great pleasure the good work done by Nos. 1 & 2 Sections of the 23rd (oy) R.E. on North & Harrison Craters and the soldierly spirit which induced these two Sections to volunteer to continue the work rather than be relieved so as to avoid the waste of time involved in carrying out such Relief.

Special Credit is due to the two Officers Commanding the above Sections viz Lieuts Potterton & Salmon.

A Holland
Major General
Comdg 18th Division

20/3/16

1st Divisional Engineers

23rd FIELD COMPANY R. E. :: ~~MAY~~ *April* 1916.

23rd (FIELD) COMPANY
No. 64
MAY 1916
ROYAL ENGINEERS

D.A.S.
G.S.O.

War Diary, 23rd (Field) Co. R.E., for month of April 1916 herewith.

1st May, 1916.

Humphrey
Captain R.E.
Commanding 23rd (Fld.) Coy. R.E.

Army Form C. 2118.

Instructions regarding
War Diaries and Intelligence Summaries
are contained in F.S.Regns, Part II,
and the Staff Manual respectively.
Title pages will be prepared in manuscript

War Diary
or
INTELLIGENCE SUMMARY

23rd Field Coy. R.E.
April 1916

Hour, date, place	Summary of Events and Information	Remarks and references to Appendices
Les Brebis - Loos		
1/4	Loos Defences contd. Support Alley Dug out M6 B59½ } Continued. Sapt. St. Dug out M5 B9-28 } Road maintenance ch. contd.	Lt. Cohen, C.J. No 3 relieve " Lt. Pilkerton C.J No 1 in Loos.
2/4	As above. Bakerloos Ry extended from Artillery Row. maure towards Loos.	
3/4	As above	" Lt. Bradey to Loos to relieve " Lt. Orr.
4/4	Loos Defences contd. Dug out contd. Bakerloos Ry up to Old British Line. Shifting cellars in maure for use of Gorrie Lector. Road maintenance contd. French name plates, trench boards etc contd	" Lt. Vanston C.J No 4 relieve " Lt. Salmon C.J No 2 in Loos
5/4	Loos Defences Contd. Then work as before	" Lt. Morris returns from leave

Army Form C. 2118.

Instructions regarding War Diaries and Intelligence Summaries are contained in F.S.Regns, Part II, and the Staff Manual respectively. Title pages will be prepared in manuscript.

War Diary
INTELLIGENCE
or
SUMMARY

23rd Field Coy. RE
April 1916

Hour, date, place	Summary of Events and Information	Remarks and references to Appendices
Les Brebis – Loos		
4/4	Loos Defences Cont'd. Seaforth Alley dug out M6 B 57½ Cont'd South-SI. dug out M5 B 49. Waterloos Ry about 250' beyond O.B.1. Cast-iron pushing piece inside in Road No 2 Road at L 34 B 72. Shutting & minor Reserve Lieut Allens continued Trench hunter plates, front lines at cont'd	4/4 Capt Leyton O/C & adjt at Intelligence Headqrs at Loos. " 2/Lt Bradley paying his Batln in Loos. " " Slater to Le Brebis. " Smith returning from leave
7/4	Loos Defences Cont'd. Firing charges laying leads for mining Wrexham Tunnel under Loos Crassier. Seaforth Alley Dug out cont'd South (J.) Dug out " Posts Start made with Listening Posts Waterloos Ry cont'd at N 34 C 85 material for Lens Crossing cont'd & Lens Road. at etc	" 2/Lt Smith to Loos. " "
8/4		Lt Cohen returns to Les Brebis " Hamilton " Le Brebis " Pritteston " Loos. Capt Mackey proceeds to Hq 1st DE to act as CRE. Capt Wilson assumes command of 23rd Coy

Army Form C. 2118.

Instructions regarding
War Diaries and Intelligence Summaries
are contained in F.S.Regns, Part II,
and the Staff Manual respectively.
Title pages will be prepared in manuscript

War Diary
or
INTELLIGENCE SUMMARY

23rd Div Coy RE
April 1916.

Hour, date, place	Summary of Events and Information	Remarks and references to Appendices
Les Brebis & Loos		
9/4	Loos Defences contd. Reports Alley dugout M.6.6.59½ contd. South Street dugout M.5.6.48 } contd. Bakerloos Railway contd. Listening Posts Commenced {I. M.6.6.½.5 / J. M.6.6.46 / K. M.6.6.57	
10/4	Loos defences contd. Listening posts contd. {I. M.6.6.½.5 / J. M.6.6.46 / K. M.6.6.57 Trench number plates - Vent pipes for Dugouts contd. Bakerloos Ry. contd. Loos defences contd. Listening posts contd. {I. M.6.6.½.5 / J. M.6.6.46 / K. M.6.6.57	
11/4	Bakerloos Railway contd. Mining cases - Vent pipes for dugouts - Trench mortar plates etc. contd.	No 1 Section relieves No 3 Section at Loos. No 3 Section returns to Les Brebis. " Lt Smith takes command of No 4 Section " Lt Polladian " No 1 Section " Lt Smith accompanies Corps Commander on inspection of Mr 9 & E's Loos " Lt Brewis 10 D Plowden leaves Capt Whitaker's reports for attachment Black Watch

Army Form C. 2118.

Instructions regarding
War Diaries and Intelligence Summaries
are contained in F.S.Regns, Part II,
and the Staff Manual respectively.
Title pages will be prepared in manuscript.

War Diary
or
INTELLIGENCE SUMMARY

23rd Field Coy. R.E.
April 1916

Hour, date, place	Summary of Events and Information	Remarks and references to Appendices
Ex Bulin & Loos		
12/4	Loos Defences contd. Listening Posts contd. { I. M.6645 / J. M.6646 / K. M.6657.	2 Lt STEELE to Loos. " ORR to Les BREBIS.
	Bakerloos Ry continued. Completed hant junction with LENS Rd. Supervising digging of new Reserve Line from CARFAX RD to SOUTH ST. between Points. Hand number Plates - Vents for dugouts - mine cases &c. contd.	Capt MULLOCKS - Blackwatch returns to his unit.
13/4	Loos DEFENCES contd. Listening posts contd. { I. M.6645 / J. M.6646 / K. M.6657. making preparation to start. Port L.	[signed]
	Boxes of R.E.distributed too KEEPS and receipts obtained. Constructing passing places on BAKERLOOS RAILWAY. Branch line to POSE 5 commenced. mining cases, trellis &c contd.	
14/4	Loos Defences contd. Listening posts contd. { I. M.6645 / J. M.6646 / K. M.6657 / L.	Lt SPENCER and No 2 Section go to Loos relieving 404 Section and 11th SMITH who return to Les BREBIS
	Salvaging trucks BAKERLOOS RAILWAY. mining Cases contd. making frames for hand proof Shelter -	

Army Form C. 2118.

Instructions regarding
War Diaries and Intelligence Summaries
are contained in F.S. Regns, Part II,
and the Staff Manual respectively.
Title pages will be prepared in manuscript.

War Diary
or
INTELLIGENCE SUMMARY

23rd Field Coy R.E.
April 1916

Hour, date, place	Summary of Events and Information	Remarks and references to Appendices
Coy HdQrs. LOOS		

15/4	LOOS Defences cont'd.
	Listening posts cont'd. I M66b25
	                                 J M66b46
	                                 K M66b57
	                                 L	

16/4	BAKERLOO Ry. cont'd
	Junction with E way.
	Branch line FOSSE 5 cont'd
	Mine cars cont'd - Filling hole HARROW Rd
	Carting stores to LOOS
	Vent pipes fixed in new dug out SEAFORTH ALLEY
	LOOS DEFENCES cont'd
	Listening posts cont'd I M66b25
	                                          J M66b46
	                                          K M66b57
	                                          L	

	BAKERLOO Ry. Carried to CHURCH ST. LOOS. Branch line on FOSSE 5 cont'd. 50ft completed. Carting stores to LOOS.	
17/4	LOOS DEFENCES (cont'd) Listening posts (cont'd) as above. LT. EDWARDS and 28 N.C.Os and men burning CRATER party stood by in battle station (SEAFORTH ALLEY) all night. BAKERLOO RAILWAY - Putting in bridges opening places to FOSSE 5 branch cont'd Strengthening cellars in HARROW for emergency billets. Making mine cars. Carting stores to LOOS.	LT. EDWARDS, 2/2nd.O.s + 5 J.hos + 3 Sections 15 " " 3 " 18 " N.O. " 3 }LOOS Capt Sasoon. R.A report for attachment from 1st officers School.

Army Form C. 2118.

Instructions regarding
War Dairies and Intelligence Summaries
are contained in F.S.Regns, Part II,
and the Staff Manual respectively.
Title pages will be prepared in manuscript

War Diary
or
INTELLIGENCE SUMMARY

23rd Field Coy. RE
April 1916

Hour, date, place	Summary of Events and Information	Remarks and references to Appendices
LES BREBIS + LOOS		
18/4	LOOS DEFENCES cont'd Listening posts on Loos Road work continued on FOSSE 5 Railway huts excavated work commenced on M.9.E5 - LENS RD Reserve Line Central Points to LOOS	1 N.C.O. and 6 saphers of No.4 Section to LOOS relieving 2 N.C.Os " 5 " " " " " LES BREBIS " LT ORR to LOOS " LT MORRIS to LES BREBIS.
19/4	LOOS DEFENCES cont'd Listening Points I.T.K.2 cont'd FOSSE 5 Railway cont'd M.9.E5 LENS RD cont'd Making Mine Cases, Bangalore Torpedoes - Bombay Loopholes.	Lic. EDWARDS and No 4. Section returns to LES BREBIS.
20/4	As above.	
21/4	As above.	i Lt. SMITH and the 3 Section to LOOS relieving ii Lt. POTTERTON and No 4 Section who return to LES BREBIS Lt. EDWARDS and 6 men from No.4 Section go to LOOS on special duty, including forming S D Posts and R.E. Store. Capt. R.N.Mackey returning to unknown command ceasing to act as O.C. iii Lt. RAMSDEN. R.M. returns for attached from Div. Officers School.
22/4	As above. Shaeftering colliers in MAROC -	
23/4	As above.	

Army Form C. 2118

WAR DIARY
or
INTELLIGENCE SUMMARY
(Erase heading not required.)

232nd Field Coy. R.E.
April 1916

Instructions regarding War Diaries and Intelligence Summaries are contained in F. S. Regs., Part II. and the Staff Manual respectively. Title Pages will be prepared in manuscript.

Place	Date	Hour	Summary of Events and Information	Remarks and references to Appendices
LES BREBIS and LOOS	29/4		Front defences contd. Work considerably hampered again by Enemy attack on the Divison in trenches before Garrison of D Keep again fired to. Salvaging gallerie contd. M9E3 LOOS R.O. contd. Breaking trench number plates – Preparing material of O.P. to be erected in NORTH ST. to take b.ff. telescope. B.H.Q. REGENT Ry. Rails from Q.O55 & taken into LOOS – Permit fixed for trap and rails into D Keep – 3 Pole N.C.O's. Revetting claw contd.	Lt EDWARDS to hospital at Boulogne for eye testing
	30/4		Rows defences contd. Pushing party J.I.K+L contd. BRESSLIES RD Branch to D Keep contd. Work again hampered by S.O.S. call at 11.15 p.m. Work continued on M.9.E3. CENSED. Stringlaying Callers at MAPPOS contd. making trench number plates – vend pieces – & filling caps to Kola for Keeps 1st Role Revetting claws – No. 1 claw finished & midday + No 2 claw starts in afternoon	N Lt. ORR returned to LES BREBIS being relieved Lieut by Lt. STEELE.

1st May 1916.

[signature]
Commanding 232nd (T) Field Coy. R.E.

1st Divisional Engineers

23rd FIELD COMPANY R.E. ::: MAY 1916.

Army Form C. 2118

WAR DIARY
or
INTELLIGENCE SUMMARY
(Erase heading not required.)

23rd Fd. Coy. R.E.
May 1916

M 20

Place	Date	Hour	Summary of Events and Information	Remarks and references to Appendices
LES BREBIS and LOOS	1/5		LOOS DEFENCES contd. BARBEROTS RY contd mang D Knob - Bridges made & fixed in position. Listening posts { J } continued { K } not being worked. Deep dugout starts in support line about M6A 94. LENS RD. M9E5 - galleries contd. Strengthening cellars in M9F30. Dismantling Decauville track from FOSSE 2 Rd, carting to BREBIS Station and unloading to LOOS. 1st Bde Revetting Class contd. Making experimental grate for use in proposed O.P. at G.33.d.5.1½. Collecting R.S.J.s above O.P. from O.C.1. Making trench ventilator, paper for dug outs & trench name plates.	No 3 Section to LOOS No 3 Section to LES BREBIS
	2/5		LOOS DEFENCES Quarry Dugout M6A94. } LENS RD M9E5 } As above 1st Bde revetting class Listening posts { J } continued { K } { L } Transporting Decauville track to railhead. Assembling material for O.P. at G.33.d.5.1½. Making trench number plates.	

Army Form C. 2118

WAR DIARY
or
INTELLIGENCE SUMMARY

23rd Fd. Coy. R.E.
May 1916

(Erase heading not required.)

Place	Date	Hour	Summary of Events and Information	Remarks and references to Appendices
LES BREBIS AND LOOS	3/5		LOOS DEFENCES contd. Listening posts. R. & contd. Domiciling 173rd Eng. R.E. in mine Quarry dugout. M. & A.q.u. contd. LENS RD M.9.E.5 contd. O.P. G.33.d. 1½ - work commenced and half R.E.'s 1½ placed on site. Making imitation stumps and brothers. Running chapel from STD site and repeating same.	
	4/5		LOOS DEFENCES Listening posts } as above QUARRY DUGOUT } LENS RD M.9.E.5 (work) O.P. G.33.d. 1½. - work continued and remainder of materials placed on job. Building temporary canteen at LES BREBIS. Preparing revised map of LOOS DEFENCES for COMMANDANT. Preparing diagram illustrating DOUBLE CRASSIER RAID for 1st Army. Filling materials for Loos keeps. Making hinch number plates &c.	No. 2 section to 6 crypts No. 4 section to LES BREBIS. Lt. Edwards invalided from Boulogne to England
	5/5		LOOS DEFENCES. LISTENING POSTS. QUARRY DUGOUT and LENS RD M.9.E.5 as above. O.P. G.33.d. 1½. - Overhead cover completed. traverse and loophole in position. Hurried safe to farm approved commenced. Repairing damage to BRICK ROWS Ry. Causer by shellfire. 4 Airy Vaults for Loos Building temporary canteen at LES BREBIS.	

WAR DIARY or INTELLIGENCE SUMMARY

Army Form C. 2118

2nd W R/S Coy RE
May 1916

Place	Date	Hour	Summary of Events and Information	Remarks and references to Appendices
LES BREBIS and LOOS	6/5		LOOS DEFENCES Listening posts ⎫ Quarry dugouts ⎬ as before Lens Rd M9Es ⎭ O.P. North Street G33 d 1/2 - contd. Back section - making chevaux de frises for Lens Rd M9Es otherwise as before.	" Lt MORRIS (8th R. BERKS) to LES BREBIS " 2nd Lt ORR (10th GLOSTERS) to LOOS
	7/5		LOOS DEFENCES Listening posts ⎫ as before Quarry Dugout ⎭ LENS RD M9Es - Gallerie completed and chambers commenced O.P. NORTH ST. contd. and handed over to R E Battn Back Section - Cadres finished - cleaning and repairing. Parties at Brit. Baths. Making trench elements - trench number plates &c BAKERLOOS R4 - Branch to R.E. store D. Keep completed	
	8/5		LOOS DEFENCES Listening posts ⎫ as before Quarry dugouts ⎭ Lens Rd M9Es O.P. NORTH ST. G 33 d 1/2. completed and handed over to Brit Front Officer. LES BREBIS. Repairing water supply. Repairing and fitting huts - making latrine seats and meat safes.	

Army Form C. 2118

WAR DIARY
or
INTELLIGENCE SUMMARY
(Erase heading not required.)

23rd F.Coy. R.E.
May. 1916.

Place	Date	Hour	Summary of Events and Information	Remarks and references to Appendices
LES BREBIS and LOOS.	9/5		Loos Defences. Listening posts } Continued Auxiliary dugout } LENS RD M.9.E.5 6 heavily mined chambers de fruise contd up and placed on LENS RD to screen work to be undertaken. LES BREBIS- making canvas trench shires.	
	10/5		As above.	Lt. INGLIS. 1st BLACK WATCH reports for attachment from Divl officers School.
	11/5		As above.	Lt. PALMTON returns from HOSPITAL LEBOURSIERE Lt. POTTERTON goes to LOOS 11 Lt. SMITH returns to LES BREBIS. No 3 Section to LOOS No 1 Section to LES BREBIS
	12/5		Loos defences. Listening posts K.1.L. } Continued Auxiliary dugout LENS RD M.9.E.5 Sapper work commenced. LES BREBIS.- making gas alert notifications in considerable quantities. making trench boxes- preparing skins for III 2nd BDE. M.G.Coy.	11 Lt SMITH goes to LOOS 11 Lt MORRIS goes to LOOS 11 Lt STEELE returns to LES BREBIS
	13/5		As above.	11 Lt SMITH to LOOS Lt PALMTON returns to Les Brebis

Army Form C. 2118

WAR DIARY
or
INTELLIGENCE SUMMARY
(Erase heading not required.)

23rd Field Coy RE
May, 1916

Instructions regarding War Diaries and Intelligence Summaries are contained in F. S. Regs., Part II. and the Staff Manual respectively. Title Pages will be prepared in manuscript.

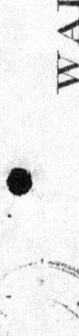

Place	Date	Hour	Summary of Events and Information	Remarks and references to Appendices
Les Brebis + Loos	14/5		Loos Defences Lens Road M.G.E.s Cont'd Listening Post K 115' / L 100' / H 10' / 13 } stopped. Quarry Dug-out - Les Brebis - making Trench frames, bomb boxes, mine cases, hand + rifle stop St.	
Les Brebis Loos + Calonne	15/5		Loos Defences cont'd. Lens Road M.G.E. Cont'd. Listening Post H - 19'6". Quarry Road Dug-out 19'. Les Brebis work as above.	Lt Pellestri + No 1 Section RE left to join to WW + Calonne to work with East Anglian RE.
	16/5.		Loos Defences. II Korps + all RE troops including M.G.E.s handed over to O.C. 11th Hants. Calonne Lotor Hocker Road. Tamworth Trench Building M.G.E.s to Angels Post Cont'd with E.A. R.E. Campbell tunnel + York St. O.P." Dug outs - 3 shafts started K 2 Dug-out in Tamworth Trench 8 " 4 Dug-out in Hocker Rd. Mazes Letov Lens Road M.G.E.s (model) landed + killed RE.	II Pellestri + Lt Smith relieve + the Brebis half Sections 2 + 3 Lt Brebis left at M. rumors "Lt" taken over + km Brebis rel. st. Mines Lt Solomon Sect No 2 + Calonne To rumors from La Brebis + Coronado. Left to La Brebis. Reconnaissance of rumors from Loos Defences handed over + 0/C 11th Hants.

Army Form C. 2118

WAR DIARY
or
INTELLIGENCE SUMMARY

(Erase heading not required.)

23rd Field Coy RE
May 1916

Place	Date	Hour	Summary of Events and Information	Remarks and references to Appendices
Les Brebis Calonne	17/5		Horton Road & Tamworth Trench Revetting Cont'd. M.G.Es - Ouget Post Cont'd. York St O.P. Cont'd Dug-outs in Tamworth Trench - Mata field Cont'd Amphill tunnel cont'd Les Brebis - Making trench frames, bomb boxes mine covers, chamber plates etc.	Pioneers moved to Calonne with lock billets in Carvenchy
	18/5		Horton Rd - Tamworth Trench mostly cont'd M.G.Es Ouget Post cont'd O.P., Dug outs & Amphill tunnel cont'd	Capt Mackeney to Calonne. Captain W. Edwards reports back from England
	19/5		As above + work on Dynamite tunnel	23rd Field Co R.E. took over work at Calonne Sector from East Anglian R.E.
	20/5		Horton Rd - Tamworth Trench mostly cont'd M.G.Es. Ouget Post 557. done Tunnel connecting above M.G.Es in hand Amphill - Dynamite tunnels cont'd York St O.P. cont'd - Dug out cont'd etc.	
	21/5		Horton Rd - Tamworth Trench mostly cont'd M.G.Es Ouget Post top down - Tunnel cont'd Amphill Tunnel driven 14'; Verbal Staff cont'd Dynamite 16'. O.P.'s Dug out cont'd Deepening front line trench to 4ft 9 Everitcho	Extra Defence Centre now up of 4 off. & 2nd Lts. & Lt Smith & Calonne with G.O. No. 3.

Army Form C. 2118

WAR DIARY
or
INTELLIGENCE SUMMARY

23rd Field Coy. R.E.

May 1916

(Erase heading not required.)

Place	Date	Hour	Summary of Events and Information	Remarks and references to Appendices
Les Brebis & Calonne	22/5		Horton Road Tamworth Trench Supply. Lt Cohen & O.R. to Bruchs instructing M.G.E.s Tunnel - Oxgells Post. 3 fire bays made 6" Welsh in Pioneer Work. O.P. York St. Cnstd Ampthill Tunnel 17' Driven - Cover over Vertical Shaft in hand Dynamite " 20 " Tamworth 1st Shaft 6' 2nd Shaft 9' Dug outs Denaston " 6' " 8' Horton Rd " 16' " 15' " 17' " 18'	
	23/5		Les Brebis Work as before Calonne Work as above Cnstd	
	24/5		Work as above Ampthill Tunnel 26' Shafts 11' and 16' Dug outs Tamworth " 9' " 11' Denaston " 16' " 19' Horton Rd. " 20 " 20 M.G.E. platf'm near Marble Arch Sapry Post started Road Tunnel started from Calonne Nord - X Calonne Sud.	
	25/5		Work as above H.Q. Street repairs in hand Western Land Defences	

Army Form C. 2118

WAR DIARY
or
INTELLIGENCE SUMMARY

23rd Field Co. R.E.
May 1916

(Erase heading not required.)

Place	Date	Hour	Summary of Events and Information	Remarks and references to Appendices
Les Brebis ↓ Calonne	24/5		Hooton Road & Tamworth Trench novelty Enft. M G E's at Orgels & Sapny Posts. O.P. York St. Made Enft M G E (Calonne N - K3 Tunnel) - 26' Ampthill Tunnel - 26' Dug-outs: Tamworth 16' + 23' / 15' 18' / Devaskin Tr. 23 23 / Hooton Rd. 21 20	Lt Vanstone Lt-Col No 2 ← Calonne relieving Lt Patterson Lt-Col No 1 who proceeds ← Les Brebis
	27/5		As above	← Lt Orr (att Honvers) goes on leave (10 : 6/60)
	28/5		As above Improving Front line Trenches near R & P.ip Corner M G E. Installed at foot of Bogan 10 Tunnel soon started to keep near Bogan 10. Gas Blanket fitted Hallard. Ampthill Tunnel 47' Dug-outs: Tamworth 19' + 23' / Devoplin Tr. 20 22 / 23 23 / Hooton Rd. 22 22 } Chambers started	

Army Form C. 2118

WAR DIARY
or
INTELLIGENCE SUMMARY

(Erase heading not required.)

23rd Field Co. RE
May 1916

Place	Date	Hour	Summary of Events and Information	Remarks and references to Appendices
Les Brebis Calonne	29/5		Hulton Road . Tamworth Trench Revetting &c. O.P. to York St. contd. Revetting Front Line near P.K. Prop. Corner + building Fire Bays. Dugout Covers near to Fire Bays Began 10. Work on Right Shaft Front Line contd. Pipe Line for Water Supply being advanced. M.G.E.s to Angels Post End of tail of Bryans 10 Contd. Gen. Haulot. York to Cellars Ampthill Tunnel driven 5' Dug outs: Tamworth Trench M 20 C 79 Right chamber started Left 3' 1½ Deviation Trench A 95 do 2½ Hulton Road M 15 A 82 Right chamber 2' Left 3' do. B 13 " 2' " 4' Road Tunnel Calonne Nord. Calonne Sud 90% done Les Brebis Section Fosse 11 Roofs (Supplying holts to Calonne &c.) being prob(?) by comoflaged(?) hutting &c. Pipe line being repaired. Tape fixed to trestle to hold it. Cutting RE. party to harness making Trench Stores &c. Painting. Lamp Maxtro(?) Photo.	11 Lt. Mannina k Calonne
	30/5		do above	herries hones from Cornado "Back Billet" to Bribis Lt. Roberts Sect. No. 1 " Ketelnne, relieving Lt. Hamelink " " Capt. Mackay k Les Brebis Lt. Edwards k Calonne Lt. Steele k hosp(?)til
	31/5		do above Staff mod bolts O.P. in Maistre Line	

1st Divisional Engineers

———————

23rd FIELD COMPANY R.E. :: JUNE 1916.

Army Form C. 2118

23rd Field Co. R.E.
June 1916

WAR DIARY
or
INTELLIGENCE SUMMARY
(Erase heading not required.)

Instructions regarding War Diaries and Intelligence Summaries are contained in F.S. Regs., Part II. and the Staff Manual respectively. Title Pages will be prepared in manuscript.

Place	Date	Hour	Summary of Events and Information	Remarks and references to Appendices
LES BREBIS CALONNE	1/6		Hoxton Road & Tamworth Trench improvements cont'd First two letters Barril Alley & Berry St. awaiting material "Burning Byng" - Revetting Durham Keep - Head Cover read at Loopholes, made in walls Rasora Line. Parapets improved, new firebays made Expt: Post - Improving trenches, entering N.G.E. Tunnel "A" Cellars in Dynamite House Started N.G.E. W. end of Bazar 10' cont'd Salt gallery Mansell bend filled & Cellars Amp.hill Tunnel driven 60' Maistre Tunnel " 7' Dug outs (a) Tamworth Trench N20 c79 Right chamber 3' Left 5' 60'. (b) Dermatin Trench H.93 5' 6' 80' (c) Hoxton Road M 15 A 82 3' 4' 90' (d) " " B.13 3' 5' 60' Les Bretons Sector Rose 11. Bomb bostts'n cont'd O.P. & Maistre Line cont'd Same numerous platters made - Trestles Cat lengths for houses Top f.H.O. Preparing trestles for light storage in Calonne Return of Coy to DN Brit'n hot water apparatus Preparing washing places at Calonne	Lt Bayliss (S N 5) from 2nd Aust'l A Troops to 23rd RE as attached Mining Officer Lt Vaseline R.J. & ? Calonne returning to N D Smith Sect 3. From Gazette of 3/6 (Capt Kilam - M.C. (S.N. Matheson - D.C.M.
	2/6		As above	
	3/6		As above Amphill Tunnel 68' Maistre " 12 Dug outs (a) Right 4'; Left 7' (b) " 7', 8' (c) " 10', 10 (d) " 4' 5	

Army Form C. 2118

WAR DIARY
or
INTELLIGENCE SUMMARY
(Erase heading not required.)

23rd Field Coy R.E.
June 1916

Place	Date	Hour	Summary of Events and Information	Remarks and references to Appendices
LES BREBIS CALONNE	4/6		As before	2Lt Stobb returns from Hospital (1st Gibro.)
	5/6		Ampthill Tunnel 72'. New tunnel at right Ls. "Maistre". Dug out (a) Tamworth Trench R. 4' L. 8' (b) Densley " 9' 9' (c) Houghton Road " 10' 10' (d) " 6' 6'	
	6/6		As above. O.P. in Maistre Line finished both going in & making Dug out for use with O.P.	
	7/6		As above	2Lt Smith & Lillie 3 returns Lt Salmon who's 2 in Les-Brebis
	8/6		Houston Road & Tamworth Trench — Revetting. Making Traverses. New Bays at "Burning Byng" Revetting with Expanded plates bricks hit Loks to sleeping Burrows deep. Bricked over & Fire Bays — two Traverses etc. R.E. batt. Store — Dynamite House improvements O.P. Maistre Line started & Seat & efforts — Dug out cont. MGEs at Angels — Begun 10 cont. & St started Ampthill Tunnel — Broken through & Calloux beyond Support Line. Maistre Tunnel — 20' from turning. Dug cut (a) Tamworth Tr. 85'. (b) Densley Tr. 70 (c) Houston Rd 90 Fort Ft. Sandbag Protection to Pump cult Div. Baths repair - Cell. Ballyelite. Racks bin Rolls — Trench Name Plate etc. making Ballyelite.	with 2Lt Stobb to Calonne relieving 2Lt Harris

Army Form C. 2118

WAR DIARY
or
INTELLIGENCE SUMMARY

(Erase heading not required.)

23rd Field Coy RE
June 1916

Place	Date	Hour	Summary of Events and Information	Remarks and references to Appendices
Les Brebis (Calonne)	9/6		Work as above.	Two Sections of 231st Coy RE (40th Div) attached to work in Calonne. [Stamp: 23rd FIELD COMPANY, JUL 1916, ROYAL ENGINEERS]
	10/6		Do. M.G.E. So stated	Capt Lumsden (1st R.H.) attended Div School.
	11/6		As above. 3 hrs day out slates. 3 hrs day out slabs	Lt Pollott, Sect No 1 & No 2 to les Brebis. Sect No 4 Calonne.
	12/6		As above. 1 hrs day out slates (see knowledge note dtd 14/6)	
	13/6		Hooton Road – Tambsitt Tunnel – Bunning Bag – Dinsdam Keep – Really out 1 cult. M.G.E.s – Bryan 10 ; So (L. Bryan 13) cult. Manetts Tunnel cult. Dug out a, b, c, d practically finished. W Maddison posn Back 9 – Maddison – Emergency Post, shot I the filled in. 3 hrs day out slabs. Work as From No 11 cult.	25 Br.
	14/6		As above. Began Thomas – Dwelling, making keep held known at. Removing more food from Amplified Tunnel. Making both held known to tunnel. Cutting New from Amplified shaft to Morgan allies. Dug out a Bancroft 1st. 5 Hugh (Bryan 12) 5/1. b Bancroft 7? 5 Rifle 3 c Hunter 7? 3 R.A. 2 3 Maneths Tunnel cult. From 11 work cult.	Capt Lumsden (1st R.H.) to 1st Bde.

Army Form C. 2118

WAR DIARY
or
INTELLIGENCE SUMMARY

(Erase heading not required.)

23rd (Field) Coy RE
June 1916

Place	Date	Hour	Summary of Events and Information	Remarks and references to Appendices
LES BREBIS CALONNE	15/6		Hulin Road, Tamwork Trench, Burning Ring, Durham Keep - Revetting etc with N.G.E. Railway Bridge over Bryan Thomas blown up	Lt Pellat Jun, Sect N°1 k Calonne Lt Vanestine Sect N°4 k Rue Brebis
			N.G.E. { S1 Tunnel S6 Tunnel cont. N°5 Emplacement founded N°3 Road in site S7 R1 Collecting materials for brick work	transferred in disposition 15/6 { Lt Estevants Lt Salmon Capt Perfitt
			Posts for Lewis Gun - Air Rifle cont from Bon Tunnel under tracks New Support Line - Cellars being cut through not finish Boyan Thomas First Final Cellars all cont Cutting through from Bangalore Shaft at Morgan French cellars. Dug out { (a) Houston Road (Bryan 12) 25' (b) 20 (c) 15	
	16/6		Frost 11 - work cont Bangalore Torpedoes. "Fred" Basket tunnel to hand	Lt Vanestine k RFC.
			As above Maistre Tunnel 70' from Maistre Line k Calonne Nord finished	
	17/6		As above Dug out { (a) 35'/ (b) 35 (c) 20 Calonne Road maintenance As above	
	18/6			Lt Vanestine returns from RFC
	19/6		Cdr. New Support Line started with 160 Inf.	

Army Form C. 2118

WAR DIARY
or
INTELLIGENCE SUMMARY

23rd Field Coy. R.E.
June 1916

(Erase heading not required.)

Place	Date	Hour	Summary of Events and Information	Remarks and references to Appendices

LES BREBIS CALONNE	20/6		Hooton Road & Tamnorth Trench - New harness Gulls & Revetting Gulls.
			Burning Byng - Revetting Gulls.
			Durham Wep. - Two bays revetted with Unolied Can.
			5 bays in hand - Revetting Gulls.
			
			Work carried on New Support Line.
			Tunnelling from Ampthill Shaft to Cellars.
			Fitting Cuts 900 planks. Morgan Tracks Cellars.
			Boyau Thomas Revetting and fire bay tunnelling trench.
			Cleaning out trench under locked Bridge.
			
			M.G.E. No 5. Tunnel Gulls.
			R. Brick walls Gulls.
			
			Dug outs (a) Boyau 12 N15a 61½ 60%
			          (B) Sap E M20B 2F 55
			          (G) R.A.2 11½ 40
			
			Ventilation pipes fitted to A.B.C & D.
			Force 11. Overhead protection to pump Gulls.
			Calonne Road maintenance Cont? - Cutting metalled.
				JUL 1916
				23rd FIELD COMPANY
				ROYAL ENGINEERS

	21/6		As above N.G.E. No 3 in hand	
	22/6		do do	

	23/6		As above N.G.Es. 3, 5 M.G. Gulls
			                        (6) 75%
			Dug outs (B) 70%
			                        (9) 60%
			
			(b) New Bttn HQ & Temple W. Shelter
				" Lt Stott from Les Brebis to Calonne
				" Lt Baylis Calonne to Les Brebis
				
				Lt Vanstone - Lt Not to Calonne returning
				" Lt Smith - Lt No 2 - to Les Brebis

Army Form C. 2118

WAR DIARY
or
INTELLIGENCE SUMMARY

(Erase heading not required.)

23rd Field Coy R.E.   June 1916

23RD (FIELD) COMPANY — JUL. 1916 — ROYAL ENGINEERS

Place	Date	Hour	Summary of Events and Information	Remarks and references to Appendices
LES BREBIS CALONNE	24/6		Burning Bring- Contt, New Support-Line Contt - Shutting Cellars in New Support Line - Filling Anti Gas Blankets. Bryan Thomas dwelling built. N.G.E. Nr B, 5 + R1 Contd. C3 start. Dug out (a) "Bryan 12" M15a 6½.4. 70% (b) "Set E." M20B 4.8 70% (g) "R.4.2." 1½ d. 55% (6) Btn HQ. M1d. 2.5 5 ? Calonne Road maintenance - Fords 11 Pumps protection Completed. Experimenting with Pipe Pushing Jack. Sawing timber for Minnie. Cutting Plates for M.G.E: Preparing latrine frames for trestle storage. Making yard where Pipes for Dugout. Preparing Cutting Stones to Calonne	
	25/6		do above	Lt. Smith to Calonne Lt. Petticrew Sub Nr1 from Calonne & Lt. Baylis relieves Lt. Bayliss Calonne
	26/6		do	
	27/6		do	
	28/6		do	Lt. Salomon Sub Nr2 to Calonne
	29/6		do	Two Lieuts 231st Field Co. report New Div. from Calonne
	30/6		Burning Bry New Support line at contd. M.G.Es Nr5 + R1 Contd - S1 finished. Dug out M15a 6½.4 95% 20B 4.F 95% 1½ d 72% 1ad 2.5 32% Sawing timber. Cutting rails, making French name plates. Ventilation pipes at Repairing Stables elsewhere. Building New Div Latrine.	[signature] R.E. Capt

1st Divisional Engineers

23rd FIELD COMPANY R.E. ::: JULY 1916.

WAR DIARY
or
INTELLIGENCE SUMMARY
(Erase heading not required.)

23rd Field Coy. July 1916

Vol 2.2.

Place	Date	Hour	Summary of Events and Information	Remarks and references to Appendices
LES BREBIS CALONNE	1/7		Burning Bug nesting contd. New Support Line – Cellar connections contd. Demolished Bridge Post – hrick stacked in new traverses at Calonne. Laid in Cressy Passage – Strengthening Dug out entrances to Hector Wood – M.G. E's contd. Dug outs { N 15½ 6½½ 98½ } { 2/3 4. 6 98½ } Complete except for gas blankets { R 4 98½ } { R. 2.5 32½ } 10d. Building of new Latrines for Sanitary Dept. – Repairing Stable Theatres. Making Ventilation pipes into Tunnels. Carrying ropes &c.	Lt's Edwards & Salmon & No 4 Section to LES BREBIS from CALONNE
	2/7		New Support Line – Butting Trench – Cellar connections contd. Demolishy Bridge Post. Work continued on new traverses & new firebay. Strengthing Dug out entrances HECTOR Rd contd. – M.G. E's contd. Dug outs { M14 1d 9.5 70% } { Reserve Lie 5% } Detail work continued as above	

WAR DIARY or INTELLIGENCE SUMMARY

23rd Fd Coy RE
July 1916

Place	Date	Hour	Summary of Events and Information	Remarks and references to Appendices
CALONNE to LES BREBIS	3/7		One Section of 23rd Coy RE to LES BREBIS. Section on to CALONNE. Officer remaining at LES BREBIS. Lt VANSTONE with No 1 Section 23rd Fd Coy RE returns to LES BREBIS	
	4/7		"Lt. HARMON " STEELE " BAYLIS } rejoined their unit. " MORRIS No 3. Section returns to LES BREBIS - Lt Smith remains at CALONNE. Coy with transport leaves LES BREBIS at noon arriving at RUITZ - 3.30 p.m.	
RUITZ	5/7		Lt Cotton rejoins Coy from Pioneer School, HOUCHIN Lt Smith returns to Coy from CALONNE.	
	6/7		Company with transport leaves RUITZ at 9.30 a.m. and marches to FOUQUEREUIL Railway station via HALLICOURT & FOUQUIERES arriving at midnight.	
HARGNIES	7/7		Company and transport finishes entraining at 2.15 a.m. Arrives at DOULLENS at 7.15 a.m. Detraining by 8 a.m. marches to HARGNIES via BEAUVAL, TALMAS, NAOUR arriving at 2.30 p.m. Heavy rain all day. Company goes into billets at HARGNIES	
MOLLIENS AU BOIS	8/7		Company with transport leaves HARGNIES about 5 p.m. and goes into billets at MOLLIENS AU BOIS via NAOUR, TALMAS, VILLERS, arriving at 8.30 p.m.	

WAR DIARY or INTELLIGENCE SUMMARY

23rd Field Coy. R.E.
July, 1916

Army Form C. 2118
JUL 1916
23rd (FIELD) COMPANY
ROYAL ENGINEERS

Place	Date	Hour	Summary of Events and Information	Remarks and references to Appendices
BAISIEUX	9/7		Company and transport leaves MOULIETS AU BOIS at 7.30 a.m. to join 1st Brigade at BAISIEUX. Transport via ST GRATIEN & MONTIGNY. Six minutes delay strict to MONTIGNY. Company and transport meet at crossroads MONTIGNY and proceed together via BEAUCOURT arriving in billets at BAISIEUX at 11.45 a.m.	
BAISIEUX	10/7 11/7		Company drilling and general routine.	
	12/7		Whole Company together with 2nd Bn. 3 mining parties and 3rd Bn. 6½ WELSH PIONEER Bn. mining front line and keeps at CONTALMAISON.	
	13/7		Mining at CONTALMAISON continued by Lt. VANSTONE and No 4 Section. Placing posts at CONTALMAISON started by party 12.85 to Lt. pts R.E.	Lt. EDWARDS & No 3 Section } proceed to BECOURT WOOD to bivouac. Lt. VANSTONE & No 4 " }
ALBERT & BECOURT WOOD			Company proceeds to HALT by ALBERT relieving 228 Coy R.E. (19th Division). Principal marches at 7 A.M. via HENENCOURT and MILLENCOURT arriving at ALBERT at 10.30 A.M. Dismounted section by motor lorry arriving at 11 A.M.	
	14/7		Work continued on CONTALMAISON KEEPS. (a) CUTTING KEEP. X.17.a.54. (b) Keep X.16.b.2.5. Reported holdable.	Lt. SMITH & No 2 Section to BECOURT WOOD.
	15/7		Capt. Hudson R.E. handed over front line work to Capt. BATEMAN R.E. 26th Fd. Coy. R.E.	No 2 section and 2/Lt SMITH to ALBERT

WAR DIARY or INTELLIGENCE SUMMARY

(Erase heading not required.)

Army Form C. 2118

23rd FIELD COY. R.E.
July 1916

Instructions regarding War Diaries and Intelligence Summaries are contained in F.S. Regs., Part II. and the Staff Manual respectively. Title Pages will be prepared in manuscript.

Place	Date	Hour	Summary of Events and Information	Remarks and references to Appendices
ALBERT & BÉCOURT WOOD	16/7		(1) Road-making - BEZENTIN RD (BÉCOURT-LOZENGE WOOD). Carrying improved across trenches to avoid batteries firing in a northerly direction. Carting brick from ruins at FRICOURT for road. (2) Carting stores from D dump BERNAFAY COURT to forward dump at BÉCOURT WOOD.	2nd Lt VANSTONE and No. 4 Section proceed to BÉCOURT WOOD. Bivouac relieving Lt POTTERTON and No. 3 Section who return to ALBERT.
"	17/7		Filling lorry to Pontoon wagon to enable cartage of road material. Road-making continued BEZENTIN ROAD. Forming wheelbarrow with broken brick from X 27 a 7½ to junction X 27 b 2.1½. Carting bricks from FRICOURT.	Lt PATTISON and No. 2 Section relieve Lt POTTERTON and No. 4 Section at BÉCOURT WOOD. No. 1 return to ALBERT on being relieved.
"	18/7		BEZENTIN RD continued - Carting bricks and fascines.	Lt EDWARDS and No. 3 Section to BÉCOURT WOOD.
"	19/7		Road-making continued. Fascines largely employed in consolidation. Bigging and wiring new KEEP at CONTALMAISON VILLA - X 11 d 5 9½. Carting road materials from ALBERT and FRICOURT. Carting wiring materials from LOZENGE WOOD to CUTTING KEEP DUMP.	2nd Lt S417H returns 2nd Lt VANSTONE & BÉCOURT WOOD & No. 4 Section relieves No. 1 Section.
"	20/7		CONTALMAISON VILLA KEEP. Trenches improved and fireways slopped. Extra bay added and loose wire/rabbit entanglement in rear.	2nd Lt VANSTONE relieves Lt EDWARDS who returns to ALBERT after work. No. 4 Section relieves No. 2 Section while returning to ALBERT.

WAR DIARY or INTELLIGENCE SUMMARY

23rd Field Coy. R.E.
July 1916

Army Form C. 2118

Instructions regarding War Diaries and Intelligence Summaries are contained in F. S. Regs., Part II. and the Staff Manual respectively. Title Pages will be prepared in manuscript.

(Erase heading not required.)

Place	Date	Hour	Summary of Events and Information	Remarks and references to Appendices
ALBERT AND BECOURT.	22/7		Marking Battle Station for Bde Ad Ors in Lower Wood X.18.a.58. Repair and maintenance of cutting road from Cross Roads X.17.a.54 in an Easterly direction towards MAMETZ WOOD. Officers making front line reconnaissances.	
ALBERT BECOURT AND QUADRANGLE TRENCH MAMETZ X.12.c.50	22/7		Established Bde Dump of R.E. material at VILLA WOOD X.12.c.56. Battle Station for Bde HQrs continued. Bridging 0.9½" – 0.9½" at head of VILLA WOOD VALLEY. Reconnoitring for shelters in BE AVENUE.	Capt. WILSON. Lts EDWARDS. POTTERTON. VANSTONE. MSMITH with sections 1.3 + 4 move up to QUADRANGLE TRENCH Lt SARGENT + No 2 section to BECOURT WOOD
"	23/7		Working on new advanced line and making strong point working with BLACK WATCH at S1.c.66. S1.c.47. Trench made in existing trench S.2.c.17. also firesteps drills. Brest/support digging from S1.c.7b to S.10.55. Computing batteries material. Strong point at X.L.c.17 uniformed. Sap made under Railway from this point to connect with trench E of same. Trench dig by 6th WELCH PR.B.N. from LANE'S TRENCH to S2. C.17.47 Strong point made at S2.c.47. Compass Survey made of WELCH TRENCH from B.E. AVENUE.	Lt POTTERTON killed Early morning 23?/45 at S2.c.17. No 3 section relieves No 3 section which returns to BECOURT No 2. Lt VANSTONE severely wounded about midnight 24/25. position. No 4 section goes to BECOURT WOOD
"	24/7.			
"	25/7		Capt WILSON + Lt EDMONDS to officers guiding 70th Bde working parties to directing their work. Handing over works to representatives of 101st Fd Coy. R.E. Spots dug out for H. Qrs 70th Bde in VILLA WOOD	

WAR DIARY
or
INTELLIGENCE SUMMARY

(Erase heading not required.)

Army Form

25th ROYAL ENGINEERS

July 1916

JUL 1916

Instructions regarding War Diaries and Intelligence Summaries are contained in F.S. Regs., Part II. and the Staff Manual respectively. Title Pages will be prepared in manuscript.

Place	Date	Hour	Summary of Events and Information	Remarks and references to Appendices
ALBERT BECOURT WOOD AND BUMONTANGLE TRENCH	26/7		Sunday urgent works. Remainder of Company 4B hrs Divisional Rest.	O.C. hands over works and forward billets to O.C. 101st A. Coy RE. All sections return to ALBERT.
BAIZIEUX	27/7			Coy with transport proceeds to billets in BAIZIEUX
"	28/7		Supervising works on HENENCOURT-BAIZIEUX Rd. Sundry carpentering works for Brigade HdQrs. Water supply.	
"	29/7		Sundry carpentering works for 11th Bde Sports. Supervising road work at HENENCOURT. Water supply. Physical Exercises. Carting material for water supply.	
"	30/7		Constructional work at Bde Sports. Small jobs for Bde. Church Parade. Sports in afternoon. Company training. Supervising roadwork at HENENCOURT	
"	31/7		Making washing troughs for Bde. Company training, entrenchments & wiring. Physical Exercises, sports. Supervising roadwork at HENENCOURT.	

E.G. Esher Lt/Ko
for Major, R.E.
Commanding 23rd (Fld.) Coy. R.E.

1st Divisional Engineers

23rd FIELD COMPANY

ROYAL ENGINEERS

AUGUST 1 9 1 6

WC23

Army Form C. 2118

WAR DIARY
or
INTELLIGENCE SUMMARY
(Erase heading not required.)

23rd Field Coy. R.E.
August 1916

233rd (FIELD) COMPANY
SEP. 1916
ROYAL ENGINEERS

Place	Date	Hour	Summary of Events and Information	Remarks and references to Appendices
BAIZIEUX	1/8		Training troops continued in BAIZIEUX WOOD. Improving dugouts at Divl. baths BAIZIEUX. Laying out Divl. Sports ground. Making jumps - driving gates &c. Painting wagons. Improving billets. Company training - Route marching.	
"	2/8		Company was inspected with 26th Howitzer Fd. Coy & 65th Welch Fd. Coy by C.R.E Coy Anzac and C.E. III Corps. Working on Divl. Sports grounds. O.E. sports at HENENCOURT. Making flags for same.	
	3/8		Training troops continued. Carpenters jobs for Bde. Repair & Strengthening Divl. Baths, BAIZIEUX. Company training - Company drill.	
	4/8		Training troops to complete for 3 battalions. Company Training - mining & hackwork. Trial Sports. Carpenters jobs contd.	
	5/8		Carpenters jobs contd. Company training - drill parades. Football held.	
	6/8		Church parade. Company training - Pontooning (dry) and wire entanglement.	
	7/8		Repairing & Improving BAIZIEUX - HENENCOURT ROAD. 1 Section with technical vehicles inspected by C.R.E. Company training - 1 section Lewis gun. Shoeing smith with trades continue wire. Route marching.	

WAR DIARY
or
INTELLIGENCE SUMMARY

23rd Field Coy. R.E.
August 1916

(Erase heading not required.)

Army Form C. 2118

Place	Date	Hour	Summary of Events and Information	Remarks and references to Appendices
BAIZIEUX	8/8		Fieldwork BAIZIEUX-HENENCOURT RD Water supply BAIZIEUX Sundry carpentering jobs for Divn HQts. Training. St-Hocking model Kept. section Lewis gun Entanglements with barbed concertina wire Route marching Inspection of guns by G.O.C. Divn - R E	Lt A J PARKES RE joined Company for duty. [stamp: 239 (FIELD COMPANY) No. SEP 1 1916 ROYAL ENGINEERS]
"	9/8		BAIZIEUX - HENENCOURT RD contd. Also repair BEHENCOURT RD Stopping model kept ?? Training as before.	
"	10/8		Repair BEHENCOURT - BAIZIEUX-HENENCOURT roads contd. Training contd as before	
"	11/8		Roadwork BAIZIEUX-HENENCOURT RD contd. Repairing Wells Carpentry work for B/a. Training. B.E. spark at HENENCOURT WOOD Mining new Kept.	
"	12/8		Road work BAIZIEUX - HENENCOURT RD contd. Repairing Wells Company Training Squad drill ½ Day unallotted in finishing by Brigade MATCH Bombing officer WELDON trestle bridging	

Army Form C. 2118

WAR DIARY
or
INTELLIGENCE SUMMARY

(Erase heading not required.)

23rd Field Company R.E.
August 1916

Place	Date	Hour	Summary of Events and Information	Remarks and references to Appendices
BAIZIEUX	13/8		Company attended 1st Bde. Church parade in morning.	
	14/8		Company training contd.	
FRICOURT to ALBERT	15/8		Officer & Section Recce forward to take over billets and works from 208th Field Coy R.E. Marching and packing up by men. Company marched in forward billets and became attached to 1st Bde. for duty.	Lt. Shaydon and No 2 Section report up to take line to take over.
			Making reconnaissance of front line. Failing to trace tabands (new advanced front line) S.2.d.3.2 to S.3.c.1.6 50' East of frontage in intermediate line. About 100' N.E. from S.2.d 3.2 was hoped to digging commenced by Infantry under R.E. Supervision but from S.3.c.16 S.M. nothing could be done. Very heavy casualties caused to both the Sappers & Infantry.	Captn Wilson goes to 1st Bde HQrs about S.13 b 49 nr BAZENTIN LE PETIT WOOD Lt Pankes EDWARDS) with 4 Section to billets JAYDON) X 27 & 62 nr FRICOURT 2nd Lt SMITH Lt Cohen with transport and H.Q Qrs to E11a 98 - at BELLE VUE FARM, ALBERT
	16/8		Carpenters making shelving and tables for 1st Bde Adv HQrs. at old German dugout. Sappers starts digging new cut and comn dugout for Bd 14.D Qrs. and worked continual reliefs. Mines carried to MAMETZ WOOD - 2 Section rendered useless through bad work of Infantry guide.	
	17/8		Work continued on excavation for Bde dugout. Excavation finished by morning of 18th. 2 Sections digging handed S.2.d 10.3 - S.3.c.6.33 distance of 80". 40' of this being new and 40' partially dug. Traverse made at No 2nd. Carpenters carts to MAMETZ WOOD and carried in frames & to size of dugout.	
	18/8		Carpenters erected in cut & covn dugout (note 8 ft deep x 18' x 10') Work commenced on internal hutlike construction. No Coy. training by for consolidation work. The attack failed and therefore the Sappers were not required.	

WAR DIARY
or
INTELLIGENCE SUMMARY

23rd Wd. Coy. R.E.
August 1916

(Erase heading not required.)

Army Form C. 2118

Place	Date	Hour	Summary of Events and Information	Remarks and references to Appendices
FRICOURT to ALBERT	1918		Additional timber carts up for Bde dugout & framing carried – Sawing & carrying tree from BAZENTIN LE PETIT WOOD to form hutting cover. Dwelling & revering submerge. Breaking holes bombs – turning seats re. Carting R.E. stores to MAMETZ WOOD.	
	20/8		Work continued in extension & reforming of Bde dugout. Trade at MAMETZ WOOD DUMP dugout and carted to FRICOURT WOOD for repairs. Trestle boards. La Briar Pearl. Lostphile loaves re camb. Carting stores to MAMETZ WOOD DUMP.	
	21/8		Bde dugout completed by evening, including trenches, tables, & frame revelling &c. Various trench boards made and painted for D.E. 1st Bde relieved by 3rd Bde in evening. Odd jobs for 1st Bde Hd Qrs – rear.	Capt Pillsworth R.E. gone to FRICOURT billets X 27 c 6.2.
	24/8		Repairing Tramway in MAMETZ WOOD VALLEY. Making concertina barbed wire. Repairing 2ft gauge railway line where damaged by aeroplane bomb at E 11 a 99. Making trestle bombs. Salvaging trestle for railway.	
	20/8		Repairing Tramway in MAMETZ VALLEY and altering line to suit broad gauge truck. Making entrance road to 1st D.A.C. Am. Dump. Burying GERMAN dead near FRICOURT billets, and generally improving same position. Carpenters working at Hd Qrs. 1st Bde. Cooking Shelters. Cartry fence.	

Army Form C. 2118

WAR DIARY
or
INTELLIGENCE SUMMARY

(Erase heading not required.)

23rd Fd. Coy. R.E.
August 1916

Instructions regarding War Diaries and Intelligence Summaries are contained in F.S. Regs., Part II. and the Staff Manual respectively. Title Pages will be prepared in manuscript.

Place	Date	Hour	Summary of Events and Information	Remarks and references to Appendices
FRICOURT ALBERT.	23/8		Work continued on D.A.C. road - Shelters (carpenters) for an unused mine shaft. Repairing MAMETZ road tramway. Fixing shutters — making holes & loopholes for 1st Bde. Carrying to PETERPAN and 1/B BRITISH SOLDIER (not identified, obliterated) Pumping up PETERPAN dugout containing 9 GERMAN corpses. Sealing up PETERPAN dugout, carrying back to MAMETZ DUMP. Filling tap to bricked parapet, centring tanks to MAMETZ DUMP and fixing it in ground. Making covers for tanks. Preparing material for canteen for 1st Bde. Making 3 [strikethrough] plate hovers (loopholes) Cutting stone.	
	24/8		As above.	
	25/8		Repair to MAMETZ Railway contd. 1st D.A.C. Ammunition Dump Shelters and road completed. Experimental work with English steel shelters. Returning mine generators. Surveying and platting positions of railways from PRISONERS found. Earliest floor -	
	26/8		MAMETZ Ry contd and handed over to 14th Divn. Railway R.S.S. and ladder from old GERMAN LINES. Extension & hut work with low side shelters. Carpenters working at 1st Bde H.Q. Bns. R. Battery H.Q. Making 3 plate loophole boxes.	Lieut SMITH to see party go to BAZENTIN le GRAND to make preliminary arrangements for taking over from 11th Fd Coy R.E.

WAR DIARY
or
INTELLIGENCE SUMMARY

(Erase heading not required.)

Army Form C. 2118

23rd Field Coy. R.E.
August 1916

Place	Date	Hour	Summary of Events and Information	Remarks and references to Appendices
ALBERT– BOUZINCOURT – BAZENTIN	27/8		Getting over billets wrecked in Daours in passes 11.E. Fr. Coy. R.E. Troubling from billets implied even. Officers & N.C.Os reconnoitring new front central point to forward lines Dy. Preparing and filling in Bangalore Torpedoes. Barbed steel "helices" at 1st Field As Rgs. S.19.b.6.30 Instruments and stores issued on R.E.Bn. As Rgs.	Lt Edwards and Men 1–3 Sections to Bazentin to HQ. Select S15.b.2.4 Bazentin Le Grand Capt Wilson N.E. (Sec) to Ride over S19.b.30.
	28/8		Officers reconnoitring routes for carrying parties. Sets drawn for parades. Parties working R.E.Bn. As Rgs. Improvements and fitting up of Bde Battle Statin. S15.b.2.4. Returning 3 carrying parties of 100 men each & lamp-posts intended for skeleton entanglement to forward dump Pig. Both Battalion As Bh Hq. As Rgs. S19.b.30. Carrying GS & DS 07 Dumps.	Lt. Spencer Jr Z Section to Bazentin Le Grand On Billets
	29/8		Officer N.E. O reconnoitred route to front line trenches tomorrow. Switch Line, Lt Spencer in charge of S.R.E. Organisation working on Bde Battle station. Two sections selected for & preparing material for special operation. One section Bivouac stores shelters at F.d. Hq Qrs. S.19.b.6.30. Gits, E&D to D2 and D7. Making trench number plates.	

Army Form C. 2118

WAR DIARY
or
INTELLIGENCE SUMMARY
(Erase heading not required.)

23rd Field Coy R.E.
August 1916

Instructions regarding War Diaries and Intelligence Summaries are contained in F. S. Regs., Part II. and the Staff Manual respectively. Title Pages will be prepared in manuscript.

Place	Date	Hour	Summary of Events and Information	Remarks and references to Appendices
HENCOURT PRICOURT BECOURT LA BOISELLE	3/8		Lt. Bris. to Bris. Commanding chambers - B.R. - Bde. Battle station - 2 Plns - cleaning out, making roads attempting in. 2 sections on Bde. H.Q. Rs at 59¢30 - musical shelters constructed. Reving Emplacements: Made in for H.Q. - Railway from Pozu to mine Plate Unloading Siding to 59¢30 - - Unloading office Buildings for Bde HQ R.S. - 1 Section loading or clearing our subways loading slab to D7.	
	2/8		Lt. Brs. to Brs. Commanding Lealonois roads on to Br. H. QRs. troth or two shelters R. Br. two sections at R. Br. H. QRs. Commander Carrying made to Bruno, hut & Dumps hoye convened on Bde. Advr. Head Qrs. Cutting slab to D7 -	Section 1 & 3 under Lt. Connors & Lt. Smyth return to Pricourt Capt. Preston R.E. taken Bde & gave 15 Prisoners

E. Usburn Lieut.
for Commanding 23rd [?]

1st Divisional Engineers

23rd FIELD COMPANY R.E. :: SEPTEMBER 1916

Army Form C. 2118

WAR DIARY
or
INTELLIGENCE SUMMARY

(Erase heading not required.)

Vol 24 — 23rd Field Coy. R.E. September 1916

Place	Date	Hour	Summary of Events and Information	Remarks and references to Appendices
ALBERT FRICOURT and BAZENTIN LE GRAND	1/9		Working on D.H.Q. Road, FRICOURT. Work carts on 1st Pdr Adv. Dvs. - S 19 d 30. Officers training over us front line. Camp improvements at HORSESHOE, ALBERT	Lt SAXTON with No 2 Section returns to FRICOURT having handed over to 1st Lowland Fd Coy RE
	2/9		Work carts on road. Making preparation for the attack.	Lt EDWARDS No 1 Section to BAZENTIN LE GRAND S 15 b 20 Capt HILSON RE (acty OC) to 1st Bde Bomb Station S 15 b 24
	3/9		The 1 Section under Lt EDWARDS R.E. arrived in 1st Bde attack on H 19 H hours. Work was done towards consolidating trenches Sect 12 6½ which was taken at zero. The enemy bombarded heavily at 3.30 pm and we were driven out and back to our front line. Lt EDWARDS R.E. reorganized garrison and troops retaken and with the arrival of BLACKWATCH officers the remaining section were standing by in shelter ready to consolidate during the night. The attack having failed No 2 section arrived in repairing own front line trenches. Trunks in Sator C.L.E. O ri Dr. Bandstand W Rft. Stores carts to BAZENTIN LE GRAND D 7.	Lt SAXTON - PARSONS - 70 SMITH with No 2, 3 & 4 Sections to Adv shelter S 15 b 24
	4/9		Working on TRISTLE ALLEY from Bank to front line - bagging out - dressing batter. ALLOWATER ALLEY and front line - Trying ducked boards in front line and communication trenches.	Lt EDWARDS SMITH with No 1 & 3 Section returns to FRICOURT Capt HILSON RE returns to FRICOURT

23rd (FIELD) COMPANY
No. ....
OCT. 1916
ROYAL ENGINEERS

Army Form C. 2118

WAR DIARY
or
INTELLIGENCE SUMMARY
(Erase heading not required.)

23rd Field Coy. R.E.
September 1916

Stamp: 23rd (FIELD) COMPANY, OCT. 1916, ROYAL ENGINEERS

Place	Date	Hour	Summary of Events and Information	Remarks and references to Appendices
ALBERT & FRICOURT (Bray)	5/9		Reconnoitring reserve trenches.	
	6/9		Tracking road near BOTTOM WOOD. Coy. transport employed on above. Making mine covers at 4 DUMP. Transporting concertina barbed wire from FRICOURT WHEAT to O.G. DUMP FRICOURT. Salvaging R.E. Stores and R.E. material from O.G. lines.	Pts PARKER + PARSONS R.E. with No. 2 + 4 sections hand over to 265 Coy R.E. and return to FRICOURT. Lt EDWARDS R.E. and No 1 Section to bivouac on HORSESHOES, ALBERT. E.11.q.9.8.
	7/9 8/9 9/9 10/9		As above.	
	11/9 12/9 13/9		As above. Roadwork handed over to 4yth Divn.	10/9. 2 Sapper go forth to MEAULTE WOOD with 11 Bde to act on guides for BEHENCOURT WOOD. 11/9. Lt SAYTON R.E. with No.2 section go to BEHENCOURT to act as advance party.
BEHENCOURT	14/9		Company (less 1 section) marches into Rest Billets at BEHENCOURT.	
	15/9		Improving billets. Preparing additional billets to receive pioneer class (14th Bde). Company training.	
BRESLE WOOD	16/9		Company marches to bivouac in BRESLE WOOD.	

Army Form C. 2118

WAR DIARY
or
INTELLIGENCE SUMMARY
(Erase heading not required.)

23rd Field Coy R.E.
September 1916.

Stamp: 23rd (FIELD) COMPANY, No......, OCT. 1916, ROYAL ENGINEERS

Place	Date	Hour	Summary of Events and Information	Remarks and references to Appendices
BRESLE WOOD	17/9		Church Parade. Company Training. Improving bivouacs. Parker Class (1st Field) was started but was abandoned and the men returned to their respective units in the afternoon.	
	18/9		Reinforcements drilled under Coun. Training the bivouacs. Very heavy rain precluded any useful Company training.	
	19/9		Striking tents and bivouacs. Returning tents to Town Major BRESLE. Cutting down trees.	Lts PARKES and EDWARDS with Section 3 + 4 proceed to bivouacs in FRICOURT. (F 3 c 09)
FRICOURT & BAZENTIN LE GRAND	20/9		Company (No 2 Section) marched to FRICOURT and bivouaced at (F 3 c 09). Officers reconnoitring front line. Locating new Adv. R.E. Dump. &c. 9.10 a.m. 3. Two forward Sections affiliated to 8th Bde. Improving R.E. Bn. Hq. Dug-outs and cleaning up approach trench.	Lts PARKES + SMITH with Sections 3 + 4 proceed forward billets at BAZENTIN LE GRAND (S9d00)
	21/9		Building a traverse to protect entrance to dug-outs in SWITCH LINE (S a 43). Entrance improved to receive steel shelter. Stores parade - Coy H-DRo. M 36 a 74 - Shield fixing - making M.G.E. M 35 a 83 - Digging out trench obstructed by enemy shellfire. Nailing artillery boards. Salvaging R.E. material FRICOURT. Improving Camp.	

Army Form C. 2118

WAR DIARY
or
INTELLIGENCE SUMMARY
(Erase heading not required.)

23rd Field Coy RE
September 1916

[Stamp: 23rd (FIELD) COMPANY, OCT. 1916, ROYAL ENGINEERS]

Place	Date	Hour	Summary of Events and Information	Remarks and references to Appendices
FRICOURT to BAZENTIN LE GRAND	22/9		Set out new trenches dug by 10th Glousters M 34 - 98 to M 28 d 91 + M 28 d 91 to M 29 c 51. Two shelters erected near Br. H.Qrs in PEAKE LINE - M 36 a 28. Salvaging mine cases from B. GERMAN dugout. Carting them to D 8 - new R.E. Adv. dump. S.10 a 43. Improving camp	
	23/9		Elephant shelters carried up and erected at Br. HQ's M 35 c 64. in the STAFFSH. Erecting steel shelter for forward section billets at D 7. Salvaging mine cases from O.G. dugouts making trench mantlets and delivering same to R.E. making trench footbridges. Carting store to D 7.	Lt COMMAS with No.1 section proceeds to BAZENTIN billets and relieves Lt SMITH & No 3 section which returns to FRICOURT.
	24/9		Advanced Dressing Station S.10 a 8.6. (a) Excavating for ELEPHANT shelter roof (b) Excavating for framed trench dressing station. Deep dugout for Bn. H.Qrs. M 35 c/4 started in conjunction with 26th Inf bry RE. making gunners lodges. Trench bridges (nos) placed in position near BRIGHTON. Salvaging mine cases from O.G. dugouts making trench mantelpiece. Carting stores to D 8	Lt SALMON with No 2 section relieves No 4 section (Lt PARKER'S) at BAZENTIN

Army Form C. 2118

WAR DIARY
or
INTELLIGENCE SUMMARY

(Erase heading not required.)

233rd FIELD COY RE
September 1916

Place	Date	Hour	Summary of Events and Information	Remarks and references to Appendices
FRICOURT + BAZENTIN LE GRAND	25/9.		Sect dugout M 35 c 74 contd. Making artillery bivvys. Salvaging wire cores near Plateau Sheltering from O.G. dugouts. Adv Trenching Stn. S10 a 86 contd. Making bench number plates, trench plates, etc. Carting steel to D.8. Camp improvements. Filling shelters.	
	26/9.		Work contd on dugout M 35 C 74 and Adv. Trenching Stn. S10 a 86. Large returboard "yet intotrench" found at Lutherne COKER ALLEY Carting guncar bridges + salvaged mining material to D.8. Filling shell holes FRICOURT Camp contd.	2/Lt SMITH with No 3 section proceeds to Mealy Maillet - BAZENTIN - 2nd Congress with No 1 section return to FRICOURT.
	27/9.		Adv Trenching Stn. S10 a 86. One chamber completed. 3 dugouts on pit all over. Steps cut + revetted. Excavation complete to 7ft for framed head hospital. SYMPFISH Dugout M 35 c 74 contd. Making Ruffrones Repairing pontoon wagons.	2/Lt PARKER R.E with No 4 section proceeds to forward billets BAZENTIN. Lt Thompson R.E. with No 2 section return to FRICOURT.
	28/9.		Dugout at SYMPFISH M 35 c 74 hands over to 2/3rd London Pro Coy R.E. Advanced trenching Station S10 a 86 Completed. Building additional huts for section returning to FRICOURT. Carting stores from G Dump. Draining and improving camp. Repairing pontoon wagon.	2/Lt PARKER + SMITH with nos 3 + 4 section return to FRICOURT after handing over work + billets to 2/3 London Fd Eng R.E. (47th Div). Lt GILLESPIE R.E reports for attachment from 26th Fd Coy R.E.

Army Form C 2118

WAR DIARY
or
INTELLIGENCE SUMMARY
(Erase heading not required.)

23RD FIELD COY. R.E.
SEPTEMBER 1916

Instructions regarding War Diaries and Intelligence Summaries are contained in F.S. Regs., Part II. and the Staff Manual respectively. Title Pages will be prepared in manuscript.

Place	Date	Hour	Summary of Events and Information	Remarks and references to Appendices
FRICOURT	29/8		Building additional huts to accommodate "Brigade" Pioneers. Casting floors from G dump. Draining and improving camp. Training in Pioneer training ground. Reconnoitring road work near BAZENTIN LE GRAND.	
	30/8		2 sections road making between road junction S10 c 30 on Longueval Rd and HIGH WOOD. Casting bricks from BAZENTIN LE GRAND and for trench from D.5. Casting floors from G dump. Completed hut for the Pioneers. Camp drainage & improvement contd. Filling shell holes on parade ground. Building drawing office.	

E. Cohen Lieut. R.E.
for Commanding 23rd Field Coy R.E.

[Stamp: 23rd (FIELD) COMPANY ROYAL ENGINEERS OCT. 1916]

1st Divisional Engineers

23rd FIELD COMPANY R.E. :: OCTOBER 1916.

Army Form C. 2118

WAR DIARY
or
INTELLIGENCE SUMMARY
(Erase heading not required.)

23RD FD COY R.E
October 1916

Vol 25

[Stamp: 23 (FIELD) COMPANY OCT 1916 ROYAL ENGINEERS]

Place	Date	Hour	Summary of Events and Information	Remarks and references to Appendices
FRICOURT	1/10		Roadmaking - Road junction S10c 30 to D8 S10a 43. (COMPSTRE - BAZENTIN) Coy working under C.R.E. 47th Div. Erecting huts - Camp. Draining Camp. Painting wagons.	
	2/10		S10c 30 to S10a 43 road continued. Erecting hut for Officers Mess. Draining Camp. Filling shell holes on parade ground.	Capt. P.J. HACKETT R.E. evacuated to England Sick. and shown as attached to G. of Company
	3/10		Road as above cont'd. Hutting cont'd at FRICOURT Camp. Shelters - office filling & in - Marking sentry box.	
	4/10		Road as above cont'd. Collecting and carting bricks to Camp. Carting stone from G Dump. Making stoves - sheets etc.	
	5/10		Road as above cont'd. Collecting DECAUVILLE TRACK & TRUCKS - and laying line from FRICOURT village to Camp. Carting slate from G Dump.	
	6/10		Road as above cont'd. Carting bricks on Kaskie and laying horse lines. Making CROSTER base for pontoon wagon. Making stove. Hutting cont'd. Painting Coy wagons.	

Army Form C. 2118

WAR DIARY
or
INTELLIGENCE SUMMARY

23RD FD COY. R.E.
October 1916

(Erase heading not required.)

OCT. 1916 ROYAL ENGINEERS

Place	Date	Hour	Summary of Events and Information	Remarks and references to Appendices
FRICOURT	7/10		HIGH WOOD road as above contd. Horsestandings contd. Artillery. Carting stores from G. dump. Improving Camp drainage - Fitting stoves to painting wagons.	
	8/10		As above.	
	9/10		As above.	Lt EDWARDS, R.E. reports to D.E. for detachment
	10/10		HIGH WOOD RD contd. Horsestandings contd. Carting stores from G. Dump. COOPER plates from pr position wagon contd. Painting hutments.	23rd Fd Coy R.E. attached 9th D.E. for duty
	11/10		Track examined in OLD FRICOURT RD between X29 b 55 + X 30 a 58. Horsestandings contd. Carting stores from G. Dump. Building footbaths.	23rd Fd Coy R.E. attached 50th D.E. for duty in environs.
	12/10		Road improvement & maintenance from X 29 b 55 to S.14.b.18. Hutments FRICOURT Camp as before. Stain stoves from G dump.	

Army Form C. 2118

WAR DIARY
or
INTELLIGENCE SUMMARY

(Erase heading not required.)

23 Field Coy RE
October 1916

[Stamp: 23 FIELD COMPANY ROYAL ENGINEERS OCT. 1916]

Place	Date	Hour	Summary of Events and Information	Remarks and references to Appendices
FRICOURT	13/10		2 Sections on road improvements & maintenance from x 29 6 55 to S/14 6 18	
	14/10		Work in FRICOURT camp as before. Stores carted from G dump.	
	15/10		3 Sections on road as above. Horestanding contd. Painting tool carts.	
	16/10		4 Section on roads. Horestanding contd. Painting of tool carts contd.	
	17/10		do.	
	18/10		do.	
	19/10		do & making mud scrapers for road	
	20/10		do.	
	21/10		Work on road as above. Painting of tool carts. Erection of permanent huts in FRICOURT CAMP. Stores carted from G dump.	
	22/10		Devices improving horestandings etc. do. above	
	23/10		do. above	

Army Form C. 2118

WAR DIARY
or
INTELLIGENCE SUMMARY

23RD F.Coy. R.E
OCTOBER 1916

(Erase heading not required.)

Instructions regarding War Diaries and Intelligence Summaries are contained in F. S. Regs., Part II. and the Staff Manual respectively. Title Pages will be prepared in manuscript.

Place	Date	Hour	Summary of Events and Information	Remarks and references to Appendices
FRICOURT	24/10		4 Section on road S.25.a.30 to S.14 b.18. Painting huts/tents and repairing pontoons. Carting stores. Hutting in camp.	Company attached 9th D.E. for Corps roads.
	25/10		As above.	
BAZENTIN FRICOURT	26/10		2 Section on road as above. Officers looking over BATH HORSE at BAZENTIN (S.8.d.85) and looking over forward billets.	9.O.R. to occupy new forward billets. BAZENTIN S.15.b.58. 2 Section attached 50th D.E. " " 1st D.E. Remainder Hdqr of Coy attached 50th D.E. 3 sections - Nos 1.2 (less 10 O.R.) + No 4 with Lts. PARKES, SAMPSON + GILLESPIE proceed to forward billets S.15.b.58.
	27/10		O.C. and officers reconnoitring front line work. Work commenced on new Bn. Hd Qrs. M.23.d.58. Carrying stores forward for above work. Work commenced on BATH HORSE (S.8.d.85) Carting stores from G. dump to FRICOURT + B.P Dump (S.8.d.9.1).	
	28/10		Work huts on Bn. Hd Qrs. and evening Stn. M.23.d.58. w/ 3 shifts - Erecting small steel shelter. BATH HORSE (S.8.d.85) cont. Carting stores from FRICOURT camp and BOTTOM wood. Fittings for BATH HORSE being prepared at FRICOURT.	Remainder of No.2 Section proceed to BAZENTIN. (S.15.b.58)
	29/10		Work cont. at M.23.d.58 + S.8.d.85. Night shift commenced at forward front. Carting stores from FRICOURT camp and BOTTOM wood. Also from G. dump. Improvements to forward billets.	O.C. proceeds to forward billets S.15.b.58

WAR DIARY
or
INTELLIGENCE SUMMARY

23rd FIELD Coy. R.E.
OCTOBER 1916

Army Form C. 2118

Place	Date	Hour	Summary of Events and Information	Remarks and references to Appendices
FRICOURT AND BAZENTIN	30/10		Bn. H.Q. Bus to Dressing Station M.23.d.58. conts. 1 dugout shaft down 5 steps each. 2 shelters completed - 4 E. longeretted. Revetting 2&3 not 1st mine craters. BATH HOUSE E. (S.9 & 35) C.9 widening to BOILER HOUSE emplts. FRICOURT Making mine cases, fainting wagons, repairing pontoons with R.E. Canvas - making fittings for BATH houses - Carting stones from G pump and also from BOTTOM WOOD to FRICOURT.	No 2 Section proceeded to BAZENTIN and relieved No 2 " which returned to FRICOURT.
	31/10		Bn. Hd. Qrs. to Dressing Stn. M.23.d.58. conts. Lift shaft down 8 steps further - shelter. Rifle - ". Gallery commenced. Bath House (S.9 & R.?) conts. Prisoner to hospital.	2 Lt. F. CONVEY. R.E. joined Company.

E. Sheen
for Commanding 23rd (Field) Coy R.E.

1st Divisional Engineers

23rd FIELD COMPANY R.E. ::: NOVEMBER 1916.

Army Form C. 2118

WAR DIARY
or
INTELLIGENCE SUMMARY
(Erase heading not required.)

23rd FIELD COY. R.E.
NOVEMBER 1916

Place	Date	Hour	Summary of Events and Information	Remarks and references to Appendices
FRICOURT F.3.b.6.9 & BAZENTIN S.15.c.58	1/11		Br. Hd Qrs and Stores Sn. HEXHAM RD. M.23.d.58. Working on Chamber from lost steps. Infantry encamped for Stores Sn. BATH HOUSE. BAZENTIN. S.8.d.58. Carting Stone from 6 dump and from FRICOURT to BAZENTIN.	Capt W.R. Nelson R.E. (T.C.) assumed command of the 23rd Field Coy R.E. vice Capt. P.J. Mackesy R.E. on 3rd October 1916.
	2/11 3/11		As above. HEXHAM Rd Dugour - chambers connected up - BATHHOUSE BAZENTIN contd. FRICOURT Section making mine covers. Training Parties for BRYANT.	No 4 section relieves No 1 at BAZENTIN
			SHED to be sent forward to BATH HOUSE. Making water fittings for BATH HOUSE. Recavating pontoons. Carting materials to BAZENTIN. 1 Officer making reconnaissance for CORPS DEFENCE LINE.	Lt Damon R.E. gone to 7th D.E. as assistant Adj.
	4/11		Work on HEXHAM RD. DUGOUTS 3 contd. BAZENTIN BATH HOUSE 3 Improvements to forward camp. FRICOURT Section as above. Carting Stone to BAZENTIN.	1 section to work under corps arrangements on DEFENSIVE LINE
	5/11		Work on HEXHAM RD. dugouts cease during local operations - "BATH HOUSE" contd. "DRYING SHED commenced. FRICOURT making fittings for BATH HOUSE. Framing DRYING SHED.	
	6/11		Carting Stone. As above.	No 1 section proceeds to BAZENTIN and relieves No 3 section which returns to FRICOURT

Army Form C. 2118

WAR DIARY
or
INTELLIGENCE SUMMARY

23RD FIELD COY R.E.
NOVEMBER 1916

(Erase heading not required.)

Instructions regarding War Diaries and Intelligence Summaries are contained in F. S. Regs., Part II. and the Staff Manual respectively. Title Pages will be prepared in manuscript.

Place	Date	Hour	Summary of Events and Information	Remarks and references to Appendices
FRICOURT F.3.B.0.9 & BAZENTIN S.15.b.58	7/11		HEXHAM RD dugouts 14.2.3 et S.8. no work done. BATH HOUSE S.8d.85 contd. Forward to dep't improved. FRICOURT Preparing material for DRYING SHED. Collecting firebricks & clinkers for DRYING SHED furnace. Salvaging Lanoury huts for cvrs use between B.P & CHARGES DUMP. Carting Stores. Work commenced on BLOCKS – CORPS DEFENCE LINE M.29.d.22 M.29.c.94 M.28.b.33	
	8/11		As above.	
	9/11		CORPS DEFENCES contd. BATH HOUSE. Making shelter at BAZENTIN for 149 Bde Infantry. Excavation 15'x6' finished and kitchen framing commenced. Making permanent HEN COOP joists to h.82.9 3 men. Carting Stores to BAZENTIN from G. Dump.	2/Lt. P.L. FORWOOD R.E. joins Coy for duty from Bℰ PONTOON PARK.
	10/11		HEXHAM ROAD dugouts. Work resumed. DRESSING STATION. Excavation completed. CORPS DEFENSIVE BLOCKS. Work contd. by night. BATH HOUSE Complete except for fittings. DRYING SHED. Roof covered. Work contd. on same. FRICOURT making h.a. cups pattern finner. Carting Stores to BAZENTIN.	2/Lt. FORWOOD R.E. proceeds to BAZENTIN relieving Lt PARKES R.E. who returns to FRICOURT. No 3. Section proceeds to BAZENTIN and relieves No 4 Section which returns to FRICOURT.

Army Form C. 2118

WAR DIARY
or
INTELLIGENCE SUMMARY
(Erase heading not required.)

23RD FIELD Co 87. R.E.
NOVEMBER 1916

Place	Date	Hour	Summary of Events and Information	Remarks and references to Appendices
FRICOURT F 36 d 09 & BAZENTIN LIS B 58	11/11		HEXHAM RD dugouts. M 1 2 3 & 58 - 2 Right - Right hand shaft finished 8 steps Left " " " 5 " DRESSING STN. Erection of steel shelters commenced - CORPS DEFENCES work conts on Blocks E (M. 28 b 33) & L (M 28 d 08). BATH HOUSE. S 8 d 8.5 contd DRYING SHED - Chimney finished. Wire netting completed - fettling nearly finished FRICOURT making 'hencoop' pattern trivies. Existing S.Line is BAZENTIN	Lt. H. A. PARKES. R.E. proceeds to No 6 PONTOON PARK for duty.
	12/11		HEXHAM RD. } conts CORPS DEFENCES } BATH HOUSE - Seating accommodation completed and BATH HOUSE handed over in working order. Pullboxes - Excavation completed ready for concreting. DRYING SHED Wire netting clothes rack over fire. Brickwork inside flue nearly finished. FRICOURT. Sheeting huts & making 'hencoop' trivies - Carting slate from G Dump and to BAZENTIN.	
	13/11		HEXHAM RD dugouts - { Right shaft finished ¾ chamber commenced. { Left " " " CORPS DEFENCES - Working on Blocks E and L. BATH HOUSE - work conts on filler for Drying Shed &c FRICOURT. making trivies. Existing S.Line to BAZENTIN.	No. 4 Section proceeds to BAZENTIN and relieves no 2 Section which proceeds to FRICOURT. Capt. W. R. WILSON. R.E. returns to FRICOURT.

Army Form C. 2118.

WAR DIARY
or
INTELLIGENCE SUMMARY.

(Erase heading not required.)

23rd Co. Coy R.E.
NOVEMBER 1916

Instructions regarding War Diaries and Intelligence Summaries are contained in F. S. Regs., Part II. and the Staff Manual respectively. Title pages will be prepared in manuscript.

Place	Date	Hour	Summary of Events and Information	Remarks and references to Appendices
FRICOURT F.36.d.09 BAZENTIN S.15.d.58.	14/11		HEXHAM RD dugouts M.23.d.58 - work contd. CORPS DEFENCE line - work contd on Block E. M.28.b-33 } nightwork " L M.28.d-08 } BATH HOUSE S.8.d.85 Framing timber for filter tanks. Gangway over flue in DRYING SHED - 50% completed. Pugging flue joints with clay. Painting roof. Repairing spare timber. Cleaning foundation for WAITING SHED FRICOURT: making "Haircord" hivers " material for Topographical model for Divn " Carting stores from G. dump and to BAZENTIN.	
	15/11		As above but no work done HEXHAM RD.	
	16/11		HEXHAM RD dugouts, no work done - CORPS DEFENCES Block E } Straight shoots and loopholes Block L3 } timbers.	Capt W.R. Wilson R.E. proceed to BAZENTIN. No 2 section proceed to BAZENTIN and relieve no1 section which return to FRICOURT
	17/11		BATH HOUSE BAZENTIN S.8.d.85 Waiting Shed. Framing bents. Filter beds. Concreting. FRICOURT old Jobs in connection with forward work Carting Stores	

Army Form C. 2118.

WAR DIARY
or
INTELLIGENCE SUMMARY.
(Erase heading not required.)

23rd FIELD COY. R.E.
NOVEMBER 1916

Place	Date	Hour	Summary of Events and Information	Remarks and references to Appendices
FRICOURT F.36.c.9 to BAZENTIN G.15.B.59	17/11		HEXHAM RD & Regent no work done. CORPS NESTS Block E. M.28 & 2.3 " F. M.28 & 0.8.3. Making some bunks and loopholed Traverses and digging shrapnel proofs - work on faelings commenced. BATH HOUSE. BAZENTIN. S.8.d.8.5. Work on two Waiting Rooms - BAZENTIN CAMP. Excavation for splinterproof shelter. Making arrangements for handing over HEXHAM Rd jobs to 26th Div R.E. Casting stone & NISSEN huts	
	18/11		CORPS NESTS - work started on Block A. M.29 & 20 B. M.29 & 04. progress much hampered by bad weather. BATH HOUSE, BAZENTIN. Making shafts continued. Excavating to Unloosed cents. Fittings to Boy Shed shed. BAZENTIN CAMP. Erecting NISSEN huts Excavating for shelter cents. FRICOURT Section (i) making fittings for BATH HOUSE (ii) Re-anchoring pontoons (iii) making new cook Lines	No 1 Section proceeds to FRICOURT encamp to work on Dud School pressures No 3 Section returns to FRICOURT from BAZENTIN
	19/11		As above.	

Army Form C. 2118.

WAR DIARY
or
INTELLIGENCE SUMMARY.

(Erase heading not required.)

2 N.Z. FIELD COY (N.Z.E)
NOVEMBER 1916

Place	Date	Hour	Summary of Events and Information	Remarks and references to Appendices
FRICOURT F.3.b.09 & BAZENTIN S.5.b.58.	20/11		Work continued on CORPS NESTS; A = M.29.d.20 & B = M.29.d.04	
			Constructed Ravens hut to with bomb-proof overhead cover. Slaining shoot dug Wind deflector erected Old traverses filled in.	
			BATH HOUSE BAZENTIN- Washing Room finished in cpt for windows "Walls of filter bed - Cementing finished + floors up.	
			BAZENTIN CAMP - Erecting NISSEN huts Splinter proof tents-	
			FRICOURT- Making various fittings for frame work Ceiling Joists	
	21/11		CORPS NESTS } as above - BATH HOUSE &c }	
			FRICOURT (i) One + detachments (ii) making gunner turn 95 (ii) Trench handrails (iii) BATH HOUSE fittings Ceiling joists	
	22/11		As above -	No. 3 section proceeded to BAZENTIN & No. 12 Coy returned to FRICOURT for duty (from BAZENTIN)-

Army Form C. 2118.

WAR DIARY
or
INTELLIGENCE SUMMARY.

(Erase heading not required.)

23rd FIELD COY RE
NOVEMBER 1916

Place	Date	Hour	Summary of Events and Information	Remarks and references to Appendices
FRICOURT 9 b 6 9	23/11		CORPS NESTS:- Work conts on Mock A. M29 d20? B + M29 d04. Digging and moving thought sheets new fillings commenced.	Capt H.R. Wilson R.E. returned to FRICOURT
BAZENTIN 9 15 c 58			BATH HOUSE. Work on filter beds contd. BAZENTIN CAMP. Erecting NISSEN hut commenced FRICOURT:- (1) making French number plates (2) making stoves (3) " PENSTOCK (4) Recovering pontoons. Casting stoves.	
- do -	24/11		Work continued on CORPS NESTS. (A and B. Posts) " " DIV: BATH HOUSE. Three NISSEN huts erected at advanced billets, BAZENTIN. Repairing company equipment + vehicles at H.Q. Billet. FRICOURT.	
- do -	25/11		As above.	No 19910 Spr T.E. Barnes, Cook, HQ Section and No 24757 Sr W. Kennedy, Cooks Mate, slightly burnt when legs stove swung to throw out ashes, fire. The fire was extinguished by the Staff Sergeant.

Army Form C. 2118.

WAR DIARY
or
INTELLIGENCE SUMMARY.

(Erase heading not required.)

23rd FIELD COMPANY.
NOVEMBER 1916

Instructions regarding War Diaries and Intelligence Summaries are contained in F. S. Regs., Part II. and the Staff Manual respectively. Title pages will be prepared in manuscript.

Place	Date	Hour	Summary of Events and Information	Remarks and references to Appendices
FRICOURT F.3.b.0.9 and BAZENTIN S.15.4.58	26/11		Work continued on CORPS NESTS. (A and B Posts) M.29.d.28 and M.29.d.0.t " " " DIV. BATH-HOUSE } BAZENTIN " " " NISSEN HUTS Repairing company equipt & vehicles at HQ Billet FRICOURT	NOV 1916
-do-	27/11		As above. DIV. BATH HOUSE finished. Work commenced on DIV. GUM BOOT SHED and SOUP KITCHEN. (S.9.f.37.)	
-do-	28/11		CORPS NESTS — Work continued on "A" and "B" Blocks. DIV. GUM BOOT SHED and SOUP KITCHEN — work continued. One NISSEN Hut finished, one other commenced. (S.9.f.3.7) BAZENTIN — Erected latrine cupboards and fourth NISSEN Hut erected. FRICOURT — Repairs to Company equipment & vehicles.	Lieut S.J. Colson proceeded on leave to England 28/11/16. Capt W. Nelson took over charge of all "Hutting" in the BAZENTIN Area.
-do-	29/11		CORPS NESTS. Work continued on A and B Blocks. DIV. GUM BOOT SHED and SOUP KITCHEN — work continued. BAZENTIN LE PETIT. Hutting Infantry Commenced. FRICOURT — Repairing Company vehicles and Equipment.	

Army Form C. 2118.

WAR DIARY
or
INTELLIGENCE SUMMARY.
(Erase heading not required.)

23rd FIELD Company
R.E.

Place	Date	Hour	Summary of Events and Information	Remarks and references to Appendices
FRICOURT F.3.b.6.9 BAZENTIN S.15.b.58.	30/1/1		CORPS NESTS. Work continues on "A" and "B" Blocks. BAZENTIN-LE-PETIT - Hutting continues. Gum-BOOT-SHED - Work continues. SOUP KITCHEN. Finished. FRICOURT - Repairing Company vehicle and equipment.	
			Extract from Corps Routine Orders No 2273 by Brigadier General A.J. Kelly D.S.O. Commanding 71st Infantry Brigade. 1. OPERATIONS. The Brigadier Commanding wishes to express to all ranks of 71st Brigade yesterday, the fact that they did not obtain the objective they had set themselves was not in the least hearing counter-attacks, was not in the least effort on the part of all ranks with which they succeeded. The Brigadier desires to express his keenest satisfaction with the manner in which all the preparations and fighting of yesterday. In addition to having no rest the three weeks now being in the trenches (for the greater part of the time in close touch of the enemy) and were subjected to very heavy shelling both before and after their fine dash into the enemy's lines. The Brigadier in must regret the heavy casualties incurred (on the Canadian front) and hopes would be arranged by the first batch upon the same spirit which has already rendered such a service to the Empire, to get back for the present from the Divisional Commander. Signed T.A. Aston Major Brigade Major 71st Infantry Brigade P.T.O.	

4/9/16

Army Form C. 2118.

WAR DIARY
or
INTELLIGENCE SUMMARY.

23rd FIELD COMPANY ROYAL ENGINEERS

(Erase heading not required.)

Place	Date	Hour	Summary of Events and Information	Remarks and references to Appendices
FRICOURT F.8.4.0.9. BAZENTIN S.15.6.5.8.	30/11		(Continued) Dear Wilson, Your support order – mistake, I take the opportunity to express my gratitude for the good work done by your Company, especially the Covering party under Lieut EDWARDS, and for the valuable information. The 23rd FIELD COMPANY is always been most willing to help me in emergency and we couldn't have a better one. Yours 6/9/16. Signed E.J. Roodie. Morley. Lt. RE. for OC 23rd Field Coy RE 30/11/16	

1st Divisional Engineers

23rd FIELD COMPANY R.E. :: DECEMBER 1916

Army Form C. 2118.

23rd Field Company R.E.
DECEMBER 1916

Vol 2

WAR DIARY
or
INTELLIGENCE SUMMARY.
(Erase heading not required.)

Place	Date	Hour	Summary of Events and Information	Remarks and references to Appendices
FRICOURT F.3.b.9. BAZENTIN S.15.b.5.6.	1/12	—	CORPS NESTS- (A and B. Posts) M.39. d.2.0. and N.39.d.0.4. All work holds harrow strought sheets, and wire pickets to both "Keeps" finished — HUTTING - BAZENTIN-le-PETIT- One and a half sections employed under LIEUT. BOWMER R.E. GUM BOOT SHED. Material for sheeting and shelves conveyed to Site and sixth Cammerales FRICOURT- Repairing Company vehicles and equipment.	
—	2/12		CORPS NESTS- (A and B. Posts) Revetting, draining and wretting as finished in "Keeps". HUTTING-BAZENTIN-l-PETIT- One and a half sections employed under LIEUT. BOWMER R.E. GUM BOOT SHED. Cowhi seats and shelves one side finished. FRICOURT. Repairing company vehicles and equipment.	
—	3/12		CORPS NESTS - as above. HUTTING-B-l-P- as above - GUM BOOT SHED - finished. FRICOURT - as above.	

Army Form C. 2118.

WAR DIARY
or
INTELLIGENCE SUMMARY.

(Erase heading not required.)

23rd Field Company R.E.
December 1915

Place	Date	Hour	Summary of Events and Information	Remarks and references to Appendices
FRICOURT F.3.b.o.g. BAZENTIN S.15.b.5.6.	4/12		CORPS NESTS. (A and B Posts.) M.29.d.2.0 and M.29.d.0.4. Retaining, draining, repairing and making fire bays in old french fireing traps. HUTTING - BAZENTIN-L-PETIT - One and half sections employed under Lieut BOVIMER RE. Gun Boot Shed - Sounds. One Armian Hut - finished - Soup Kitchen - Tables & forms added. FRICOURT - Repairing Company equipment & vehicles	
— do —	5/12		CORPS NESTS - As above HUTTING - B.L.P. - " - SOUP KITCHEN - Finished. FRICOURT - As above.	
— do —	6/12		CORPS NESTS - Work continues. HUTTING. B.L.P. Two sections employed. BAZENTIN CAMP. Reclaiming old fascines from disused road and making entrance to camp. FRICOURT - As above.	
— do —	7/12		CORPS NESTS - Work continues. HUTTING B.L.P. Two sections employed. BAZENTIN CAMP. As above FRICOURT. As above.	

Army Form C. 2118.

WAR DIARY
or
INTELLIGENCE SUMMARY.
(Erase heading not required.)

23rd Field Company R.E.
December 1916.

Instructions regarding War Diaries and Intelligence Summaries are contained in F.S. Regs., Part II. and the Staff Manual respectively. Title pages will be prepared in manuscript.

Place	Date	Hour	Summary of Events and Information	Remarks and references to Appendices
FRICOURT P.3.b.6.9 BAZENTIN S.15.b.5.8	8/12		CORPS NESTS (A and B Posts) M.29.d.20. and M.29.d.0.4. Redrawing, draining, revetting and making for traps in o.4 trenches. Leaving Kips. HUTTING. BAZENTIN PETIT. Three Sections employed FRICOURT- Dugout, hidden traps, superstructure & huts. R.E. Dump. Repairing Coy Vehicle, equipment.	Advance Party (Officers and 2 O.Rs raub of N[?]4. A.T. Co other ranks of N[?]4. A.T. Co R.E. arrived for Hut[?]
—do—	9/12		CORPS NESTS. As above. HUTTING B.& P. As above.	No 147 A.T. Co. R.E. arrived (Major TRENCHARD and his 12 other ranks Surveying). Three Sections proceed to BAZENTIN and remain in FRICOURT.
—do—	10/12		FRICOURT. Repairing Coy.Vehicle & equipment. BAZENTIN CAMP. One Officer & 2 L.D. Horses attached. Horse transport	
—do—	11/12		CORPSNESTS. As above HUTTING. B.& P. As above. FRICOURT — As above.	Promotions. Lieut E.F.[?] Afton is acting Captain and 2nd in Command of Company with effect from 3.10.16. Captain Coker reverts from [?]
—do—	12/12		— — do — — — do — —	

Army Form C. 2118.

WAR DIARY
or
INTELLIGENCE SUMMARY.
(Erase heading not required.)

23RD FIELD COY. R.E.
DECEMBER - 1916

Instructions regarding War Diaries and Intelligence Summaries are contained in F. S. Regs., Part II. and the Staff Manual respectively. Title pages will be prepared in manuscript.

[Stamp: 23 FIELD COMPANY No. ... DEC. 1916 ROYAL ENGINEERS]

Place	Date	Hour	Summary of Events and Information	Remarks and references to Appendices
FRICOURT 73 b.6.9 BAZENTIN S.15 b.5.8	13/12		CORPS NESTS "Post A". Digging out fallen trenches. Revetting. Digging short hut road. HUTTING. BAZENTIN LE PETIT. Three sections employed. BAZENTIN CAMP. (S.15.5.B). Petrol bin sleeping hut for men practically completed. Work in shelter contd. FRICOURT. Drawing entrance road. Wagon repair.	
	14/12		CORPS NESTS. As above working in CAMPS. 1, 2, 3 & 4. HUTTING working in CAMPS. 1, 2, 3 & 4. DIVL. BATH HOUSE. Lining contd. BAZENTIN CAMP. As above. FRICOURT. Making doorwork - wagon repair &c.	
	15/12		CORPS NESTS } As above HUTTING } DIVL. BATH HOUSE } BAZENTIN CAMP. Roof to horse standing half finished. FRICOURT. As above.	"A convoy return to BAZENTIN
	16/12		CORPS NESTS. Work contd on B Post. HUTTING. 3 Section employed on Camps. 1, 2 & 3. DIVL. BATH HOUSE. Lining completed. BAZENTIN CAMP. Cementing 16 new shelter contd. Work contd on Divl. Cross. FRICOURT. New Civic shelter commenced. Repairs to waterwork and wagons.	

Army Form C. 2118.

WAR DIARY
or
INTELLIGENCE SUMMARY.

(Erase heading not required.)

23RD. FIELD COY. R.E.
DECEMBER 1916

Instructions regarding War Diaries and Intelligence Summaries are contained in F. S. Regs., Part II. and the Staff Manual respectively. Title pages will be prepared in manuscript.

Place	Date	Hour	Summary of Events and Information	Remarks and references to Appendices
FRICOURT C.3.b.6.9 & BAZENTIN J.15.6.78	17/12		CORPS NESTS - Pst. H. Sappers revetting and laying floor boards on C Frames. Infantry party of 12 carrying & digging.	2nd Lt GILLESPIE R.E. returns to FRIENCOURT
			HUTTING. Work carried on Camps 1.2.+4. - 2 sections employed	
			BAZENTIN CAMP Concreting to new shelter huts.	
			Work on Birt. ovens and stable huts.	
			FRICOURT - Drainage to latrine tents. Baths shelter coats	
			Wagon repairs - Carting stone.	
	18/12		As above.	
			Divl. SOUP KITCHEN - Fitting 3 Soyers stoves.	
	19/12		As above	
			HUTTING - has 3 r 5 camps worked on in addition.	2nd LIEUT. ………… proceeds on leave from D.E and is relieved by 2/LtGILLESPIE. R.E
			Divl SOUP KITCHEN - 2 Soyers stoves fitted	
	20/12		As above -	
			FRICOURT Salvaging bricks for cooks fireplace	
	21/12		CORPS NESTS as above	
			HUTTING - Camps 1.3 + 4 cont.	
			BAZENTIN CAMP. Cross cuts hur. 2 shelter coats	
			DIVL. SOUP KITCHEN - making Stone taller + fitting chimney	
			FRICOURT Cookhouse cont. Salvaging bricks -	
			Building new incinerator. Carting stone.	
	22/12		As above -	

Army Form C. 2118.

23RD FIELD COY R.E.
DECEMBER 1916

WAR DIARY
or
INTELLIGENCE SUMMARY.
(Erase heading not required.)

Instructions regarding War Diaries and Intelligence Summaries are contained in F. S. Regs., Part II. and the Staff Manual respectively. Title pages will be prepared in manuscript.

Place	Date	Hour	Summary of Events and Information	Remarks and references to Appendices
FRICOURT 78 Z c 9 — BAZENTIN S.15.6.58	23/12		CORPS NESTS. A POST - Revetting conts. to Infantry party. HUTTING work conts on Camps 1.3.4. BAZENTIN CAMP - Bde. Cross ready for erecting — brown shelter conts. FRICOURT - Work on Cookhouse conts - new incinerator conts - Canteen Stores -	
	24/12		CORPS NESTS. A POST - Revetting and flooring conts - 180" of trench completed - 140' of which floored HUTTING. Work conts on Camps. 1.2 + 4. BAZENTIN CAMP - Bde. Cross conts - brown shelter conts - FRICOURT - New cookhouse conts. Fireplace and Chimney nearly completed - Canteen Stores BE 18 BAZENTIN	C.R.E. and Company officers with mens huts at dinner time and distributed contributions to dinner fund -
	25/12		No work performed excepting that demanded by ROUTINE	
	26/12		CORPS NESTS. as above HUTTING. Work conts on camps 1.2 + 3. Remainder on fur 24th	
	27/12		As above - BAZENTIN CAMP Bde Cross finished. Cementing to mens shelter (2 layers) conts. Relaying trench board paths - FRICOURT - Improving driver's cook shelter -	

Army Form C. 2118.

WAR DIARY
or
INTELLIGENCE SUMMARY.
(Erase heading not required.)

23RD FIELD CO. R.E.
DECEMBER 1916

[Stamp: 23RD FIELD COMPANY / DEC. 1916 / ROYAL ENGINEERS]

Place	Date	Hour	Summary of Events and Information	Remarks and references to Appendices
FRICOURT 72.b.6.9 and BAZENTIN 51.5.58	28/12		CORPS MESS & A. POST. Resetting walls & framing and X P.M. Laying out rough landings on D. Rooms.	Maj. W.R. WILSON R.E. & FRICOURT
			HUTTING CAMPS 1.2. 4 & worked on monthly allotion - laying sheds and hutting stores.	
			BAZENTIN District memorial cross taken to High Wood and erection commenced. Making tables for Divn. Laying numerous cables to division. Fitting bunks & cubicle shelter. Repairing one hut for General Gore.	
	29/12		As above.	
	30/12.		As above.	Major W.R. WILSON R.E. proceeds to BAZENTIN. Transport by 147 A.T. Coy R.E. Hands FRICOURT
	31/12.		CORPS MESS A POST. Sizing new bench and readjusting roof.	Lt. R.L. FORFORD R.E. returns to BAZENTIN.
			Utranca 4 P.M. Portion of wood between C-D posts slightly altered.	11 Lt F. CONLEY R.E. proceeds to FRICOURT with No 2 Section for training.
			HUTTING Camp 4. Allotion shifts cont'd	Half of No 1 Section proceeds to FRICOURT
			BAZENTIN CAMP Improving drainage - finished tables for Division - Fencing to Divl. Cross commenced.	to act as duty section. Major W.R. WILSON to FRICOURT. From midnight 31.11. 3 sections minus C.R.E. To Divn
			FRICOURT New hut commenced for attached officers Flooring to mens hut cont'd. Small wood baths cont'd	& for training

E. Slater. Capt.
~~Commanding~~ ~~Major~~ 23rd Field Coy R.E.

Army Form 2118.

1ST DIVISION
ROY. ENGINEERS

23RD FIELD COMPANY, R.E.

JAN - DEC 1917

WAR DIARY.

23rd. Field Coy. R. E.

1st. DIVISION.

JANUARY. 1917.

Army Form C. 2118.

War Diary C 2118

23rd Field Coy R.E.
January 1917

WAR DIARY
or
INTELLIGENCE SUMMARY.
(Erase heading not required.)

Instructions regarding War Diaries and Intelligence Summaries are contained in F.S. Regs., Part II. and the Staff Manual respectively. Title pages will be prepared in manuscript.

Place	Date	Hour	Summary of Events and Information	Remarks and references to Appendices
FRICOURT 23 c 6.9 & BAZENTIN 57 d 5.4.5.8	1/1		CORPS BLOCKS A POST. Sappers digging new trench and revetting with U frames & pickets. 10 sappers put in - portion of wire abatis and wire 15 mid way between C & D.	
			HUTTING CONTD. Mebium sheds Coy H.Q.	
			BAZENTIN. Improving main shelter. Drainage - making tables for D[?].	
			FRICOURT. New hut for orderlies officers T.R.[?]	
			Carting stores.	
	2/1		CORPS BLOCKS Contd A POST. 15 yds ? deepened & revetted.	
			HUTTING CONTD. Abbution sheds Coy H.Q.	
			BAZENTIN. Four Br. Div. Cross ambs.	
			FRICOURT. Flooring new hut contd.	
			Carting stores.	ii Lt PALIN 10th Glosters attached for Pioneer Course
			Officers Mess Crane Stand - Section Washery commenced.	
	3/1		CORPS BLOCKS. Work contd A POST A.	
			HUTTING. Abbution sheds contd. Coy H.Q.	
			Commenced removing Bde H.Q.s from J 8 & J 9 to S 14 Central.	
			BAZENTIN. Watering Entrance Road. Camouflaging.	
			FRICOURT. Flooring main hut.	
			Section Washing - Officers Mess Crane contd.	
			Carting Stores.	

Army Form C. 2118.

WAR DIARY
or
INTELLIGENCE SUMMARY.

23RD FIELD COY.
JANY. 1917

(Erase heading not required.)

Instructions regarding War Diaries and Intelligence Summaries are contained in F. S. Regs., Part II. and the Staff Manual respectively. Title pages will be prepared in manuscript.

Place	Date	Hour	Summary of Events and Information	Remarks and references to Appendices
FRICOURT BAZENTIN 28.M.9 BAZENTIN S.15.b.58	4/1		Corps BILLETS Conts - POST A - Scratcoat + revetting trenches WIRING. About 300' apron finished. HUTTING. Filling stoves in CAMP. Running Pole to Rly cont. Drainage conts. BAZENTIN. Extending entrance road - Sundry running jobs. FRICOURT. Improving + repairing substance Rd. Lecture Raising + Officers Pioneer class conts. Casting Stores	
	5/1.		As above.	
	6/1.		As above.	
	7/1.		As above.	
	8/1.		CORPS BILLETS. (Nightwork), 150' high wire trestles - 450' long dug with apron 1 side. Relief screens unto 50' long. (Rue C Pose W). Two large Infantry parts Employed. Work hindered by very bad weather.	No. 2 Section completed training + proceeded to FRICOURT 15 BAZENTIN - N. 3 Section + No. 3 section to FRICOURT for training - No. 1 Section to BAZENTIN + No. 4 Section to FRICOURT for duty.
			HUTTING - Pole Hut Area. Running conts FRICOURT Lecture training to officers Pioneer course conts. CORPS BILLETS Over 300' entanglement completed. 2 Ind. parties.	
	9/1.		HUTTING. As above - BAZENTIN. Drainage improvement - Canvas Screen stables erected. FRICOURT. Improvements to substance Rd conts. Lecture training + Officers Pioneer class conts. Casting Stores	

A5834 Wt. W4973/M687 750,000 8/16 D. D. & L. Ltd. Forms/C.2118/13

Army Form C. 2118.

WAR DIARY
or
INTELLIGENCE SUMMARY.
(Erase heading not required.)

23RD FIELD Coy. R.E.
JANY 1917

Place	Date	Hour	Summary of Events and Information	Remarks and references to Appendices
FRICOURT F.3.b.09 & BAZENTIN P.15.6.58.	10/1		CORPS BEFERS. WIRING - Wire west of C Post completed (Intermediate line) between Br. & Pnts. 2.50" L.W. ready for fastening. Infantry working/carrying parties 300 men.	
			HUTTING. Hole H.Q. Rn SABOT COPSE cont'd	
			BAZENTIN - Sundry repairs (obs)	
			FRICOURT. Estaminet road repairs - Section training cont'd Officers Pioneer Course (1st class under Capt COHEN R.E.) concluded - Carting Stones -	
	11/1		CORPS BEFERS. INTERMEDIATE LINE. Wiring between Posts A, B & C completed.	Lt PAUN. 10th Gloesters rejoin run sent 2nd Lt R.B. MACLEOD 1st Eastern Highlanders } attached for lt. G. MEREY. 8th R. Berks } Pioneer Course
			HUTTING as above	
			BAZENTIN " "	
			FRICOURT. Estaminet road repairs. Section training contd Officers 'PIONEER' Course (2nd class) started under Capt COHEN) throwing Abt D. men.	
	12/1		CORPS BEFERS. Repair damage by shellfire to Post A.	
			HUTTING Pole H.Q. R.E. SABOT COPSE completed	
			FRICOURT Section training and Officers 'Pioneer' course contd Erecting new Aviation Shelter 2 Carpenters working of FS Dim. HQ Rm.	
	13/1		CORPS BEFERS. Repairs to A Post finished	Major WILSON R.E. returns to 7th Corps RE
			HUTTING Aviation Sheds in CAYPS 11 - 4	
			BAZENTIN Posts and rails to Burl Cross erected High Wood	
			FRICOURT. Section Training + Officers Pioneer Course cont'd Carting Stone.	

Army Form C. 2118.

WAR DIARY
or
INTELLIGENCE SUMMARY.

(Erase heading not required.)

Instructions regarding War Diaries and Intelligence Summaries are contained in F. S. Regs., Part II. and the Staff Manual respectively. Title pages will be prepared in manuscript.

23rd Field Coy. R.E.
Jany 1917

Place	Date	Hour	Summary of Events and Information	Remarks and references to Appendices
ALBERT 7.31-0.9 BAZENTIN 9.15.b.58	14/1		HUTMENTS. Hut. huts in CAMPS. 1, 2 & 3. Ablution sheds in Nos 1, 1 & 2 and lining in 3 - BAZENTIN. Repairing kennel and draining latrines - FRICOURT. Repairs to entrance road contd. Section training and officers Pioneer course contd.	Section No. 4 commences repairing "3" duty section FRICOURT Lieut Smyth R.E. proceeds to BAZENTIN - 15 Feb 1917 returns to FRICOURT. Mr. MILSON R.E. returns to BAZENTIN
	15/1		HUTMENTS. Hut. huts in CAMPS. 1, 2, 3 & 4. Fixing water tanks in HIGH WOOD CAMPS E & W. BAZENTIN RAILWAY STN. A.S.C. platforms commenced FRICOURT. Road repair contd. Raising T.B. hutt. Section training and officers Pioneer course contd.	
	16/1 17/1		As above.	
	18/1		HUTMENTS. Stores now total 56 all huts in CAMPS 1, 2, 3 & 4. (with exception of wind R.M. & M. stores camp 1). About 16 stores required to complete camps. Hut huts in CAMPS. 3 but. HIGH WOOD. E & W. BAZENTIN RLY STN. Contd. FRICOURT. Wagon repair - Section training contd - Officers Pioneer class contd - Lasting stone -	Major Wilson R.E. proceeds to FRICOURT
	19/1		HUTTING. Hut huts in CAMPS 3 & 4. BAZENTIN RLY STN. 4nd. Platform. 180' x 13'-6". Completed - 2nd " 35' x 18'-6" - ½ " FRICOURT. Raising T.B. huts. Section training & Officers Pioneer course contd.	" Lt GILLESPIE R.E. proceeds to BAZENTIN

WAR DIARY
or
INTELLIGENCE SUMMARY.
(Erase heading not required.)

23rd FIELD Co. R.E.
JANy. 1917

Army Form C. 2118.

Place	Date	Hour	Summary of Events and Information	Remarks and references to Appendices
FRICOURT P.3.b.a.9. BAZENTIN S.15.c.5.8.	20/1		HUTTING Work carried on in CAMPS 2, 3 & 5. BAZENTIN RY. STN. 2nd Platform (for R.S.O) Post & finished. FRICOURT. Raising T.B. butts. – Building new dismantls to wagon line road – Section training contd. Officers Annex – 2nd etage finished – Note This annex was composed of 2 etages – each consisting of 6 officers from Bria + 2 from 5th WELCH PIONEERS. By this means 1 officer from every Infantry Bn. in the Bria attaches his Coronet + from the 6th WELCH. Pioneers Bn.	Maj. W. R. WILSON, R.E. R.E. proceeds to 1st D.E. as acting C.R.E. Capt. E.G. COHEN R.E. assumes acting command in his absence. 2 Lt. J. SMITH R.E. appointed HUTTING OFFICER. 2/Lt. MACLEOD, 2/Lt. CAMERON S. & 2/Lt. MELBY, 8th R. BERKS, & rejoin their unit. [stamp: 23rd FIELD COMPANY No. ... FEB 1917 ROYAL ENGINEERS]
	21/1		HUTTING 6th WELCH CAMP + No 2. Water supply contd. BAZENTIN RY. STN. 2nd Platform & hut for R.S.O completed. FRICOURT Carting heavy stones to 9 Dump preparatory to moving. Section training contd.	Lt. FORWOOD R.E. and Sections 3 + 4 moved to BAZENTIN. Sections 1 + 2 proceed to FRICOURT. 2/Lt. GILLESPIE R.E. returns to FRICOURT.
	22/1		CORPS BLOCKS Pvt. A. Ruckling adds to dugouts and commencing Russian 3cm. BAZENTIN RY. STN. Improvements. HUTTING water supply contd. in CAMP 2. FRICOURT Carting heavy stones to 9 Dump preparatory to moving.	
	23/1 24/1		As above.	Work under 50th D.E. ceased on evening of 24/1/17.

Army Form C. 2118.

WAR DIARY
or
INTELLIGENCE SUMMARY.
(Erase heading not required.)

23rd FIELD COY. R.E.
JANUARY - 1917

Instructions regarding War Diaries and Intelligence Summaries are contained in F. S. Regs., Part II. and the Staff Manual respectively. Title pages will be prepared in manuscript.

Place	Date	Hour	Summary of Events and Information	Remarks and references to Appendices
GRIVCOURT to BAZENTIN 51.S.6.5.8.	25/1.		Handing over forward billets and work. Hutting & trolleys supply handed over to C.R.E. 50th Divn. handed over CORPS Works to 3rd A.E.Coy. A.E. 25 Galv. over Company billets - Australian Barn.	
MARLOY	26/1.		Lt. FORWOOD.R.E - 1st Lt. SMITH. R.E. and section 3rd to RICOURT - 1st Lt. GILLESPIE and No.1 section proceeds to 1st Lt. GILLESPIE and No.1 section proceeds over Company billets - 25 Galv. over Company billets - 11 Lt COWLEY R.E proceeds to MARLOY -	(stamp: COMPLETED 15 MAR 1917 ROYAL ENGINEERS)
			CAPT COHEN. R.E. Lieut FORWOOD R.E. Lt SMITH with Company (less 1 section) march to billets at MARLOY via ALBERT. MILLENCOURT - HENENCOURT. arriving at 1pm.	
	27/1.		Cleaning up and informing billets. Repairs at Brit School FREMENCOURT.	
	28/1. 29/1. 30/1. 31/1.		Company training. Repairs at Brit School FREMENCOURT. " to BATH HOUSE BAIZIEUX.	
	31/1/		Lt. B. B. EDWARDS. M.C. R.E return to the Company for duty.	ELE

E.D. Oehrenzift
Major R.E.
Commanding 23rd (Fld.) Coy. R.E.

WAR DIARY.

23rd. Field Coy. R.E.

1st. DIVISION.

FEBRUARY. 1917.

Army Form C. 2118.

WAR DIARY
or
INTELLIGENCE SUMMARY.
(Erase heading not required.)

Vol 29
23rd FIELD Coy. R.E.
2nd-3rd JANUARY 1917

FEB 1917 — FIELD COMPANY — ROYAL ENGINEERS

Place	Date	Hour	Summary of Events and Information	Remarks and references to Appendices
MARLOY	1/2		Company training – Company drill under 2 Lieut. T.R.E. Paperchase for whole company afternoon. Lecture to N.C.O.s on WIRE ENTANGLEMENTS by Capt E.J. COHEN. R.E.	Lt EDWARDS M.C. R.E. proceeds to BECQUINCOURT to live with the Chef de Génie 24ᵉ Divn (FRENCH) to take over Engineer work generally.
	2/2		Company training – Details, major, Company, with exception of orderlies and guards at LA PLAQUE – Packing up for move.	Major H.R. WILSON M.C. R.E. rejoins company.
MARLOY & MERRICOURT sur SOMME.	3/3		Sunny march Section 1, 2 & 3 went forward and rendered passable portion of road between RIBEMONT and BAILLY which was flooded and holding up the column.	Company marches from MARLOY at 9.30am for MERRICOURT SUR SOMME via BAIZIEUX, RIBEMONT pt 105, BAILLY, CERISY and MORCOURT. Company marches with 2ⁿᵈ Bde and bombing starting point at AMIENS-ALBERT main road at 11. A.M. Arrives in billet camps at 7. P.m.
MERRICOURT SUR SOMME	4/5		Men cleaning wagons.	
MERRICOURT, MOULIN DE BECQUINCOURT 116 L.I. FONTAINE DE CAPPY Mad 27. Map references Sheet 62 C. J.M 1/40	5/5			Company marches from MARLOY with 2ⁿᵈ Bde to billet at MOULIN DE BECQUINCOURT passing horselines at Chateau FONTAINE DE CAPPY. Pass starting point at 11.15am. Route: CHUIGNOLLES, CHUIGNES and DOMPIERRES. The Bde with company marched past Gen. HIRSCHAUER G.O.C. 18ᵉ French Corps, and Gen. PULTENEY G.O.C. III Corps near CHUIGNOLLET. Lt Lt GILLESPIE R.E. with M. JEUDET (Interpretér) 3 N.C.O.s and 2 sappers proceeds to BOIS DE BOULOGNE (N16 central) to reconnoitre line and work to be taken over from the FRENCH GENIE. Details sent to take over dumps.

Army Form C. 2118.

WAR DIARY
or
INTELLIGENCE SUMMARY.

(Erase heading not required.)

23rd FIELD COY. R.E.
FEBRUARY 1917.

Place	Date	Hour	Summary of Events and Information	Remarks and references to Appendices
BEAUMCOURT BOIS DE BOULOGNE & FONTAINE DE CAPPY	6/2		Company improving billets at BEAUMCOURT and FONTAINE DE CAPPY. Officers reconnoitring dumps &c. " Lt. W.G. SMITH. R.E. reconnoitring CORPS DEFENCE LINE with C.E. III CORPS (Brig. Gen. HEPPENBERG) — L.E.	No. 1 Section forms with Lt GILLESPIE. R.E. in forward billets at BOIS DE BOULOGNE.
Map 62 C. S.W. 10.000	7/2		Work as above in billets. All officers taking over from the French —	Lt. FORWOOD. R.E. and No 4 Section proceed to forward billets at BOIS DE BOULOGNE. Lt. B.B. EDWARDS. N.C.R.E. rejoins Company. " Lt SMITH. R.E. detached for work on 2nd line under III Corps
	8/2		Work commenced on partially completed dugout M3 and M4 in TRANCHÉE DU POIVRE. Repairing pump near B. DE GUADALOUPE H16b.6.5. Improving billets. B. DE BOULOGNE. Work commenced on horse shelter at FONTAINE LES CAPPY. Building workshop. BEAUMCOURT DUMP. Carting stores —	
	9/2		Dugouts. M.3. Iron mining sides, shaft and sheeting — M.4. SS4. complete Installing new pump & spring B.L. 7th Gns in QUARRY. H16a.8.3. Back Section. Stabling contd. Making and delivering hinds notice boards. Moving into new billets M6d.S3. Carting stones from LA NEUQUE to BOIS LE BOULOGNE.	

Army Form C. 2118.

WAR DIARY
or
INTELLIGENCE SUMMARY.
(Erase heading not required.)

23rd FIELD COY. R.E.
FEBRUARY 1917

Place	Date	Hour	Summary of Events and Information	Remarks and references to Appendices
BECQUINCOURT. M6 d.5.3. BOIS DE BOULOGNE N16 a.8.3. FONTAINE LES CAPPY M9 d.2.8.	10/2		Dugouts. M9 (N23 a.1.6) Sheeting to sides of shaft 80% completed. M4. 70% completed Rock sections. Roofing to horse standing finished. Improvements to billets contd. Cooking stoves.	
	11/2		Dugouts M3 - (N23 a.1.6) completed. M4. (N22 b.27) 80% completed. Bull section Roof to side sinkle FONTAINE LES CAPPY completed. Improvements to billets M6 & S3 contd. Cooking stoves. Repairs to pump near Bosjois NOUVIEZA about N22 c.36.	
	12/2		Dugouts. M4. (N22 b.2.7) 85% complete. Repairs to pump N22 c.36 in conjunction with the French GENIE. BACK SECTIONS Improving horselines and billets. Cooking stoves.	Lt EDWARDS R.E. proceeds to B. DE BOULOGNE and GILLESPIE R.E. returns to BECQUINCOURT.
	13/2		Dugouts. M4. 90% complete. Officers making reconnaissance of M.G. Dugout in Reserve line at N16 & 05. BACK SECTIONS. As above.	

Army Form C. 2118.

WAR DIARY
or
INTELLIGENCE SUMMARY.

(Erase heading not required.)

23rd Z.E.Z.P. Coy. R.E.
FEBRUARY 1917

Instructions regarding War Diaries and Intelligence Summaries are contained in F.S. Regs., Part II. and the Staff Manual respectively. Title pages will be prepared in manuscript.

Place	Date	Hour	Summary of Events and Information	Remarks and references to Appendices
BECQUINCOURT M6 d 53 BOIS DE BOULOGNE N16 a 8.3 FONTAINE LES CAPPY M9 d L8	14/2		DUGOUT. M.4. (N22 b 2.7). 95% completed. Work commenced on repairs to Bn. H. Qrs (173 BDE Hd Qrs) at BOIS DE BOULOGNE, badly damaged by shellfire on 13/2. BRICK SECTIONS work on Stables contd Carting stones to BOIS DE BOULOGNE. Party improving AV West.	Capt E.G. COHEN assumed command of Company during absence of O.C. 2nd Lt GILLESPIE R.E. performs duties of Capt.
	15/2		DUGOUT M.4 (N.22 6 2.7) 98% completed. Commenced M.G. Post. N22 a 1.9. Capt COHEN R.E. made a reconnaissance with Recd. No. DUBBIE (J.S.O.1) and work commenced in the evening. Heavy hand dug at right angles to proposed entrances. BRICK SECTIONS as above. Party improving and widening AV West.	No 2 Section proceeds to BOIS DE BOULOGNE to relieve No 1 which return to BECQUINCOURT
	16/2		Work commenced on 3rd entrance to M.G. Dugout near GUADALOUPE AVENUE (N16 d o 5). DUGOUTS N 16 d o 5. Shaft 10% completed. N.22 a 1.9. Trench as above deepened to 8 ft. except where works now commenced. BRICK SECTIONS as above. Carpenters working at Bde HQrs (Right) at ASSEVILLERS.	
	17/2		DUGOUTS. N22 a 1.9. Work commenced on humid trench communicating with REUNION AVENUE. frost very severe making it frozen condition of ground 3 ft down to 1 ft. BRICK SECTIONS as above.	No 3 Section relieves No 4 which return to BECQUINCOURT

Army Form C. 2118.

WAR DIARY
or
INTELLIGENCE SUMMARY.
(Erase heading not required.)

232nd Field Coy. R.E.
February 1917

Instructions regarding War Diaries and Intelligence Summaries are contained in F.S. Regs., Part II. and the Staff Manual respectively. Title pages will be prepared in manuscript.

Place	Date	Hour	Summary of Events and Information	Remarks and references to Appendices
BECOURT ALT. M.6.d.53. BOIS DE BOULOGNE N.16.a.83. FONTAINE LES CAPPY N.9.d.2.8	18/2.		DUGOUTS N.16.d.08 - Shaft 15% complete. Concealed Post N.22.a.19 - contd - hodging party employed riving to Relief. Sappers carrying up camouflaging material and making frames for revetting. Gas Helmets being fitted to Adv billets - 6 men and N.C.O go forward to Adv billets each day to Details and inspect them. BATH SECTIONS. Improving stables and service billets - Carting stores -	
	19/2		DUGOUTS H.16.d.08. 20% complete at shaft. Concealed M.G. post N.22.a.19. Party of 50 Black Watch digging. Hindered C.T. Ground very hard + frozen shaft driven down to 18". Sappers camouflaging after work. Filling gas Helmets to advanced billets. BATH SECTIONS as above. Carpenters finish at Bde HQrs ASSEVILLERS.	
	20/2.		DUGOUTS N.16.d.08. Third shaft at 50% complete. Concealed Post N.22.a.19. Blinded trench contd - Now 3 ft in depth. 50% complete. 50 BLACK WATCH digging. Trestle Pump for 1st Bde. Bath Section as above - N.C.O attending bungalow Torpedo practice - at TELEGRAPH CAMP. N.C.O making Road Reconnaissance. BOIS DE BOULOGNE RD H.C.O. 1577 Bde ra pumps giving trouble. Repairing damage to trestle billets caused by contraction of Thaw and rain. Lt. SMITH with C.E. N.E. R.E. over CORPS LINE	Lt COMPOS. R.E. to 1st Report at FRESHENCOURT to lecture.

Army Form C. 2118.

WAR DIARY
or
INTELLIGENCE SUMMARY.

23RD FIELD COY, R.E.
FEBRUARY 1917

(Erase heading not required.)

Instructions regarding War Diaries and Intelligence Summaries are contained in F.S. Regs., Part II. and the Staff Manual respectively. Title pages will be prepared in manuscript.

Place	Date	Hour	Summary of Events and Information	Remarks and references to Appendices
BECQUINCOURT M6 d 53 BOISSE BOULOGNE N 16 a 83 FONTINELET CAMP M 9 d 28	2/1/2		M.G. POST (N22 a 19) Blinded C.T. about 60% complete. SUGDT. (N16 d 05) cont₅. Air Billets Party continue returning (from Ram billets) Reconstruction. Clearing mud from track leading to hill. Carting stores to Bois de Boulogne.	2 Lt M.G. SMITH. R.E. hands over CORPS LINE to Officer of 409th (London) Fd. Coy. R.E. and proceeds to Adv. billets.
	22/2		As above.	2 Lt COMPASS. M.C. R.E. returned for duty from PREVENGUEY proceeds to Avenue billets
	23/2		" "	" " " " " "
	24/2		M.G. POST (N22 a 19) - Approved width run 4'6" dept. Corn hutch widened to take new steel frames. M.G. POST (N16 d 05) Shaft 90% finished. Pump at GUADALOUPE AVENUE repaired. BRICKSECTIONS. One section on roadwork between half village and ASSEVILLERS. Table improvement cont⁴. Carting stores to Bois de Boulogne.	
	25/2		M.G. POST (N22 a 38 ?) Approved width down to 5'0". M.G. POST (N16 d 05) Shaft finished. BRICKSECTIONS - 1 section on ASSEVILLERS RD. with party of 50 Infantry. This section was relieved by section of 26th Fd Coy R.E. Transport loading tents x c. + bully sticks & coverings.	Lt HARWOOD. R.E. with section 1 & 4, being relieved by section of 26th Fd Coy R.E. 2 Lt EDWARDS with that section return to BECQUINCOURT

FEB. 1917
ROYAL ENGINEERS

A.S. 834 Wt. W 4973/M687 750,000 8/16 D. D. & L. Ltd. Forms/C.2118/13.

WAR DIARY or INTELLIGENCE SUMMARY

Army Form C. 2118.

23RD. FIELD COY. R.E.

FEBRUARY - 1917

Place	Date	Hour	Summary of Events and Information	Remarks and references to Appendices
CHUIGNOLLES	26/2		Packing up and moving to Reserve Billets. Carpenters working at D.A.H.Q.s. erecting NISSEN hut. Officers reconnoitring works.	Company less Section 1 & 4 marched to CHUIGNOLLES leaving BECQUINCOURT at 10 a.m. - Lt. C.H. WALES. R.E. reports for duty - attached from Lb'th R.E. Coy. R.E. Lt. J.F. ECHLIN. R.E. (T.F.) attached from 428th (E.LANCS) F.D. COY. R.E. 4.25 p.m.
"	27/2		CHUIGNES. Sir Balthorne - Excavation for fuel tank 4'-6" x 8'-0" x 3'-6". 1000 bricks salved and cleaned for above. Drying huts erected for socks. Plan to this enabled for washing machines. Drains cleared & repaired. SAN. MLLE. Officers & party to CERISY dismantled engine and boiler for removal to CHUIGNOLLES. CHUIGNES RAILHEAD. Officer supervising drainage party (Infantry). CHUIGNOLLES (1) Surveyor & Plumber - visiting water points. (2) Carpenters at D.A.H.Qrs. erecting NISSEN hut. (3) Road Hands loss in sundry items of work. (4) Road sweeper fetched from MERRICOURT. R.E. Park No 6. (5) Improving harnessing and carting stones from PROYART. CHUIGNES. BATH HOUSE : as above. CAMP : Flooring to Officers hts commenced. RAINIERS. Working road sweeper.	
"	28/2		CHUIGNOLLES (1) Erecting Saw mill. (2) Workshop. Sundry repairs (iii) D.A.H.Q. hut. (iii) Surveyor & Plumber repairing water points CHUIGNOLLES. (iv) Carting material to CHUIGNOLLES.	D.C.M. ribbon presented to C.S.M. J.E. SUMMERS R.E. by Corps Commander. (Gen. Sir W. PULTENEY).

[signature] Major R.E.
Commanding 23rd (Fld.) Coy. R.E.

WAR DIARY.

23rd. Field Coy., R.E.

1st. DIVISION.

MARCH, 1917.

Army Form C. 2118.

WAR DIARY
or
INTELLIGENCE SUMMARY.
(Erase heading not required.)

23RD FIELD Coy. R.E.
MARCH 1917.

Vol 20

Place	Date	Hour	Summary of Events and Information	Remarks and references to Appendices
CHUIGNOLLES	1/3		Officer reconnoitring with TOWN MAJOR CHUIGNOLLES, all photo-stereoscopes - Fire precaution - Reg. CHUIGNOLLES Girl Battn. work home for sucks completed. Brick drain laid connecting same with filter trenches. Extensions and improvements to soakpit. Stand for waste-oils cleared and half bricked - CHUIGNES CAMP. 3 bays of officers hut floored + partitioned 6 Bustles erected	New green devilly dries issued to all ranks.
	2/3		Road surface at work - CHUIGNES RAILHEAD. Enquad and saw benches transported from CERISY. Bag plates & joists placed in position for stamping. Smithy carpenters Etc. CHUIGNES reconnoitred as above for full precaution. Report sent to D.E. Ramp built from main road with level crossings over railway tracks to give access to halfway man RAILHEAD. Pont-à-flare NISSEN hut - 5/9/0 - Road surface at work - Repairs required Saw mill works. Horse standings ends - Sundry carpenter work - Partitioning + flooring CHUIGNES CAMP huts	i/c Lt Sgt 114. having attains below on how Box RESPIRATOR detailed to fit all helmets for which he is responsible.
	3/3		As above -	Maj. W.R. WILSON returns from leave and resumes command.

WAR DIARY
or
INTELLIGENCE SUMMARY.

Army Form C. 2118.

23rd Fd Coy R.E.
MARCH 1917

Place	Date	Hour	Summary of Events and Information	Remarks and references to Appendices
CHUIGNOLLES	4/3		CHUIGNES. Bris Brdle & Bottle Brin finished. (1) 2nd Brick filled tank finished. (2) 3rd " " " " commenced. (3) Gegsen k hutter repaired. CHUIGNES CAMP (a) both light trestle forkway erected from footbridge to new platform at waterpoint. (b) 100ft footroad laid on piles. (c) Floorboarding + partitioning in Officers hut completed. (d) 16 bunks made for Officers CHUIGNOLLES (1) Gunners photo carts (2) Luminous direction boxes (3) Shots in hut - trying Tollans to render fireproof (4) Sundries -	
CHUIGNOLLES BECQUINCOURT DOMP. M.6 b & E BOIS DE BOULOGNE N.16 a 23.-	5/3		Troops as above cont'd and handed over to Officer of 409th (Lowland) Fd Coy R.E.	No 1 Section under Lt EDWARDS. M.C. R.E marched to forward billets in BOIS DE BOULOGNE No 3 Section under Lt ? & Wales R.S marched to Ho Qu. billet at BECQUINCOURT
FONTAINE LES CAPPY. M.9.c.58.	6/3		Dugouts work taken over on N.10 a 3.1 ½ N.11 c.o.5. N.11 b 4.6. Stores carted to BOIS DE BOULOGNE Officer taking over roadwork. Roadwork. MEAULTE QUARRY RD - 180 fascines laid at N.4 b.5.9 - 100' of ground cleared of mud and drained -	No 4 Section under Lt POTHRO. R.E marched 15 forward billets in BOIS DE BOULOGNE No 2 Section under Lt CONWAY. R.E and Staff marched to BECQUINCOURT billet

Army Form C. 2118.

WAR DIARY
or
INTELLIGENCE SUMMARY.

(Erase heading not required.)

23RD FIELD COY R.E.
MARCH 1917.

Place	Date	Hour	Summary of Events and Information	Remarks and references to Appendices
BEAUCOURT CAMP M6 central BOIS DE BOULOGNE N 16 a 83. FONTAINE LES CAPPY M 9 c 58.	7/3		Dugouts. N 10 d 3½ } continued - N 11 e 0.5 } N 11 7.6 } Roadwork. Half section by day laid brick and worked on drainage between BECQUINCOURT and HERBECOURT Half section by night laid 50 fascines at M 4 b 57. 230 fascines wired together in half of rebands. Threestrading for 10 horses completed - Entering huts at BECQUINCOURT and BOIS DE BOULOGNE making notice boards Carting stores to MEUDON QUARRY and BOIS DE BOULOGNE	2/Lt J.P. ECHLIN R.E. proceeds to Armd. Section at BOIS DE BOULOGNE.
	8/3		Dugouts as above - Roadwork between BECQUINCOURT - HERBECOURT and MEUDON QUARRY. Party of 200 Infantry on former - Back work as above -	
	9/3		As above -	
	10/3		As above	
	11/3		As above. Also two NISSEN huts erected to house the Infantry Road making parties unshielded.	(2/Lt Cowley relieves Lt.
	12/3		As above. No work on BECQUINCOURT - HERBECOURT Road owing to Bde. Relief.	100 men arrive forming party for Roads.

WAR DIARY
or
INTELLIGENCE SUMMARY.
(Erase heading not required.)

Army Form C. 2118.

23rd Field Coy. R.E.
March 1917

Place	Date	Hour	Summary of Events and Information	Remarks and references to Appendices
Becquincourt Dump M16 Central = Coy. H.Q. B. de Boulogne N.16.a.6.3 = Adv. L.H.P Block Fontaine le Cappy M9c.5.5 = Transport Lines	13/3		Becquincourt, Herbecourt & Heudon Quarry Roads Contd. Brickwork reform reparation & salted. Permanent Roads Part I. Vingt. of 200 being formed to work in roads with R.E. Vingt. on right. B'de Front-Shaft to Left B'de Front under R.E. Coft on Infantrie areas. Work on Dug out continued.	Capt E.G. Olen proceeds to 4" Army School at Flesicourt as instructor to attend off strength on from 13. inst. Lt Edwards takes on duties of Second in Command
	14/3		Road work as above. Dug out Contd. do —	Left half Coy. of Road party L.H.S utilisation by 23" Field Co. 11 W. Echelon reforms his unit
	15/3		do —	Major Ridduk R.E. A.2.8. R.N.Co. D.E. attached from 42" Div.
	16/3		Roads Contd. Look took a Dug out stopped at mid day Report received from Bangalore Torpedo try was same enemy to friend put in barbedwire Lt Smith with Small party R.E. reports to HQ. 1" Cams. to Lt Corsley 2nd Lt N.O. 10th Glos (Royal Bk) (Left Bk.) 10 p.m. Left Batn tried successful in by using 1 Torpedo but Right Batn failed to get through enemy wire at final attempt. Bangalore he went early in morning of 17."	
	17/3	4 a.m	One Bangalore Torpedo placed in German wire by Sergt Elcombe (N.1.8602) & Capt Byrd more men of C. Coy Artillery formed fire lifted Torpedo was fired & road arrangement for using Torpedo party ran caught in artillery barrage. did much difficulty in getting back Enemy M.G. fire found killing no 1.10.610 wounding Sgt. Elcombe 10⁺ ride full (Capt reported to following day) Having gap in German wire cit. to Div. H.Q.	Lt Smith returns & Bequincourt Sgt Elcombe evacuated wounded

Army Form C. 2118.

WAR DIARY
or
INTELLIGENCE SUMMARY.
(Erase heading not required.)

23rd Field Coy R.E.
March 1917

Place	Date	Hour	Summary of Events and Information	Remarks and references to Appendices
Do.	18/3	9.30am	Lt Smith & 2/Lt Corby meet officer 1st Cant. H.Q., braced R. Etaypigny to make reconnaissance to repair x Somme Bridges. 2/Lt Corby returns in evening with report, leaving later with S.S.L. No 2 Zimber to Etaypigny.	
	19/3	2am	2/Lt Corby, & Sect 2 L Etaypigny by 2am & work on Bridge crossings (4) Main rise at O.21.a.2/2.6/2.	Etaypigny Bridge had main[?] covered with transport, the decking having been very thin. Foot bridge had been destroyed previously at the Boyer main gate. The Beams had been mostly destroyed by [?] and part had been [?] by fire in [?]. Taxed [?] has been [?]
		8am	2/Lt Corby & Sect 3 with Lt Smith arrive at Etaypigny at 8am and to Bridging	Lering [?] Larger pit [?] Braston [?] Charges not found but that sinking La Fire packet & explosives were with Tools Engr 2 Bdy & Bro & charge Canal bridge approach range in this about 700 [?] was destroyed.
Etaypigny O.20 & 67 H.Q.s. with Transport Hop at Fontaine le Cappy Mule Beguincourt at Cappy		9.30am	Two Oxford Crops. & 1/Lt Bell cross in Single file at 9am. Sect. 1 & 4 crossed [?] and arrive in afternoon. Continue Bridging Work. Foot Bridge 300' up stream O.21.a.1.2 repaired & made passable for Inf in Single file. Hurst Carnal in [?] 7.30 pm by 3 actions. Lot 4 [?] till 10 pm in [?] hut brute Antwerp ch B de Boudgery assisted & Bre in clearing Barleux Road for Traffic.	Bottom of main has been made trackless, Holes shelving 12'.1'-15' hit the ground & extensive from wall Creating in the Canal. Gave much trouble army to Still crushing in demolition battle, and "dead" falls by pontoon train took want up
	20/3		& Lotions on Bridges from 6am till 7pm. Making of W for Field Guns. Small foot bridge (Single file) finished & not load ready. Cross houe in use daily in the cart	This O. Cops pontoon took place of main column of Somme to word the trouble of running bridge by pontoon train last went up Gorre, La Bassee Canal Etc 19/3
	21/3		Full Coy on Main Field Gun Bridge at Etaypigny O.21.a.2/2.6/2.	

Army Form C. 2118.

WAR DIARY
or
INTELLIGENCE SUMMARY.
(Erase heading not required.)

23rd Field Coy RE
March 1917

Instructions regarding War Diaries and Intelligence Summaries are contained in F. S. Regs., Part II. and the Staff Manual respectively. Title pages will be prepared in manuscript.

Place	Date	Hour	Summary of Events and Information	Remarks and references to Appendices
H.Q. Etérpigny Office Becquincourt Transfelt-Lines		O 20 b 6,7 M 6 C 5,9 M 9 C 5,8	Etérpigny (Wesbury) Bridge O 21 a 2½ 6½. Sect for field guns. Preparing in pieces at 1.30 p.m.	Sects 2 & 3 return to Bde Boulogue. Work on Villers Carbonnel Road under Duties of Brig-Gen 2nd Rate
	22/3		Sects 1 & 4 improving Etérpigny Bridge & Removing Demking piles clearing old decking etc	
	23/3			H.Valio to Etérpigny from 3rd de Boulogue Sects 2 & 3 return to Etérpigny Road working "B" Major Riddick RE 425 Field Co RE (42nd Div) supervises this work Captain met the CRE 48 Div 23/3 Visit 23 Fd Coy Took over Construction of Lamire Bridge from 23 Fd Coy towards attrition HQ Office Staff from Becquincourt to Etérpigny
	24/3	5 a.m	Lt Forward Sect 4 start on Lamire Bridge under orders CRE 48 Div - but was relieved about 11 am	
			Sections 2 & 3 working on Brie Bridges 6 a.m - 2 p.m. 2 p.m - 6 p.m	
		Sects II 1,4	Parties - turning shaft digging at Gap No 3. Searching for foundation piles of old French Bridge Re-approached Balance of turning Staff throwing up old cart system on Road to Estrain at main Somme channel (Bridge No 6)	
		O 27 C 2 3½	A removing Dam Afternoon Staff started excavating for pounds at Bridge 5 + during Slast pulse on timber say abutment protection maintenance squad B R on Etérpigny Bridge	

Army Form C. 2118.

WAR DIARY
or
INTELLIGENCE SUMMARY.
(Erase heading not required.)

23rd Feb Corps R.E.
March 1917

Instructions regarding War Diaries and Intelligence Summaries are contained in F. S. Regs., Part II. and the Staff Manual respectively. Title pages will be prepared in manuscript.

Place	Date	Hour	Summary of Events and Information	Remarks and references to Appendices
HQ = Etérpigny Transport Lines Fouterre le Capp. M9 C58	25/3	D 20 B 17 M9 C58	Worked on Stocking selection 2 + 3 on Brie Bridge 6am-2pm. 11 Fd Coy V Nahs 1 - 2pm 2pm-10pm. Continued excavation for tumble & started laying timber footings for end work of abutments. Steel work of one girder of 60' Through Bridge (Portable Type 3) erected. 50 men of 1st Northants Collecting materials. Lancashire Girders Section. Lt Gillespie from Beguinvert to Fontaine l'Etapp in charge. (7 Remounts arrived leaving Coy at 5 under strength 70 men to (including Transport) 2 mios 2nd Grider erected on First End of Bridge. Enclosing SGT Willis Derrick failing launching, all of East abutment Complete. Arrangement of supports as above.	Bridge used is to clear span (Through) Portable Bridge Type 3. Each girder & section rolled boards. Foundation has started recently construction of Cpn Briggs beginning 20' × 14' view taken Fin high. Timber for laying was ready 16 × 10" memorandum A letter from Majr Laxd his been placed. Girders were assembled on Needle also launched singly - no trestle experienced. [Both worked a bank girder trestle would have mounted bed-plank of bridge in the two marks. Plank Piers] field only available for launching [to place] into field Cpn 1 were they ready Hun paper will probably make Great Dam nonetheless under
	26/3		10	
	27/3	7.30 am	1st Girder launched by 7.30 am based on Course of the morning. Four whip lines cross girders above each abutment. Second whip complete Cross girders away bracing girder struts, dismantled all launching gear. Timber road hand at bolts in position. Timber decking laid but not spiked.	in completion of Filling in l Flanks (m) Embankment by 26th Re left a large return of rates wants to the old main channel (Bridge 5) removed of the girders driven from channel found upstream hanged

Army Form C. 2118.

WAR DIARY
or
INTELLIGENCE SUMMARY.
(Erase heading not required.)

23rd Field Coy RE
March 1917

Place	Date	Hour	Summary of Events and Information	Remarks and references to Appendices
Etrepigny O 20 B 6.7 to Aire	28/3		Chiefs tents & stores. Picketing completed. billets spoiled Abutments filled in with broken brick stone well rammed. Rotunda Curbs & billets. Bridge ready for traffic by mid day. Afternoon relay engaged in improving road approaches clearing ground from all stores & returning same by Delainville road to West end of crossing.	3rd Corps messaging. Army Commander expresses his high appreciation of every and able work in early completion of BR.E crossing Corps Commander endorses the above & to be conveyed to the O.R.E. Field Engineer Brigade attachments and Field Coys, 1st Battalion North'd Fusiliers R.E. and Royal North Lancs whose efforts have attained this result. (Sgd) C. Ransome Brown Lieut Colonel R.E. C.R.E. 15 Div 11.30 am 29/3/17
	29/3		Baths rigged up by Canal bank. Brick tub at myocarted wrecks 1/2 Coy got hot bath Sect 1 - 2 working on pits of adv'd A.H.Q. O 31 a 7.2 in afternoon putting in piles for Nissen hut etc & also moving approaches returning road of No 6 Bus Bridge.	
	30/3		Below 1/2 Coy billet A.H.Q. 3rd m. (and 1/4 H.Q. Camp from O 26 c 7.4 - O 31 a 7.2 fallen in still late it. Two Nielson trestles (ing. equipment) put in Etrepigny Bridge.	
	31/3		Sect 1+2 7am - 1pm dismantling hill timber bridge parallel to No 6 (60' through) at Bois V stack piling for here dismantled light bridge Sect 3 1pm - 7pm continue piling Sect 3 continue re-decking of Etrepigny Bridge.	

WAR DIARY.

23rd. Filed. Coy., R.E.

1st. DIVISION.

APRIL. 1917.

Army Form C. 2118.

WAR DIARY
or
INTELLIGENCE SUMMARY.
(Erase heading not required.)

23rd F Coy RE
April 1917

Vol 31

[Stamp: 23RD FIELD COMPANY, MAY 1917, ROYAL ENGINEERS]

Place	Date	Hour	Summary of Events and Information	Remarks and references to Appendices
ETERPIGNY 4000x S. of PERONNE on R. SOMME. Horse lines at FONTAINE-LES-CAPPY.	1/4/17		Replacing No 6 Goff temporary bridge at BRIE. Piling to form basis of bridge continued. No 2 Section 7.30 a.m to 11 p.m. No 4 Section 1 p.m to 7 p.m. No 1 & 3 Sections inspected in marching order (with toolcarts) by C.E. III Corps. Br. General A.h. Schreiber C.M.G.	
Same	2/4/17		No 2 & No 4 Sections continue work on BRIE Bridge working same hours. No 1 Section work erecting huts to hold Advanced 4th Army H.Q at D.31.a.7.2. near VILLERS-CARBONNEL (2 p.m to 8 p.m hours of work) No 3 Section drawing bridging equipment from No 4 Pontoon Park at the first bridge outside PERONNE on main VILLERS-CARBONNEL - PERONNE road (Route Nationale No 17)	
Same	3/4/17		No 1 Section training (Squad & Section drill) in morning & cleaning waggons in the afternoon. No 2 Section continues morning shift on BRIE Bridge. No 3 Section works on Army H.Q. as above, No 4 No A so called off. BRIE bridge by C.R.E. to assist.	

Army Form C. 2118.

WAR DIARY
or
INTELLIGENCE SUMMARY.
(Erase heading not required.)

23rd Field Coy. R.E.
April 1917

Place	Date	Hour	Summary of Events and Information	Remarks and references to Appendices
As above	4/4/17		No 1 & 3 Sections working on a short piece of roadway at Eastern end of BRIE Bridge to make a siding to admit of lorries turning. No 2 Section continued the work on the MEDIUM BRIDGE in No 6 gap BRIE. No 4 section in camp training, drill use of explosives etc.	Start painting tentcarts & fixing up drag-ropes & petrol tins for water.
	5/4/17		No 1 & 3 Sections as above undermining & unloading the portion of roadway. (v. bad weather, heavy snows blizzard) No 4 Section carry on No 6 gap BRIE Bridge completing it with the erection of some bracing & handrails. No 2 training, drill, use of explosives etc.	
	6/4/17		Company as now directed to work on LAMIRE FARM Bridge. No 2, 3 & 4 commence work. No 1 resting & training as above, detachments of No 4 putting bracing on BRIE Bridge as above, & collecting boats, punts etc. from the river. Condition of bridge very bad. The former German Bridge had been comp[ose]d part of piles, across the two main channels the	18 new-pattern steel helmets with chain mail visors to protect eyes issued experimentally to sections. 111 men 7th Manchesters 42nd Div[isio]n attached for work on Bridge.

WAR DIARY
or
INTELLIGENCE SUMMARY.
(Erase heading not required.)

Army Form C. 2118.

23rd F.? Coy. R.E.
April 1917

[Stamp: 23rd (FIELD COMPANY) ROYAL ENGINEERS MAY 1917]

Place	Date	Hour	Summary of Events and Information	Remarks and references to Appendices
As above	6/4/17	mount'd	Remainder of cribs piers of stringers & square timbers laid on fascine rafts. The demolition had been very thoro' & the bridge had been worked on by at least six different companies in the preceding fortnight. The result was that the bridge was one great tangle of shattered timbers. Work commenced to make Bridge good. A new line was set out avoiding the worst portions & straightening off various curves. A 20' pile driver with ½ ton monkey brought down from BRIE Bridge & two small pile drivers made out of 7"×3" & the counter-weights of the level crossing (Monkey about 1cwt.) Work continued by all four sections on LAMIRE Bridge. 20' Pile driver brought down from BRIE & re-erected on a raft of two pontoons. A deviation foot-bridge made to keep the traffic off the main bridge so as not to hinder work. Pontoons in bridge over eastern main channel taken out so as to allow of piling. First 24' pile is driven right home by the weight of the monkey with no drop [range pile driver]	Two 20' piles butted & trapped together driven to 1" subsidence with 4' drop of ½ cwt monkey. Then two piles in main stream only.
As above	7/4/17			

Army Form C. 2118.

WAR DIARY
or
INTELLIGENCE SUMMARY.
(Erase heading not required.)

23rd F.d Coy. R.E.
April 1917.

Place	Date	Hour	Summary of Events and Information	Remarks and references to Appendices
As above	8/4/17.		Work continued as above on LAMIRE Bridge. Big pile driver driving piles in main eastern channel, & on picane raft foundation with brick rubble filling built on eastern bank of eastern main channel.	No 3 section commences 2nd days training under section officer Lt. Smith.
	9/4/17		Orders received to stop work on making LAMIRE FARM Bridge into a Medium Bridge & to make it only a foot bridge. All pontoon equipment to be taken out. Pontoon equipment to be also taken out of ETERPIGNY Bridge & replaced by piling. Rush order received to have all pontoons in water about 10 a.m. which was cancelled by C.E. in person about noon. 2.0' pile driver towed up stream to ETERPIGNY Bridge.	
	10/4/17		Work continued on both bridges. No 4 section commences piling at ETERPIGNY Bridge. No 2 work on LAMIRE FARM foot-bridge collecting baulks from an old German bridge downstream & improving old footway over western main channel.	No 3 section does 2nd day of training under section officer.

Army Form C. 2118.

WAR DIARY
or
INTELLIGENCE SUMMARY.

(Erase heading not required.)

23rd F? Coy R.E.
April 1917

Place	Date	Hour	Summary of Events and Information	Remarks and references to Appendices
Go above	11/4/17		Same work. No. 1 & 2 continue making KAMIRE foot bridge fit for traffic. No. 3 takes over filing operations on ETERPIGNY bridge.	No 4 does 1st day of section training under Lt Forrest
"	12/4/17		Same work. No. 1 Section alone works on KAMIRE Bridge. No 3 carry on filing on ETERPIGNY bridge in relief from 6 a.m. to 6 p.m. This bridge now finished & ready for traffic again.	No 2 does 2nd days training. Coy pontoons removed from Eterpigny Bridge & replaced by 4 pile trestle. Coy pontoon trestle left in bridge. Coy pontoons taken back to Coy Dump & ready move supervn K Pullen R.E.
"	13/4/17		No 2 Section carries on KAMIRE Bridge removing some land piers that had sunk & replacing them with piled trestles. No. 4 section carries out experiments with German floats salved from the river. No. 3 training on WELDON trestling.	No 1 tomorrow his class training under Lt Wales.
"	14/4/17		No 2 Section continues on KAMIRE Bridge; No. 3 Weldon trestling and painting waggons; No. 4 erects foot bridge over SOMME canal near ETERPIGNY Foot Bridge.	No 1 Section do 2nd day of section training.

Army Form C. 2118.

WAR DIARY
or
INTELLIGENCE SUMMARY.
(Erase heading not required.)

23rd Field Coy RE
April 1917.

Instructions regarding War Diaries and Intelligence Summaries are contained in F.S. Regs., Part II. and the Staff Manual respectively. Title pages will be prepared in manuscript.

Place	Date	Hour	Summary of Events and Information	Remarks and references to Appendices
As above	15/4/17		No 1 Section practises WELDON trestles & night wiring. No 3 work about camp. No 4 continue footbridge over canal.	No 2 does first day of Section training
	16/4/17		No 1 & 4 Sections work on "cover" at stone siding on PONT LES BRIE station. No 3 works in camp.	No 2 does 2nd days training Lieut Cowley moves to Aveluy
On the march	17/4/17		Coy. moves to MERICOURT sur SOMME via VILLERS-CARBONNEL, FOUCAUCOURT, CHUIGNES & CHUIGNOLLES. Adv. party moves from FONTAINE-LES-CAPPY during morning under Lt. COWLEY on cycles.	
MERICOURT SUR SOMME.	18/4/17		Company inspections of arms, accoutrements, equipment, clothing, feet etc. carried out. Billets improved.	
	19/4/17		Company Route march, Drill, Knotting & lashing etc. etc.	

Army Form C. 2118.

WAR DIARY
or
INTELLIGENCE SUMMARY.
(Erase heading not required.)

April 1917

23rd F.d Coy. R.E.

Instructions regarding War Diaries and Intelligence Summaries are contained in F. S. Regs., Part II. and the Staff Manual respectively. Title pages will be prepared in manuscript.

Place	Date	Hour	Summary of Events and Information	Remarks and references to Appendices
MERICOURT SUR SOMME	20/4/17		Coy. training carried out as follows:-	
		Morning	Gas Helmet Drill & Laying out kits. Section Drill.	
		Afternoon	½ Coy on range; ½ Coy on Weldon trestles.	
	21/4/17	Morning	Extended order drill, Bayonet Fighting & Judging Distance	
		Afternoon	½ Coy on Weldon trestles; ½ Coy on range.	
	22/4/17	Sunday	Church Parade	
	23/4/17	All day	Bombing under C.I. 42nd Divn Bomb School.	Sergt. W.V. Elcombe awarded M.M. by Corps Commander.
	24/4/17	All day	Rafting, gun & horse etc etc in conjunction with Bde of R.F.A.	
	25/4/17	Morning	Marching Order inspection & Company Drill	
		Afternoon	Route march & filling dummy charges to bridges in the neighbourhood.	
	26/4/17		Inspection by C.R.E. 1st Divn	
	27/4/17		Inspection by G.O.C. 1st Divn	
	28/4/17		Inspection by C.E. XIV Corps.	
	29/4/17	Sunday	Church Parade & Bathing Parade	
	30/4/17	Morning	Wiring (Men III Army Wire), Musketry, Bridging Expedients, Works, Section work	
		Afternoon	The same as morning.	

[Signature]
Capt.
Commanding 23rd (Fld.) Coy. R.E.

WAR DIARY.

23rd. Field Coy., R.E.

1st. DIVISION.

MAY. 1917.

Army Form C. 2118.

WAR DIARY
or
INTELLIGENCE SUMMARY.
(Erase heading not required.)

23rd F.Coy. R.E.
May 1917

Place	Date	Hour	Summary of Events and Information	Remarks and references to Appendices
MERICOURT SUR SOMME	1/5/17		Training resumed on above scheme. No 1 Section. Practise in laying out WELDON trestle & stores for night work. Also bridging expedients & rafting for new men. No 2 Section. N.C.O's & some men map reading. Remainder work around camp. No 3 Section. Practising wiring & working on Coleman hut for Divisional Baggage Store at MERIGNOLEZ. No 4 Section. — Rifle Practice & Bayonet Fighting.	Revd A.W.M. Cowan C.F. (att'd) proceeds to 55 DMER. Major W.R. Wilson M.C. R.E. proceeds to PERONNE.
	2/5/17		No 3 & 4 Sections under Lts. FORWOOD & SMITH proceed toMARU to work on a new aerodrome for No 9 Squadron R.F.C.	MURLU on main PERONNE-CAMBRAI road about 5 miles from PERONNE.
	3/5/17		No 2 Section under 2/Lt. COWLEY proceeds to MARICOURT to demolish XIV Corps Main Dressing Station.	
	4/5/17		No 1 Section under Lt. WAKES moves to CARNOY to demolish XIV Corps H.A.H.Q.	

2353 Wt. W2544/1454 700,000 5/15 D. D. & L. A.D.S.S./Forms/C. 2118.

Army Form C. 2118.

WAR DIARY
or
INTELLIGENCE SUMMARY.
(Erase heading not required.)

23rd F.d Coy R.E.
May 1917

[Stamp: ROYAL ENGINEERS MAY 1917]

Place	Date	Hour	Summary of Events and Information	Remarks and references to Appendices
As above	4/5/17		Nothing to report	
"	5/5/17	"	Remounts:- 1 Rider 6 mules.	
"	6/5/17	"	2nd Lt. Gillespie to PARIS on leave.	
"	7/5/17	"	Major Wilson returns from leave at Paris.	
"	8/5/17	"	Lt: Walso to IV Army Infantry School of Instruction.	
"	9/5/17	"		
"	10/5/17	"	2nd Lt. Gillespie returns from leave	
"	11/5/17	"	No 1 Section rejoins H.Q. from CARNOY.	
"	12/5/17	"	No 2 Section move from MARICOURT to FRISE	

Army Form C. 2118.

WAR DIARY
or
INTELLIGENCE SUMMARY.
(Erase heading not required.)

23rd F.d Cy R.E.
May 1917

Place	Date	Hour	Summary of Events and Information	Remarks and references to Appendices
Méricourt sur Somme	12/5/17 13/5/17		Nothing to report.	
	14/5/17		" " "	No 2 Section training 3rd Bn. in use of Bridging Equipments. Refitting. [Lt. Forwood moves in from NURLU by Cavalaire] [Lt. Forwood to PARIS on leave] Pontooning, & Swimming of Horses. Also teaching non-swimmers to swim. Beaten at Water-Polo by team from 1st Gloster Regt.
	15/5/17		No 3 & 4 Sections rejoin H.Q. from NURLU by motor bus	
	16/5/17		Nothing to report.	
	17/5/17		No 2 Section with bridging waggons rejoins from FRISE.	
	18/5/17		Nothing to report.	
	19/5/17		Company moves to BAYONVILLERS via PROYART.	
BAYONVILLERS	20/5/17		Company moves from BAYONVILLERS to a camp just to the S.E. of the town.	Lt. Forwood returns from leave.

Army Form C. 2118.

WAR DIARY
or
INTELLIGENCE SUMMARY.
(Erase heading not required.)

23rd F⁵ Coy. R.E.
May 1917

Place	Date	Hour	Summary of Events and Information	Remarks and references to Appendices
BAYONVILLERS	21/5/17		Cleaning new camp & checking equipment.	
	22/5/17		Complete marching order inspection of Coy.	1st D.E. Shots.
	23/5/17		Training. Night work with Very lights.	
	24/5/17		Training	1st Div⁸ Shots.
	25/5/17		Special tactical inspection of the three Field Coys. by C.R.E. lasting all day.	
	26/5/17		Inspections & training.	
	27/5/17		Company entrain at MARCELCAVE → move at 1.10 p.m towards the North.	

Army Form C. 2118.

WAR DIARY
or
INTELLIGENCE SUMMARY.
(Erase heading not required.)

23rd F⁴ Coy RE
May 1917

[Stamp: 23rd (FIELD COMPANY) ROYAL ENGINEERS MAY 1917]

Place	Date	Hour	Summary of Events and Information	Remarks and references to Appendices
On the mar [Map. 27 1/40,000] W.5.a Central	28/5/17	4 a.m	Detrain at GODEWAERSVELDE & march to new billets a farm near THIEUSHOUCK.	(Map 27 1/40,000 W5.a central midway between Caestre & Flêtre)
THIEUSHOUCK	29/5/17		Coy. Route March to the Mt. des Cats. to see the country	
	30/5/17		Training. Route march. Welden tractor g-	
	31/5		Training Cont. - Physical drill in morning. Two lectures being instructed in Vickers M.G. by 1st Div. M.G.Coy. Two lectures on Welden trestle drill.	

Victoria NE
Lt. 23 [?] Coy [signature]

WAR DIARY.

23rd. Field Coy., R.E.

1st. DIVISION.

JUNE. 1917.

CONFIDENTIAL.

1st. Division.
───────────

        Herewith War Diary of the 23rd. Field Co. R.E. for the month of June 1917.

                                                    Mellop Capt RE
                                                    ACRE 1st DIV.

1.7.17.

Army Form C. 2118.

WAR DIARY
or
INTELLIGENCE SUMMARY.

(Erase heading not required.)

23rd Field Coy. R.E.
June 1917

Instructions regarding War Diaries and Intelligence Summaries are contained in F.S. Regs., Part II. and the Staff Manual respectively. Title pages will be prepared in manuscript.

Place	Date	Hour	Summary of Events and Information	Remarks and references to Appendices
Thirlstock Sheet 27 1/40,000 W.3.a. Central	1/6/17		Training continued. A.M. Route March. P.M. Map reading, Knotting & Lashing. Judging distance & Wilson Trestling.	
	2/6/17		Training continued. A.M. Route March. P.M. as above	Company Concert in afternoon in grounds of farm.
	3/6/17		Training continued. A.M. Church Parade. P.M. "Intake & Thread".	Lt. Smith returns from leave in England.
	4/6/17		Training continued. A.M. Laying out tool cart & Wilson trestling. P.M. Instruction by Section Officers	1 Secⁿ working at 1st Div Bomb School
	5/6/17		Training continued. A.M. Route March. P.M. Semaphore, tracing trenches & laying out toolcart equipment	As above

Army Form C. 2118.

WAR DIARY
or
INTELLIGENCE SUMMARY.
(Erase heading not required.)

23rd F² Coy. R.E.
June 1917

Place	Date	Hour	Summary of Events and Information	Remarks and references to Appendices
As above	6/6/17		Training continued. A.M. Physical training & work in camp. P.M. Semaphore & Gas Helmet Drill	1 Sec working on Posts. Bomb School. 15" Rifle Range
	7/6/17		Training continued. A.M. As above P.M. As above.	2 sec now working as above
	8/6/17		Training continued. A.M. Physical Training & Squad Drill P.M. Gas Helmet Drill & making straw mats	As above
	9/6/17		Training continued. A.M. As above P.M. Gas Helmet Drill & Judging Distance	As above
	10/6/17		Training continued. A.M. Church Parade P.M. Coy. clean arms instruction	No work.

Army Form C. 2118.

WAR DIARY
or
INTELLIGENCE SUMMARY.

(Erase heading not required.)

23rd 1st Coy. R.E.
June 1917

JUL 1917 — ROYAL ENGINEERS — [FIELD COMPANY] stamp

Place	Date	Hour	Summary of Events and Information	Remarks and references to Appendices
On the move from Winnezeele	11/6/17		Company marches via CAESTRE & main road to STAPLE to 3 small farms in the QUEUE de BAVINCHOVE about 2 miles S. of Mount CASSEL. March off 8.0 a.m. Coy. follows 5th Berks down a side road in CAESTRE putting them behind school all the Division & delaying their arrival by 3 hours.	
O.27.B.3.0 (Sheet 27 1/40,000)				
Queue de BAVINCHOVE	12/6/17		Training continued A.M. Route March P.M. Wiring & Semaphore Drill	
	13/6/17		Training continued	
	14/6/17		Training continued. Two sections move to a bridging camp on Northern Edge of FORÊT de CLAIRMARAIS (No 3rd Sec.) (M.19.9.0.2) Bridging Lecture erecting field trestle, lacing & repairing hut trestle. Lecture by Lt. Colling of Company by Lts.	Lt. Walrond joins from IV Army Infantry School of Instruction
	15/6/17		Training continued	

Army Form C. 2118.

WAR DIARY
or
INTELLIGENCE SUMMARY.
(Erase heading not required.)

23rd F. Coy R.E.
June 1917

Place	Date	Hour	Summary of Events and Information	Remarks and references to Appendices
QUEUE DE BAVINCHOVE 27.0.27.B.20 No HOOR	16/6/17		Training Continued. No 192 Sections relieve 32A in Bridging Camp.	
	17/6/17		Sunday. Church Parade for 3rd A in Camp.	Sections 1 & 2 march back to HQ Camp in evening
	18/6/17		Preparing for move & resting.	
WORMHOUDT 27.C.10.B. (Av.ovo)	19/6/17	4.30a.m	Company marches with 1st Bde. via ZUYDPEENE to WORMHOUDT & spend the day there. H.Q. 47 Rue d. Bergeurs	
TLEEGERVELT 19.I.11.C (Av.ovo)	20/6/17	5.0 a.m	Company marches with 1st Bde. via la RREULLE, WYLDER & GARGDEN to TLEEGERVELT & spend day there	
11. R.35 a&c near Coxyde les Bains	21/6/17	7.0 am	Diamond formation march with 1st to KAFFRINCHOURE station 9.00 a.m detraining at COXYDE Stn. & marching to Camp LEFEVRE [R.35 a & c. Sheet 77 1/40,000] trans had moved by Road	Informed yt Inroad to Newport before taking over today. O.C. now CRE 32 Div. about taking over from 2/5 Field Coy

Army Form C. 2118.

2,3rd F³ Coy. R.E.
June 1917

WAR DIARY
or
INTELLIGENCE SUMMARY.
(Erase heading not required.)

Instructions regarding War Diaries and Intelligence
Summaries are contained in F. S. Regs., Part II.
and the Staff Manual respectively. Title pages
will be prepared in manuscript.

Place	Date	Hour	Summary of Events and Information	Remarks and references to Appendices
Camp NF FEUWE R.35.a.9.c.	22/6/17		Standing by in Camp	
R.32 (OXYDE) (1/20000)			1/5 Fresh. Coy to move up to Nieuport les Bains M.13.d.63.	Horse lines in sand dunes from M.13 d 63 Finish huts in rear of sand dunes all horse tied up to picket lines.
			lunch. 2/2nd Platoon.	Any horses lost are tethered next to trees.
			Platoon 3. 4 fellers in lorry relieving 2 Lilso 210.NE	Armed watches posted behind all horses.
			Much done back to R.32.	
M.13. d. 63.	23/6		Lt Carley Sect 2 have found a M.13 d 63.	O.C. goes forward relieving from Sept 1.
			Lt Smith Sect 3 in maintenance of Bridges including handling of Deauville	Lt Webb to hospital
			foot acorn bridge – Lorries used 1 Deauville been took	O.C. takes up quarters at M.13 d.6.3.
			Salved + returned 1 THR. Lorries used for Stove Dumps	
NIEUPORT les BAINS M.13 d 63.	24/6		Lt Callaghan Recon of L.J. #1 evening – Remarks of 218 TM.	G.O.C. 1st Div takes over at 7am.
			Came over at —	H.Q. moves into huts M.13 d.6.3
			L.J. 3. D members of Deauville foot bridge like USER supply	
			+ dump of Deauville foot bridge also.	
			L.J.2. Collecting Stone at lorry indent for Dw Dump AR. Called USER DUMP	
			O.C.	

Army Form C. 2118.

WAR DIARY
or
INTELLIGENCE SUMMARY.

23rd Field Coy R.E.
June 1917

(Erase heading not required.)

Place	Date	Hour	Summary of Events and Information	Remarks and references to Appendices
HQ at NIEUPORT-BAINS Hut d 6 3 Transport Lines M 32	23/6		Bridge below Refinery damaged 100 pairs waterproof kbl at W.Colleges returns R & L Bk Comts installed. Work took to be done by the Section preparing for evening work. Staff pack hooking forward received & alloc. OC Groups Tools & Stores. 10 Lines & Infra Comp. knee nr. 146. Tree Bridging undertaken at YSER DUMP M 19 B 19 – The above started & done by 23rd Field Coy adds Decauville system formed. All Div. arrangements can be made. Barrel cart trials at N°1 bridge. 1st & 2nd hand plug for hand Bridge – 2 fours of 2 kbl steel v. 5 fours of 2 kbl. made for footbridge. Later on Stores returned to be Party bebre start could. Trial below could also turning of Sec. Advanced HQ Shot Work carried on at Advanced Post - Rgt.W. left bank. 13Ptns	H. Fawcett on leave England 23/6 -1/7 On Sectn. preparing platelog & Bridge frame below defences. On Sectn. on Lua Bridge framing timber. Mr. Letham & Stores Decauville formed. Mr. Letham preparing twill & Dec. in fois lines for be.
	24/6		Transfer Lines moved to OOST DUNKERQUE BAINS Camp de la Corrette	23/6

Army Form C. 2118.

WAR DIARY
or
INTELLIGENCE SUMMARY.
(Erase heading not required.)

23rd Field Coy R.E.
June 1917

Place	Date	Hour	Summary of Events and Information	Remarks and references to Appendices
HQ at NIEUPORT BAINS M.14 d 6.3				
Transferred from DUNKIRK	27/6/17		Bridge Work - Civil Contr - Drocourt work f'sshd up. Running of R.E. adv Dump. Dn YSER BUMP still in hand. Placing to'd into YSER BUMP.	Officers: Transfrom Coy improve. Worked late on Drocourt. Had militia operations.
	28/6		Bridge work. Civil – making shore legs for footbridge a down stream. Told of existing bridge. Front line – Const of front trench, not of adv trench cont'd. N.C.Os from 1st Divn taking over running of YSER BUMP	
	29/6		As above.	
	30/6		Bridge Work. Heavy sea making it impossible to lay trestle in trestle bridge for certain weeks. Bridge Const: - Section taken off Civic Locaville. Evans bridging - Shore piles completed on West side of flex footbridge. All tell piles completed. Beach retained for launching. Piecedoith Down by 2 offrs & shore coln to get timber on raft to Regtl suff Centre, making timber shelters. All steel trimming carried cont.	

WAR DIARY.

23rd. Field Coy., R.E.

1st. DIVISION.

JULY. 1917.

"A" Form.
MESSAGES AND SIGNALS.

Army Form C. 2121
(in pads of 100).

TO 1st D²

Sender's Number: P.S.385
Day of Month: 1/8/17

AAA

War Diary for month of July 1917 forwarded for disposal

B.B. Edwards Capt.

Army Form C. 2118.

WAR DIARY
or
INTELLIGENCE SUMMARY.
(Erase heading not required.)

23rd Field Coy RE
July 1917

Instructions regarding War Diaries and Intelligence Summaries are contained in F.S. Regs., Part II. and the Staff Manual respectively. Title pages will be prepared in manuscript.

Place	Date	Hour	Summary of Events and Information	Remarks and references to Appendices
NIEUPORT BAINS M13 d 63 Transport Lines. OOST DUNKERQUE BAINS			Bridge Works. Heavy seas prevent track being laid on Leerand bridge. Bridge Construction East Shore from complete Bridge and King barrel fast to jetty on East bank. Landing anchor for Barrel bus bridge. Making Landing slope for Ferry. First Line Section Right Bath front Shelter at N° Pole N°2 Cmdt. Left Bath front Shelter at N°3 Pol (purple) Cmdt. Loading Bridging Stores. Providing RE Stores across YSER RIVER to from advanced RE Dumps.	Two men wounded by Shell fire # Two men on sick in hospital
	2/7		Bridge Works – Raft laid on N°1 Bridge to front line. Bridge travel gear broken and repaired. M.14 a 7.6. 14ft long & 6ft. Bridge assembled alongside, masking Covered bridge and floated out and made fast parallel to all alongside Eastern slip First Line front construction of Shelters in front cont.	U. Lt Williams (late CRE 1 Div) took over 6.5.0.1 Mg Div + CO. DCLI Armist from 2nd Div CRE 66 Div
	3/7		Bridge Works as usual. Bridge Const Leerand Coffr & barrel bus Footbridge floated into Eastern jetty. Preparing landing slope for Ferry between New bridge, Leerand bridge. First Line Work Prepared Bangalore Torpedo for Raid Torpedoes carried up & placed and successfully fired M15 B 53	Bangalore Torpedo. Lt Jackson RE Cpt Forster and 5 men 1st E. Yorks under Lt Baird 1st York's Carry out Raid at 11pm. We were reported opposed too, new the Enemy Sapping through after no Enemy was not for one 2 hours many party being out working on modern improvements of wire. Difficulty in making RE Station 6 yds. Zero hour September at 1.20 am + n preparing Signal (whistle) from stopped Torpedo successfully fired 15ft long Infantry raiding party P. 16 long killed 2 Enemy and forward dug out. Some of Sleeping party got through but wire after Sleeping Shelter by party. No further success.

Army Form C. 2118.

WAR DIARY
or
INTELLIGENCE SUMMARY.
(Erase heading not required.)

23rd Fd Co RE
July 1917

238 (FIELD) COMPANY
ROYAL ENGINEERS

Instructions regarding War Diaries and Intelligence Summaries are contained in F.S. Regs., Part II. and the Staff Manual respectively. Title pages will be prepared in manuscript.

Place	Date	Hour	Summary of Events and Information	Remarks and references to Appendices
NIEUPORT BAINS M13 d.6.3	4/7		No 3 Bridge - Pont Studey - Mortlake Bridge. Direct hit ruptured by hvy howitzer. White a small. Anchor block to protect Nos Pigmont Bridge. Hard cores erected landing stages being made at W bank for Ferry between No 1 Bridge & causeway. No 1 Bridge. Pumps on left Bank Flemish repaired. Work done on Pad 2 & left Bk. Ford. Pontoons Pad 3 Right Bk. Ford.	
	5/7		Bridge patrol as usual. Ferry landing stages made E. W. Side. Lower Water Bridge. No 1 Pont Bridge hit. Float trestle used as ferry, attended & river call? by travelling pulley - Haulage & ferry boat. Left Flemish Pumps repaired. Entrance to No 2 Pad repaired ? Right Ford. No 2 Pad shelter finished - new shelter started at No 3.	Capt Neilson O.C. 43rd Field Co RE appeared & arrange taking over.
	6/7		Bridge Patrol as usual. True Salem 43rd Fd Co RE arrive 8:30 pm. Relieved Bridge Patrol. Bridge E.W. side over. On & from relieve Bridge Patrol picks on relieve Bridge trapeze Salem took Glenn & Gorey Garrisons. No 2 D.L. hands over bridge hurt at 12 p.m. unclear out. No 3 - & hits slide hut over 2:30 keys clouded. Clipse to no bridge to wilson shelter handed over 2 a.m. 7/7 No 1 Salem hands over 10 pm.	Major J. A. J. 43rd Fd Co RE arrive 8:30 pm delivery & received trees kits. C.R.E. reported had bridge & no ferry with Co. 23rd Fd Co. Had not handed in at 10 pm. L. Colliges
Camp La Panne Coupé la Port	7/7	9 am	O.C. 43rd Fd Co RE taken over. 23rd Fd Co RE less Salem & mail & Carpt & Eqpt from Harfort Section to hutted mr 10 p.m. Leaving. Relieved by Unnamed Sec 1 / 43rd Fd Co RE.	Lt Smith & 2 Jenkins return Newport Bains to Boynton. Hydrophoid made over. 2nd Batt O.C. 1 Corps Baths. Lt Forward returned from leave.

Army Form C. 2118.

WAR DIARY
or
INTELLIGENCE SUMMARY.
(Erase heading not required.)

23rd Field Coy. RE
July, 1917

Place	Date	Hour	Summary of Events and Information	Remarks and references to Appendices
Camp le Ferte Cozyde Bains				
Le Clipper	8/7		Transport by Road 6 a.m. to Le Clippon arriving 8 p.m. O.C. & Dismounted by Motor lorries 9am arriving 12 midday. 25 tents drawn Hutments for Coy Camp.	
	9/7		Erecting tentage in shelter in Camp. Started erecting of Hut in Camp. On Lectine – Finding + erecting Nissen Huts. Setting out Sites for Bth Camp Capt Edwards leaves "Huckville Camp"	Lt. Smith & Sappers on reconnaissance of Route from Lefferts Light Bth. Newport Bains 6 Sappers & Bugle mastered hut at passing sidings before Setting on & Railing Point. spare type platoon Road & front. 9th-10th Party consisting of Lt. Smith, Cpl. Vick 2 Sappers with Workshops party & 10 carrying Sappers - 3 length Tripods used trying and Bridge across field. Placed Trestles, made stretching Foreman Tape, offer, to find friction time Tensil to find. - 2 sofs gut from close tire hou condeth of 2 hours Chinese de Frise took on 1/2 ft of start from parapet. Lined 11.30 p.m.
	10/7		Erecting Nissen Hut for Div. Camp. – 9 in hand Well sinking contd. in Coy Camp. (A "Guns Well" of Cor. iron.) 2 Trestle wagons and set of 8 horse harness Ceiling Huts & sites	Lt Smith & Cpl Vick – 2 Sappers return from Newport Bains. Capt Edwards on leave 11.19.
	11/7		Nissen Huts 9 completed – 8 neter shelter – 2 trestle wagons cooking huts. Well in Coy Camp 9' deep.	ii Lt. J.L.Kelly Inland R.E. temporarily attached to 23rd Field Co. R.E.
	12/7		14 Nissen Huts finished – 6 in hand. 5" Armstrong Hut erected. 2 8 Horse team harness began to use.	
	13/7		20 Nissen Huts completed + 7. Armstrong + J. Armstrong hut transported to Bv. H.Q. & Road formed to same through front material carted to site of three lorries outside Le Cloppen Camp	

Army Form C. 2118.

WAR DIARY
or
INTELLIGENCE SUMMARY.
(Erase heading not required.)

23rd Field Coy. R.E.

July 1917

AUG 1917

Instructions regarding War Diaries and Intelligence Summaries are contained in F. S. Regs., Part II. and the Staff Manual respectively. Title pages will be prepared in manuscript.

Place	Date	Hour	Summary of Events and Information	Remarks and references to Appendices
Le Clipbon	14/7		Started work on Horse Lines East of Loon Plage. 3 platoon troops made to cover flange – (6 loose troughs erected) Fitting latches & doors to J. Mason Huts – (horse supplied with huts) Started 3 wells for 2nd Bde Camp West of Le Clipbon, average depth 9'	
	15/7		Repairing cook line. Drains for Bell Sailing. 6 wells in hand – 3 average 12' deep – 3 9' Buying out Cooks to Transport Camps – Cooking Stoves Feet.	
	16/7		3 wells founded on 12' No 5 trate – Tank pumps etc fitted. 3 ¼ new 4' trate.	
	17/7		Work to Transport Camps Cont. Repairing horse tubs. Above 6 well complete with pumps (water timber levered & mixed on Cart top tables & Transport Lines Bridges – hose troughs transferred. Below. A few wells started. Work to East of Bde Camp to test work.	Grease supplied for horsey
	18/7		1 well complete with tank pump etc. 3 in hand. Transport Lines 6 hole tank erected – 6 hose troughs.	
	19/7		3 wells founded water supply to R.E. – Carpenters at N.B.C.M. work in Transport Lines Cont.	

2353 Wt. W2544/1454 700,000 5/15 D. D. & L. A.D.S.S./Forms/C. 2118.

Army Form C. 2118.

WAR DIARY
or
INTELLIGENCE SUMMARY.
(Erase heading not required.)

23rd Field Coy RE
July 1917

Place	Date	Hour	Summary of Events and Information	Remarks and references to Appendices
Le Clippon	20/7		Cradle from Segment drawn from Dunkerque for well sinking. No new huts started. Interior East 1/Kings Mess Hut being fitted to Transport Lines. Tanks etc completed. Cutting Nissen Huts to suction sites. 1st Bde Latrines finished. Patent Shrine @ Notre Dame. Nissen Huts. 1st Bde 70. 2nd Bde and P.O.	
	21/7		Well Re 10'6" depth. New buried line 6 steam pipes 3'. Div Q. Canvas Boards Contd. Nissen Hut. 1st Bde HBd Amb finished 2 o'clock 75 p. 2nd Bde 109. 3rd Bde finished.	
	22/7		Wells. M.M.G. well finished 5' water. Circular iron well sunk 11'6". Divisional notice boards contd. All Nissen huts (30) finished. Nissen Huts.	Lt Gillespie on leave
	23/7		Circular iron well now down 14ft. Work on 1st Bde. Obstacle course completed. Enforcement with small collapsible hand carts. Four Carpenters making fittings in huts at 2nd & 3rd Bde HQ.	Capt Edwards returns from leave

Army Form C. 2118

23rd Fd Coy R.E.
July 1917

[Stamp: 23RD (FIELD COMPANY) ROYAL ENGINEERS]

WAR DIARY
or
INTELLIGENCE SUMMARY.
(Erase heading not required.)

Instructions regarding War Diaries and Intelligence Summaries are contained in F. S. Regs., Part II. and the Staff Manual respectively. Title pages will be prepared in manuscript.

Place	Date	Hour	Summary of Events and Information	Remarks and references to Appendices
Cooxyde	24/7/17		Well at junction of Coxyde-Bains & Casino Road sunk to full depth. Tank erected, cover fitted & pump fixed. 1st Bat. Obstacle course nearly complete. Experimenting with hand carts.	
	25/7		Kit inspection of Coy by O.C. Obstacle course completed.	
	26/7		Training commenced. Drill. Moving under cover thro' sand dunes. Semaphore signalling. Use & fixing of mobile charges.	
	27/7		Drill. Target practice on beach. Knots & lashings & Demolitions.	

Army Form C. 2118.

WAR DIARY
or
INTELLIGENCE SUMMARY.
(Erase heading not required.)

23rd F'ld R.E.
July 1917

Place	Date	Hour	Summary of Events and Information	Remarks and references to Appendices
As above	29/7		Sunday. No work. Church Parade put off by rain.	
	30/7		Training continued as above. Much interfered with by rain.	Major Dibben proceeded to Villey my arms not by RE
	31/7		As above.	

B.B. Grant
Lt. Col.
Major, R.E.
Commanding 23rd (Fld.) Coy. R.E.

WAR DIARY.

23rd. Field Coy., R.E.

1st. DIVISION.

AUGUST, 1917.

Army Form C. 2118.

WAR DIARY
or
INTELLIGENCE SUMMARY.

(Erase heading not required.)

23rd Field Coy. R.E.
August 1917

Place	Date	Hour	Summary of Events and Information	Remarks and references to Appendices
St Athan Camp	1/8/17		Training continued practically staffed by men.	
Aston St Pol-sur a suburb of DUNKERQUE	2/8/17		Full "Landing Order" Inspection of Coy. held on Limb.	
	3/8/17		As above. only one (Drill) Parade owing to rain.	
	4/8/17		As above. Drill. Live Bomb throwing. 2 sections on works at Bde. Practice on Wall.	
	5/8/17		Sunday. Church Parade. Tailors & Shoemakers shops erected for 1st Bde. Temperature on wooden frame.	
	6/8/17		Climbing Wall in Musketry Order. Training under Section Officers Full Landing Order inspection.	

Army Form C. 2118.

WAR DIARY
or
INTELLIGENCE SUMMARY.
(Erase heading not required.)

23rd F¹ Coy A.E.
August 1917.

Place	Date	Hour	Summary of Events and Information	Remarks and references to Appendices
As above	7/8/17		Training continued. Obstacle Course in early morning	SEP 1917
	8/8/17		Drill. Extended Order work in sands. Wire Bombing & Beach firing.	
	9/8/17		As above. Physical Training. Drill. Marking out- Monitors for Bn. Over Wall in full Landing Order. Lecture on New Gas by M.O.	
	10/8/17		As above. Obstacle Course. Drill. Wiring. Wire Bombing.	
	11/8/17		As above. Over wall in Landing Order.	
	12/8/17		Landing scheme under 1st Bde. in Dunes near Camp.	
	13/8/17		Sunday. Church Parade & Gas Helmet Inspection.	
			Combined Scheme with 1st Bde. on Wall.	

2353 Wt. W2544/1454 700,000 5/15 D. D. & L. A.D.S.S./Forms/C. 2118.

Army Form C. 2118.

23rd Fld Coy R.E.
August 1917.

WAR DIARY
or
INTELLIGENCE SUMMARY.
(Erase heading not required.)

Place	Date	Hour	Summary of Events and Information	Remarks and references to Appendices
As above	14/8/17		Training continued. Obstacle course. Drill. Bayonet-Fighting. 1st Bde. Scheme on Wall.	
	15/8/17		As above.	
	16/8/17		As above. Also Night Operations in Dunes.	
	17/8/17		As above.	
	18/8/17		As above. Working on Wall under 1st Bde. Drill. Bayonet Fighting.	
	19/8/17		As above.	
	20/8/17		As above. Wiring on Wall for Canvas.	
	21/8/17		As above.	

Army Form C. 2118.

Instructions regarding War Diaries and Intelligence Summaries are contained in F. S. Regs., Part II. and the Staff Manual respectively. Title pages will be prepared in manuscript.

28th Div 2 Coy R.E.
August 1917

WAR DIARY
or
INTELLIGENCE SUMMARY.
(Erase heading not required.)

Place	Date	Hour	Summary of Events and Information	Remarks and references to Appendices
Cassel	22/8/17		Training continued. Coy & Command drill in morning.	SEP. 1917 ROYAL ENGINEERS
	23/8/17		3 Field Coys. & Signal Coy. formed as a Bn. for ceremonial route to G.A.C.	
	24/8/17		Inspection (Ceremonial) of Divn (less transport) on the sands by G.O.C. 1st Divn.	
	25/8/17		Inspection by G.O.C. 4th Army of whole Division on sands. Presentation of Medal Ribbons & march past. About 15,000 men troops on parade.	
	26/8/17	Sunday	Church Parade & rest	
	27/8/17		Training continued. Route March. Working parties at Disposal of G.	
	28/8/17		Very heavy storm all day. 2 sections doing a Range at Div H.Q. Returned in afternoon by others, two sections Working till dark when round up.	

Army Form C. 2118.

WAR DIARY
or
INTELLIGENCE SUMMARY.
(Erase heading not required.)

23rd Coy. R.E.
August 1917

Place	Date	Hour	Summary of Events and Information	Remarks and references to Appendices
As above	29/8/17		Training continued. Physical training. Pounds & Levers. Making obstacle refuse changes. Drawing Bill Obstructions etc. &c	SEP 1917
	30/8/17		As above. Route march. Signalling.	
	31/8/17		As above. Route march. Pt. each night Cinema (destroyed by storm on 21/8/17)	

Signed, Major, R.E.
Commanding 23rd (Field) Coy. R.E.

WAR DIARY.

23rd. Field Coy., R.E.,

1st. DIVISION.

SEPTEMBER. 1917.

Army Form C. 2118

WAR DIARY
or
INTELLIGENCE SUMMARY.
(Erase heading not required.)

23 Field Coy RE
September 1917

WO 36

Place	Date	Hour	Summary of Events and Information	Remarks and references to Appendices
Le Clipon Camp	1.9.17		Brigade Scheme. Making shed to replace hangar. Works in Camp.	
	2.9.17		Church Parade. No works. Nt. Cordy leave for England.	
	3.9.17		Route March. Making shed to replace hangar. Works in Camp. Bathing Parade. Trenching Mortars for 1st Brigade.	
	4.9.17		Company Drill. Live Bombing. Landing Order Parade. Practice on Wall.	
	5.9.17		Field Operations with 1st Brigade at W. end of Camp.	
	6.9.17		Musketry on Bench. Bayonet Fighting. Work on shed to replace Hangar.	
	7.9.17		Musketry (firing practice on beach). Demolitions on German 77mm Field Gun. Lt Smith leave for England.	

2353 Wt. W2544/1454 700,000 5/15 D. D. & L. A.D.S.S./Forms/C. 2118.

Army Form C. 2118.

WAR DIARY
or
INTELLIGENCE SUMMARY.
(Erase heading not required.)

2_3_3 Field Coy RE
September 1917

[Stamp: 233 (FIELD) COMPANY ROYAL ENGINEERS OCT. 1917]

Place	Date	Hour	Summary of Events and Information	Remarks and references to Appendices
As above	8.9.17		Scheme with 1st Brigade. Visit to Miraviton. Works on Shed to replace Hangar	
	9.9.17		Church Parade. Work on Shed to replace Hangar	Lt Thomas returned from leave
	10.9.17		Scheme with 1st Brigade. Small Kit Inspection	
	11.9.17		Kit Inspection. Battle near Parade. Company Drill. Bathing Parade. Erecting Divisional Mound Shed. Dismantling Ramp & Stables ensue.	Mr Gillespie came & Coy. Capt Edwards came to Coy to Engineering Institute at Paihaignac School
	12.9.17		C.R.E. Battle Drew Inspection. 3 Field Coys netted Transport parade in field near Camp.	
	13.9		Three Field Coys hot transport march out 7 miles towards Doulaique starting 9 a.m. Inspection by C.R.E of transport & mounts & Letters Practice in Pontoon Rafting and Welder Travelling. Return Camp 7 p.m.	2/Lt Gillespie proceeds for 6 days

2353 Wt. W2544/1454 700,000 5/15 D. D. & L. A.D.S.S./Forms/C. 2118.

Army Form C. 2118.

WAR DIARY
or
INTELLIGENCE SUMMARY.
(Erase heading not required.)

23rd F. Coy R.E.
September, 1917

Place	Date	Hour	Summary of Events and Information	Remarks and references to Appendices
as above	19/9		Company remains on de Clifton Camp. Standing by, doing a certain amount of training and instituting a few Bde "Field Days" until 29/9/17.	Capt Blanche rejoins Coy 19/4/17 & South Down G.H.R. 20/9/17 to 28/9/17
On the move	29/9/17		Company moves via St Pol-sur-Mer DUNKERQUE, ADINKERKE COXYDE, OOST-DUNKERQUE - OOST-DUNKERQUE to VILLA JULIETTE (an h.q. on OOST-DUNKERQUE - OOST-DUNKERQUE Bains Road. Transport moves to PERTH Camp. Horse lines killed during night. 29 horses killed 9/16 wounded	
VILLA JULIETTE X.11.a.2.v.	30/9/17		Coy in Camp. 2 Sections working on WELLINGTON Camp. 1 Section in Divisional Workshops. 1 Section standing by. Horse lines moved back to behind COXYDE (X.7.c.1.1)	

WAR DIARY.

23rd. Field Coy., R.E.

1st. Division.

OCTOBER. 1917.

WAR DIARY or INTELLIGENCE SUMMARY

(Erase heading not required.)

Army Form C. 2118.
23rd Field Coy. R.E.
October 1917

Place	Date	Hour	Summary of Events and Information	Remarks and references to Appendices
Oost-Dunkerque Villa Juliette X.4.a.26.	1/10		1 Section (No 2) under Lt. Corley on Div. workshops. 2 Sections (1 ma) Lt. Gillespie n Wellington Camp R.35.d.17 continuing work of 29th Fd. C.RE. Above ground timber sheds being demolished + put into underground R.E. 3.5 Ry head cover. Steel shelters being erected where timber not available. Arrangement being made to start work on Gunners dug out at Div. Section workshop WUS.6 in camp.	C.E. II Army, C.E. XV Corps + CREs visit inspect demonstration of French Bourginon Typhoon Island Coxyde. Lt. Fitzhard leave UK 6/10-16/10. 32nd Divn hands over 1/10 3 Divn. Coy comes under 1st Lot N. Humber Coy DSO R.E. CRE 42nd Div. Z 11 pm.
	2/10		As above. – Lt. Corley into HQ. Suppers - spare drivers building cover for mounted section here Coxyde.	
	3/10		As above	
	4/10 – 5/10		"	
	6/10		2 Sections continue on Wellington Camp R.35 d.17 - No Sections on Div. workshops. Transport Camps continued. "B" type Shelters erected for 168 Bde HQ	
	7/10		Wellington Camp, Div. Workshops, Transport Camp Guts - Billets of Latrine Blks. Taken over for Divn. L.t. – Some Concrete carried up to Billy positions 16R.	
	8/10		As above – Drop concrete squads to concrete Gun Emplacement invaded by 11th A.R. shd	
	9/10		Started work at Transport lines. Also work as before	

Instructions regarding War Diaries and Intelligence
Summaries are contained in F.S. Regs., Part II.
and the Staff Manual respectively. Title pages
will be prepared in manuscript.

Army Form C. 2118.

WAR DIARY
or
INTELLIGENCE SUMMARY.

(Erase heading not required.)

223rd Field Co. R.E.

October 1917.

Place	Date	Hour	Summary of Events and Information	Remarks and references to Appendices
Post Dunkerque X.a.2.b.	10/10		Wellington Camp R.35.a. - French hut dismantled, strip frame structures rebuilt from old timbers - hive structures being placed 12" above hut, covered with up to 3 Sand-Steel "C" type shelters erected. Standard Cubicle accommodation available to date 250 O.R. hut Guild at 3rd Brit Base. Dry out Guilt in Coy Camp. Shelters for drivers + stables Guilt at transport lines. Gum Boot Drying Hand Tools drying Room at Post Dunkerque in hand	Capt. Taylor R.E. from 233 R.E. Reinforcing Gen Wksd to hos. U.K.
	11/10		As above	
	12/10		hut at Rosendael Coal Guild also at Div Workshops Coy Camps. Erecting "B" Type Shelters at Btty bunker M.33.c.49.st. Drying Rooms Guilt	
	13/10		As above	
	14/10		Sect N°1 relieves N°2 at Div Workshops - broke as above	
	15/10		Sect. 3 at work on Hedley In Camp. N°2 on Gun positions. Gum boot Test drying Rooms completed handed over.	
	16/10		Wellington Camp. Accommodation available for 100 O.R. Stalls complete at transport lines.	
	17/10		Orders received to proceed to GHYVELDE Div.com - Took on Wellington Camp handed over to approximative of 229 Fld Co R.E.	Personnel, arms + equipment complete + established.
GHYVELDE Map 19 Abb CBD B15 B.7.6	18/10		Proceed to GHYVELDE - start from Coyde 9.30 a.m.	Lt. Forward regined Coy. Capt. Randle R.V.S. Clonez 23 R.E.
	19/10		Cleaning up Billits etc - began loading trials	
			Suffered cleaning newly arrived harness	
	20/10		Divisional mounted Inspection + marching order by which horses + reft horses Shelters in 20/9	

WAR DIARY
or
INTELLIGENCE SUMMARY.
(Erase heading not required.)

23rd Field Co. R.E.
October 1917.

Place	Date	Hour	Summary of Events and Information
GHYVELDE Map 19 1/40,000 I.15.B.7.6.	21/10		In Camp – on harvest – Packing hut's conts – Inspection of R.M's Stores etc.
	22/10		Lt. Gillespie goes forward with 2S.Platoon to fix forward billets. Capt Thoms turn U.K 23/10 – 7/11
ARNEKE Map 27 1/40,000 H.6.B.9.3.	22/10	On the move	Transport starts 3 am to ease the journey for remounts. Dismounted move by lorry to ARNEKE area, joining 1st Bde. Arrive 2 pm. Transport 3 pm.
	23/10		Coy. inspection – Sappers on new harness cleaning devices – Fixing Camp – hose insects O.C. allots C.R.E. Esperance LEDERZEELE – John Lichen-football. Full Lichens cold etc.
	24/10		Coy. route march in morning
	25/10		John Lichen Football (unfinished Lichen). Cleaning harness etc. Advance parties inspect new billets.
HERZEELE Sheet 27 1/40,000 I.15.a.3.3.	26/10		Move to Nouveau Monde area. Transport & dismounted lichens march 9.30 am to – Pouring rain in morning billets S.W. of HERZEELE.
	27/10		Cleaning out billets – preparing farm utensils and yard etc. Two Lichens on route march. Two Lichens photographed in WORMHOUDT.
	28/10		" Remaining Lichens "
	29/10		Capt Taylor R.A.M.C. hurn 23rd FA G.R.E. Sect 3 – A start anchor of to house that for 1st Bde. – Inspection of mounted lichen – harness etc.
HOSPITAL FARM CAMP Sheet 2F YPRES B.19 d central	31/10		Coy move forward – Dismounted by lorry. Mounted by route HOUTKERQUE – WATOU – SWITCH ROAD orders fr mahtunt from C.R.E. XVIII Corps Troops.

W.H. Evans Major R.E.
OC. 23rd Field Co R.E.

WAR DIARY.

23rd. Field Coy., R.E.

1st. DIVISION.

NOVEMBER. 1917.

Army Form C. 2118.

[Stamp: 23rd (FIELD) COMPANY ROYAL ENGINEERS DEC. 1917]

WAR DIARY
or
INTELLIGENCE SUMMARY.
(Erase heading not required.)

23rd Field Co. R.E.
November 1917

Place	Date	Hour	Summary of Events and Information	Remarks and references to Appendices
HOSPITAL FARM CAMP Sheet 28 B.19 d central	1/11		Lectures 3 mgs on horse standings, stables, hut 141 A.T. Coy.	Lt Gillespie leave U.K. 21/11 - 14/12
			Set 1. on kitchen huts, Hospital Camp.	Lt Call on CRE 63 Div (RND) for orders
			Set 2. on Harness Stables at - Camp.	
HILLTOP FARM CAMP O.21d.3.8. 2.F.H.40000	2/11		Dismounted Lectures. march to HILLTOP FARM	
			at HOSPITAL FARM - 2 weekly held (a building) Camp 1 Nissen Hut delivered 4th to units on unhealthy locality – (huts. H.V. etc)	
	3/11		3 Lectures work on projected Tram line from C.T.8. - Drainage	Lt Freeman from 5th Army attached for 10 days.
			or Lectures making shelland entrance to camp, building protection and walls. work hut etc.	
			work on Tram Line Camp Ct.8 a above	
	4/11		Taken off Tram line started on Road Metalledly from	Capt Schrader returns from leave
	5/11		GENOA 01.C.3.3 to YORK FARM D1.B.9.3.	
			Coys instructions. Lt Farrah. Head of GENOA but found absolutely necessary to obtain large metallers for road.	
			Track took line on road a base 1 Triangle Wood C.6.c.	

Army Form C. 2118.

WAR DIARY
or
INTELLIGENCE SUMMARY.
(Erase heading not required.)

23rd Fld. Coy. N.Z.E.
November 1917

Place	Date	Hour	Summary of Events and Information	Remarks and references to Appendices
HILL TOP FARM C.21.d.3.5 HOSPITAL FARM 13.19.d Central	6/11		Work on GENOA - YORK FARM RD continued. Heavy shell repairs required. Triangle front face 10 G.S. loads of fresh chalk carted to Triangle. Filled. Slush made not possible beyond GENOA.	CRE 1st Div. takes over from CRE N.Z. Div.
	7/11		Above Road contd. 10 G.S. loads & 8 FS carted to Alt. Foundation finished 100' extended 200' 15th Shropshires working in advance. Allotted to California Trench - digging for shelters behind "All Saints" Selected No 2 move to Rear billets in Canal Bank (N.17d)	
HQ. X Canal Bank N.17 N. Central	8/11		Road contd. 10 G.S. loads & fresh slabs carted. Foundation 15th Shrops laid 200' foundation finished - 300' drained. Work on advanced DD billets contd. O.C. Capt. Moore Roach billets - Canal Bank hers No 2 Section.	
	9/11		Work on Road & billets - Coy pulled on X GENOA - YORK FARM Tram line - 240' 5" 226" Capt. Alex all on the Tram Line under O.C. 23' O.C. also 2 Capts. moved to Remmure Front laid to STROOMBEEK D.1. G.O.	

2nd Bn. ORF. N°254/1/650 265000 6/15 D(D&L) A D&SS Forms/C.2118. March
Other work on above contd.

Army Form C. 2118

WAR DIARY
or
INTELLIGENCE SUMMARY
(Erase heading not required.)

23rd F.d Coy. R.E.
November 1917

[Stamp: 23RD (FIELD) COMPANY / DEC. 1917 / ROYAL ENGINEERS]

Place	Date	Hour	Summary of Events and Information	Remarks and references to Appendices
Adv. Sec.ns HILL TOP Farm H.Q. CANAL BANK Horse Lines HOSPITAL Farm	10/11		1st Division attack caused heavy enemy barrage of area around the TRIANGLE & GENOA no work could be done on the Railway. All Sec.ns therefore working on advance billets.	
	11/11		20 G.S. Wagon loads of rails carried forward & assembled. 9386' of track laid. Railhead now approx. D.1.d.40.35. Detachment working on Coy. advance billets in CALIFORNIA trench.	
	12/11		Same parties working on Tramline 23', 248', 5" + 226' Flat Co. & N.E. + 120 Articles Pierced and 120 32" Dir Pintles. 20 G.S. Wagon loads of rails. Sleepers Carried to C.T.R.S.D. handled 1000 yards, assembled, & pushed up to trolley. Rail laid to D.1. B.9.0. Point fixed for Tramway. Site arrived at 12/11. Sec.n No.3. working on Adv. Billets - California Trench.	No.2 Sec.n relieves No.3 who bring their A.I. with them down to CANAL BANK. Gen Godley G.E. II Corps visit work. Progress !!!.
	13/11		4 Sappers detailed as Repair Gang on Gy. tramlines at HUBNER. Work on Tramline from Ermines Castle - same parties. No.3 Section laying & Canal Bank working on Advanced Billets	Lt. Freeman Completes period of attachment.

Army Form C. 2118

WAR DIARY
or
INTELLIGENCE SUMMARY

(Erase heading not required.)

23rd Field Co. RE
November 1917

Instructions regarding War Diaries and Intelligence Summaries are contained in F.S. Regs., Part II. and the Staff Manual respectively. Title Pages will be prepared in manuscript.

Place	Date	Hour	Summary of Events and Information	Remarks and references to Appendices
HQ. East Bank of Canal	12/11		Continued GENOA - YORK FARM Tramline.	No 4 Section relieved by No 3 Section on Canal Bank East. No 3 joined.
Coy Billets HILL TOP FARM C.2.d.37 (Nissen Huts) Transport HOSPITAL FARM B.19.d.			23" 24" 5" + 228" Fd Co RE + 1 Coy Leicester Pioneers. 1 Coy 32nd Div Pioneers and 1 Coy 32 Div Infantry. The latter presented by the Divisions. Road laid to D.2.C.4.9. French tondo to D.2.C.7.7. French tondo to Dic St.	
	13/11		Tram line contd. Work in Coy billet contd by No 4 Section. 2 Sections loaned to 63 Div Gunners to assist in repair of Acinville track at Alberta.	Guns firing intermittently from front during the night.
	14/11		As above. Advanced Billets. Great of "C" type steel shelters dug in which erects PW Bridge. Work progressing favourably. Hill Top Nissen huts not popular on account of attentions of H.V. guns.	Lt Gillespie returns from leave. Officers 2 Sections have not Steel shelters erected in California French C.22.d.52.
Coy Billets → California French C.22.d.52	17/11		Rail laid to D.2.d P.B. Formation to D.2.d.8.6. French tondo to D.1.b.7.2. - (badly smashed by gun fire) (3" Pdr C.1.E) Placing additional sleeper works, packing up generally improving. Slab road from Triangle Wood East to crossing of tram line reformed. Turning point made for Genoa trams.	Lt Gillespie returns from leave Officers 2 Sections have huts Steel shelters erected in California French C.22.d.52.
	18/11		Rails laid to D.2.d.8.6. - formation 100x further. French tondo laid to D.2.b.2.9. - Packing track laying wooden sleepers. Road repaired East of Triangle - Wagon turning point improved. No 7 Section on advanced billets C.22.d.52.	No 1 Section N Canal Bank relieving No 7.
	19/11		6th & 226" Fd Co RE, (2nd Div) relieve without notification but eventually disappeared to consequences. 24th RE with Leicester Pioneer column laying 60 lb tracking. 23" RE + 32 Div Pioneers (140 men) + 100 N.F. (32nd Div) start new narrow n Slab road from GENOA N YORK FARM which has slipped in G/11 Officers, 3 Sections billeted in California French C.22.d.52. Hill Top Camp abandoned.	CE II Corps visits Tram line road.

Army Form C. 2118.

WAR DIARY
or
INTELLIGENCE SUMMARY

23rd Field Co. R.E.

November 1917

(Erase heading not required.)

Instructions regarding War Diaries and Intelligence Summaries are contained in F. S. Regs., Part II. and the Staff Manual respectively. Title Pages will be prepared in manuscript.

Stamp: 23RD (FIELD) COMPANY ROYAL ENGINEERS — DEC. 1917

Place	Date	Hour	Summary of Events and Information	Remarks and references to Appendices
HQ at Canal Bank No 63 East. Adv. B.Blt. 3 Lithos in California French C 22.d 52 Transport - Hospital Farm B 19 d.	20/11		Work continued as before on tram-line & Road.	
	21/11		As above. 5th & 226 Fd Coys. are relieved by 448 & 447 Fd Coys. Major Woon moves to England on 30 days leave.	
	22/11		Major Marshall takes over operation of railways - all the plant running de etc. under his company (R.E.) leaving 23rd Fd Coy. with 1 Coy. 14th Worcester Pioneers, 1 Coy. N.F. & 150 Coys. Red Pioneers to continue the GENOA-YORK Farm Road.	
	23/11		As above.	
	24/11		1st Divs. moves tomorrow & no 23rd Fd Coy continues road with 3 Coys. Worcester Pioneers other troops having rejoined their division (the 32nd)	
	25/11 & 27/11		As above. Road makes average progress of 50x a day.	
	28/11		Coy. hands over work to 248 Coy. R.E. & moves to rest area near PROVEN. Dismantled Nyssen hut from ELVERDINGHE. Mounted Ashton by Road.	

2449 Wt. W14957/M90 753,000 1/16 J.B.C. & A. Forms/C.2118/12.

Army Form C. 2118.

WAR DIARY
or
INTELLIGENCE SUMMARY
(Erase heading not required.)

Instructions regarding War Diaries and Intelligence Summaries are contained in F. S. Regs., Part II. and the Staff Manual respectively. Title Pages will be prepared in manuscript.

23rd Field Coy. R.E.
November 1917

Place	Date	Hour	Summary of Events and Information	Remarks and references to Appendices
Roads Camp nr OUTHOUSE	29/11		No work done	
Chaw on PROVEN -POPERINGHE Road	30/11		Capt. Edwards visits area about Malt taken over from II French Division in front of HOUTHOULST Forest with C.R.E.	Lt. FORWOOD. T.L. proceeds to G.H.Q. to join F.S. Survey Co.

[Stamp: 223rd (FIELD) COMPANY / DEC. 1917 / ROYAL ENGINEERS]

A B Edwards
Major R.E.
O.C. 223 Field Coy R.E.

WAR DIARY.

23rd. Field Coy., R.E.

1st. DIVISION.

DECEMBER, 1917.

C.R.E.

1st Dn.

War Diary
for December therewith

1/8   [signature] Capt. R.E.
       Commanding 23rd (Fld.) Coy. R.E.

Army Form C. 2118.

23rd Field Coy RE
December 1912

WT 39

[Stamp: 23 (FIELD) COMPANY No. 2025 1st JAN 1913 ROYAL ENGINEERS]

WAR DIARY
or
INTELLIGENCE SUMMARY
(Erase heading not required.)

Instructions regarding War Diaries and Intelligence Summaries are contained in F. S. Regs, Part II. and the Staff Manual respectively. Title Pages will be prepared in manuscript.

Place	Date	Hour	Summary of Events and Information	Remarks and references to Appendices
PARDO Comb on the CUT.HOVE Chau. on the PROVEN to POPERINGHE Road.	1/12		2 sections under Lt. COWLEY & Lt. GILLESPIE move by road	
	2/12		to LA MINOTERIE about 1000" N.W of WOESTAN. John Capt. Edwards visits sector with FRENCH Coy Commander	
	3/12		Remainder of Coy. moves to LAMINOTERIE. H.Q.Q.a sections move to billets of FRENCH 1/3 Coy de GENIE at PARATONNÈRE Farm near HET SAS.	
PARATONNÈRE Farm.	4/12		Transport under Lt Thomas moves into Transport lines at PARATONNÈRE Farm. Billets of Coy are improved.	
	5/12		Works Reconnaissance by Lt Smith, Lt Cowley & Lt. Gillespie, in our Divisional sector. Company improves billets.	
	6/12		The screening of the KORTEKEER Cabaret road is started. Brigade HQ is strengthened. Divisional Tramline is started.	
	7/12		Daily Patrol at BROENBEER Bridge commenced. Screening of KORTEKER-LANGEMARK road continued. Divisional Tramline continued. Strengthening of Brigade HQ completed.	

2449 Wt. W14957/M90 750,000 1/16 J.B.C. & A. Forms/C.2118/12.

Army Form C. 2118.

WAR DIARY
or
INTELLIGENCE SUMMARY
(Erase heading not required.)

23 Fld Coy R.E.

December 1917

Place	Date	Hour	Summary of Events and Information	Remarks and references to Appendices
PARATONNÈRE CAMP N° WOESTON X HET SAS	8/12		Work on Divisional Tram Line continued. Work on Screening of KORTEKEER–LANGEMARK road continued. O.P. for N°1 Group R.F.A. commenced.	
	9/12		O.P. for N°1 Group R.F.A. finished. Lt Thomas goes on leave to UK. Screening of KORTEKEER–LANGEMARK. B Screen of 125 yds camphlack ready for erection on site. Work continued on Divisional Tram Line. 300 yds laid. Daily patrol of Bridges across JANSBEEK, BROENBEEK & STEEBEEK continued. Small repairs carried out.	
	10/12		Bridge Patrol does small repairs to Bridges. Work on Screen for KORTEKEER–LANGEMARK road continued. Work on Divisional Tram Line continued. Total of 400 yds laid today.	
	11/12		Bridge Patrol does small repairs to Bridges. Screening of KORTEKEER–LANGEMARK road. Pile is being erected on site. Divisional Tram Line. 150 yds laid. Additional 50 yds of formation made.	
	12/12		Bridges repaired where damaged & remainder Patrolled. Screen for KORTEKEER–LANGEMARK road, all complete & ready for erection. Work continued on Divisional Tram Line. 100 yds laid.	
	13/12		Bridges in Divisional Sector Patrolled. Small repairs completed. Divisional Tram line laid up to, & across, KORTEKEER–LANGEMARK road. Arrangements for erection of Screen complete.	
	14/12		Screen on KORTEKEER–LANGEMARK road Erected & completed. Work on Divisional Tram Line continued. 80 yds laid. Formation for additional 75 yds prepared. Bridges Patrolled. Two damaged bays of DEVILS Bridge repaired.	

Army Form C. 2118.

23 Fld Coy RE

December 1917

WAR DIARY
or
INTELLIGENCE SUMMARY
(Erase heading not required.)

Instructions regarding War Diaries and Intelligence Summaries are contained in F. S. Regs., Part II. and the Staff Manual respectively. Title Pages will be prepared in manuscript.

Place	Date	Hour	Summary of Events and Information	Remarks and references to Appendices
PARATONNÈRE CAMP. N. WOESTON & HET SAS.	15/12		Bridges on Divisional Sector Patrolled & found correct. Screens on KORTEKEER - LANGEMARK road Patrolled & small repairs made. Remainder of Coy, less Section with Brigade in line, resting.	
	16/12		Work on Divisional Tram line continued. 100 yds laid. Wiring commenced between POSTS in Forward Area. 100 yds completed. Bridges Patrolled & found correct. Small repair to screen carried out.	
	17/12		Bridges Patrolled & repairs to ABADIE Bridge done. Divisional Tram line: 60 yds laid. Bridges over STEENBEEK commenced. Wiring between Posts in Forward Area continued. Bn relief in.	
	18/12		Wiring between Posts in Forward Area continued. Divisional Tram line: 60 yds of Bridges over STEENBEEK made. Piles driven for additional 40 yds.	
	19/12		Bridges patrolled & small repairs made. Divisional Tram line: 90 yds laid. Additional 50 yds of bridge built. Work continued on POSTS in Forward Area.	
	20/12		Bridges Patrolled & small repairs made. Two Sections work on Posts in Forward Area. Divisional Tram line 50 yds of Bridges over STEENBEEK made.	
	21/12		Bridges Patrolled. Small repairs effected. Two Sections work on POSTS in Forward Area. Divisional Tram line. 60 yds of Bridge built across STEENBEEK.	
	22/12		Bridges Patrolled - repairs to DEVILS Bridge executed. Two Sections with Infantry working on POSTS in Forward Area. Divisional Tram line. Bridge building - made bridge across STEENBEEK	

WAR DIARY
or
INTELLIGENCE SUMMARY

(Erase heading not required.)

Army Form C. 2118.

2 3 Fld Coy RE

December 1917

Place	Date	Hour	Summary of Events and Information	Remarks and references to Appendices
PARATONNERE CAMP Nº WOESTON & HET SAS	23/12		Bridges patrolled. DONCASTER & DERBY bridges found damaged. Temporary repairs made. Two sections working with Brigade on line of POSTS in Forward area. 8" Thaw sets in from heavy Divisional Tram Line; 300 yds of Formation prepared from existing Tram head to CORMORAN Dump.	
	24/12		Bridges patrolled. More extensive repairs carried out to DONCASTER & DERBY bridges. One section working with Brigade on line of POSTS in forward area. Divisional Tram Line: 250 yds of Track laid from Rail-head towards CORMORAN Dump.	
	25/12		Bridges patrolled. Remainder of Company had a holiday.	
	26/12		Bridges patrolled & final repairs to DONCASTER & DERBY bridges carried out. Two sections working on Divisional Tram Line. 150 yds laid track towards CORMORAN DUMP. Two sections sorting wire for 2nd Brigade.	
	27/12		Bridges patrolled. CEMETRY bridge damaged. Temporary repairs carried out. Divisional Tram line 60 yds laid. Work held up owing to Public misunderstanding of THAW precautions for Transport. Two sections sorting wire into 500 yds lengths for Brigade in the line.	
	28/12		Bridges patrolled. CEMETRY bridge thoroughly repaired. Two sections working on Divisional Tram Line. Track completed to CORMORAN DUMP. Two sections making arrangements for procuring 16 dumps of wiring material in Forward Area.	
	29/12		Bridges patrolled. Small repairs carried out. Divisional Tram Line: 80 yds of Track laid beyond STEENBEEK bridge. Tram Rose nearly complete. Two sections making preparations for forming dumps of wiring material in Forward Area. Water Points patrolled. Pill Box Tank at LANCIER FARM not yet complete.	

Army Form C. 2118.

WAR DIARY
or
INTELLIGENCE SUMMARY
(Erase heading not required.)

23 Fld Coy R.E.

December 1917

Instructions regarding War Diaries and Intelligence Summaries are contained in F.S. Regs., Part II. and the Staff Manual respectively. Title Pages will be prepared in manuscript.

Place	Date	Hour	Summary of Events and Information	Remarks and references to Appendices
PARATONNÈRE CAMP.	30/12		Bridges patrolled. Small repairs carried out. Divisional Tram line: Tram B ace finished. Duck board track from Tram head to IBIS track laid. Guides to Brigade dumps in forward area provided. Schemes prepared for Demolition of bridges in Divisional Sector	
Nth WOESTON & HET SAS	31/12		Bridges patrolled. Small repairs carried out. Lt Smith gone on leave to U.K. Two sections working on Divisional Tram line. Repairs to STEENBEEK Bridge carried out. Additional 50 yds of Formation made. 20 Trucks salvaged and are being repaired.	

A.A.Munro
Major, R.E.
Commanding 23rd (Fld.) Coy. R.E.

1ST DIVISION
ROY. ENGINEERS

23RD FIELD COMPANY R.E.
JAN - DEC 1918

Army Form C. 2118.

WAR DIARY
or
INTELLIGENCE SUMMARY
(Erase heading not required.)

23rd F. Coy R.E.
January 1918.

Place	Date	Hour	Summary of Events and Information	Remarks and references to Appendices
PARATONNÈRE Farm near HETSAS & WOËSTAN	1/1		Bridges patrolled daily & small damages repaired when necessary. Slit loop-hole for an M.G. cut at PAPEGOED Farm in main line of Resistance.	Lt Smith on tour
	2/1		Divisional tramway continued. light-track on bridge over STEENBEEK replaced by heavy traction building sandbags finished off.	
	3/1		Bridges patrolled. Tramway continued. Gas Blanketing of Adv. H.Q. commenced.	
	4/1		Bridges patrolled. Tramway continued. Gas Blanketing continued.	
	5/1		As above.	
	6/1		As above.	
	7/1		As above.	

Army Form C. 2118.

WAR DIARY
or
INTELLIGENCE SUMMARY

(Erase heading not required.)

23rd F² Cy R.E.

January 1918.

Place	Date	Hour	Summary of Events and Information	Remarks and references to Appendices
As above	8/1		As above. News of an off. 50 c.m. line bank commenced to run into new A.D.S. at MARRONIER HOUSE.	
	9/1		As above. Lay tubes over screening in front of CORMORAN Dump from 6th Welsh.	
	10/1		As above.	
	11/1			
	12/1		As above.	
	13/1			
	14/1			
	15/1		Heavy storm on top of thaw causes STEENBEEK & BOESINGHE to rise about 5'. Several bridges under water & a lot of small damage done. Only one bridge (ABADIE) destroyed.	
	16/1			

Army Form C. 2118.

WAR DIARY
or
INTELLIGENCE SUMMARY
(Erase heading not required.)

23rd Fd. Coy. R.E.
January 1918

Place	Date	Hour	Summary of Events and Information	Remarks and references to Appendices
As above	17/1		2 sections working on repairs to bridges in the Divisional Area. All bridges now made passable except ABADIE which is still under water. 1 section carrying out repair to Divisional Tramline. Party a the Clawn off for D.A. to enable a "camouflage" bric "le" to be established.	
	18/1		2 sections extending bridges too front above flood level. 1 section repairing Railway	
	19/1		As above.	
	20/1		Line of tramway now reaches near banks of BROENBEEK with heavy track. The whole of the main railway line to this front (about 1500ʸ) was laid with "cabiel" track & over 30 truckloads procured in a like manner.	
	21/1		As above.	
	22/1		As above. Repairs to revetting damaged by the storm commenced.	Lt. Smith returned from leave to U.K.

Army Form C. 2118.

WAR DIARY
or
INTELLIGENCE SUMMARY
(Erase heading not required.)

232nd Coy. R.E.
1918.

Place	Date	Hour	Summary of Events and Information	Remarks and references to Appendices
As above	23/1		As above.	
Banks of YPRES DIXMUDE Canal near Bridge 3. Horse Lines near SALVATION CORNER	24/1		Coy. is relieved by 219 F.d Coy.R.E. & relieves them at work on Army Battle Zone in 2nd Corps area. Work revetting pill-boxes by cutting new entrance & blocking old entrance, & thickening rear front face & reinforced. Work on O.P's (concrete) M.G.Empts. (concrete) & a certain amount of wiring.	
	25/1		As above. Locality of work. The Coy. is on the Army Battle Zone Outpost line which runs from the WIELTJE – St JULIEN Road to the YPRES – STADEN Railway near LANGEMARK, & follows the line of the W.Bank of the STEENBEEK.	
	26/1		As above.	
	27/1		As above.	

2449 Wt. W14957/M90 750,000 1/16 J.B.C. & A. Forms/C.2118/12.

Army Form C. 2118.

WAR DIARY
or
INTELLIGENCE SUMMARY
(Erase heading not required.)

23rd July RE
Jan. 1918

Place	Date	Hour	Summary of Events and Information	Remarks and references to Appendices
As above	28/1		As above.	
	29/1		Capt. Rondo over the O.Ps in the main line to the A.T. Coys. clearing the main line. This then enabled us to put a section on the left near LANGEMARK where the work is very backward.	
	30/1		As above thru new tunnels M.G.Es started on the left.	
	31/1		As above.	

Commanding 23rd (Md.) Coy. R.E.

Army Form C. 2118.

WAR DIARY
or
INTELLIGENCE SUMMARY
(Erase heading not required.)

23rd Field Coy R.E.   February 1918.

Place	Date	Hour	Summary of Events and Information	Remarks and references to Appendices
Boesinghe	1/2		Work on M.G.E's, Pill-boxes, and Wiring of Army Line continued at COWLEY Leave to U.K.	
Bank of	2/2		As above.	
YPRES-DIXMUDE	3/2		As above.	
Canal near	4/2		As above.	
Bridge 3.	5/2		As above.	
House known	6/2		As above.	Lt SELLMAN 10th Glosters rejoins from leave
as SALVATION	7/2		As above.	
CORNER.	8/2		As above. Work	
	9/2		Work on Army Line ceases, Company rejoins Division remaining in same billets.	Lt SELLMAN 10th Glosters rejoins his unit
	10/2		Work on Divisional Tramway from MINTY FARM to PHEASANT TRENCH began (converting from 9c.r. to 20 lb rail) and Major WILSON rejoins and reassumes command	
	11/2		Work on Tramway continued. Repairs to Duck boards at SIEGE CAMP carried out. 2 Armstrong huts erected at Div H.Q.	

Army Form C. 2118.

WAR DIARY
or
INTELLIGENCE SUMMARY

(Erase heading not required.)

23rd Field Coy R.E.   February 1918.

Place	Date	Hour	Summary of Events and Information	Remarks and references to Appendices
As Above	12/2		Work on front-line continued. 4 Armstrong huts erected at Div H.Q. Work on shelter at SIEGE CAMP begun.	
	13/2		Work on tramline and shelter continued.	
	14/2		As above and small repairs to REIGERSBURG huts.	
	15/2		As above and gas. blanketing dugouts at Div H.Q. begun.	
	16/2		As above	Lt COWLEY rejoins from leave.
	17/2		As above CANAL BANK huts dismantled	
	18/2		As above.	
	19/2		As above.	Capt EDWARDS leave to U.K.
	20/2		As above.	Lt T. CAMPBELL 1st Canadians joins as Officer i/c of A.T.
	21/2		As above. Erection of Batts at new HILL TOP FARM begun.	
House lines moved to	22/2		As above.	
REIGERSBURG CHATEAU	23/2		As above	Lt GILLESPIE leave to U.K.

Army Form C. 2118.

WAR DIARY
or
INTELLIGENCE SUMMARY

(Erase heading not required.)

23rd Field Coy. R.E.

February 1918.

Place	Date	Hour	Summary of Events and Information	Remarks and references to Appendices
As above	24/2		Work on MINTY FARM PHEASANT TRENCH tramway, SIEGE CAMP Theatre and HOSPITAL FARM BATHS continued.	
	25/2		As above. 2500' of proposed wiring near BRAY FARM marked out.	
	26/2		As above. Position of above wire shown to officers of the Battalion detailed to carry out the wiring.	
	27/2		As above.	
	28/2		As above.	

W. G. Smith
Lt/br Major, R.E.
Commanding 23rd (Fld.) Coy. R.E.

Army Form C. 2118.

WAR DIARY
or
INTELLIGENCE SUMMARY
(Erase heading not required.)

23rd Field Coy RE   March 1918

Place	Date	Hour	Summary of Events and Information	Remarks and references to Appendices
Bank of YSER CANAL nr. Bridge 3	1/3		Work on MINTY FARM – PHEASANT TR Tramway, SIEGE CAMP and HILL TOP baths continued, work on extension to SIEGE CAMP cleaned Annexy hut begun. 2000' of wiring worked out on night 25/26/R erected.	
House lines	2/3		As above. Wiring carried out farmers rgts duplicated. HILL TOP baths finished.	
REGERSBURG CHATEAU	3/3		Work on Tramway and SIEGE CAMP baths and CA hut continued	
	4/3		As above. Bunking in dug-outs at WILSON'S FARM LA BELLE ALLIANCE begun	
	5/3		As above. SIEGE CAMP baths finished	
	6/3		As above	
	7/3		As above	
	8/3		As above. Reconnaissance of Forward Zone made by Capt Edwards MCRE and Lt Thomas RE.	Major W.R. Wilson MC RE to hospital, sick. Capt B.B. Edwards MC RE 1/c.
	9/3		Work on forward zone taken over, from Aux Field Coy RE, and Back Area work handed over to 26 & 7 Field Coy RE. Work on wiring and shelters in neighbourhood of DELEAPPELLE begun	Reservations and reconnaissances to T.W. Thomas. 1st R Field water points as attached. Officers k/c attached strength increased to 60 O.R.

Army Form C. 2118.

WAR DIARY
or
INTELLIGENCE SUMMARY
(Erase heading not required.)

23rd Field Coy RE

March 1918

Place	Date	Hour	Summary of Events and Information	Remarks and references to Appendices
KEMPTON PARK Sheet 28 N.W. House Chao	10/3		Work on wiring and Posts of TOEICAPPELLE Defences continued. B.H.Q. shifted from CANAL BANK TO KEMPTON PARK.	
REIGERSBURG CHATEAU	11/3		Work as above.	
	12/3		Work as above.	
	13/3		As above. Posts at OXFORD and TERRIER Horses begun.	
	14/3		As above.	
	15/3		As above.	
	16/3		As above.	Capt E.T.G. Coates RE joins Coy and proceeds on leave to Paris. Capt B.B. Edwards MC RE to Foreway Coy RE as O.C. 2nd Lieut. Iolas over command. 2nd Lt J.C. Pool RE joins the Company.
	17/3		As above.	
	18/3		As above.	

Army Form C. 2118.

WAR DIARY
or
INTELLIGENCE SUMMARY

(Erase heading not required.)

23rd Field Coy R.E.   March 1918

Place	Date	Hour	Summary of Events and Information	Remarks and references to Appendices
KEMPTON PARK	19/3		As above. OXFORD and TERRIER Posts finished	
House Lines at			As above. Wiring in BRAY FARM area done on 14 and 1½ and 2/3 completed	
TREIGERSBURG CHATEAU	20/3		Work on IMBROS LOCALITY begun. Wiring on line OKRA - IMBROS marked out. As above.	
	21/3		As above. SOUVENIR HOUSE WELL - Sample of water taken from well sent to CRE for testing	Dr Smith goes on Infantry course to 4th Army School. Lt Thomas taken over command.
	22/3		As above. Post P1 at ROSE HOUSE completed	
	23/3		As above. Draining of Pill-boxes at POELCAPPELL completed	
	24/3		As above. Draining of Pill-boxes at POELCAPPELL completed with exception of H⁰ 16 & 17. Post P.2 at ROSE HOUSE completed. Bunking at WINCHESTER HOUSE completed	
	25/3			Capt E.T.G. Carlin RE rejoins Coy + taken over command.
	26/3		Handed over above work to 26 Fld Coy RE. Took over work from 409 L Coy RE. Moved into billets at ILMINSTER Camp C.27.8.23.	

2449 Wt. W14957/Mgo 759,000 1/16 J.B.C. & A. Forms/C.2118/12.

Army Form C. 2118.

WAR DIARY
or
INTELLIGENCE SUMMARY

(Erase heading not required.)

23 Field Coy R.E.   March 1918.

Place	Date	Hour	Summary of Events and Information	Remarks and references to Appendices
INKSTER CAMP C.27.B.23 Havelinn at REIGERSBURG CHATEAU.	27/3		Work on posts and dugouts in support system begun.	
	28/3		As above.	Lt Smith returns from 4th Army School.
	29/3		As above.	
	30/3		As above.	
	31/3		As above.	

W.G. Bennett
Lt. R.E.
for O.C. 23rd Field Coy R.E.

1st Divisional Engineers

23rd FIELD COMPANY R. E.

APRIL 1918.

Army Form C. 2118.

WAR DIARY
or
INTELLIGENCE SUMMARY
(Erase heading not required.)

2J 2nd Field Coy R.E.

APRIL 1918

Vol 43

Place	Date	Hour	Summary of Events and Information	Remarks and references to Appendices
ILMINSTER CAMP Sh.t 28. C.27.b.2.3.	1st	—	Coy working in support system of Forward Zone. The localities from left to right are BEAR (near YPRES-STADEN railway), EAGLE (at SOMEBOOM), LOUIS FARM, WHITE MILL, PHEASANT FARM. These are being constructed as defensive posts for all round fire. Average garrison. 1 platoon + 2 m.g's.	Capt. W.G. SMITH. M.C., R.E. no transferred to 86th Field Coy R.E. and takes over the duties of 2nd in command. 2nd unit next work 2 acting Capts.
Horse Lines at REIGERSBURG CHATEAU.	2nd	—	Work is also proceeding on a trust view artillery O.P. at DOUBLECOTT'S. and another is being started at PHEASANT FARM. Deep mined dugouts in the area are also being put up. Nobile boards are being hunted.	
	3rd	—	As above. Reconnaissance made of mined dugouts at WHITE MILL, TUFF HOUSES, DOG HOUSES, & ALOUETTE FARM, with a view to their being hunted.	
	4th	—	As above. Work proceeding on hunting of dugouts. A ferry a tank erected at the BIG WHISTLE Battalion HQ. near LANGEMARCK. A warning order of an impending move received. All nobile boards put up. Bunking at IMPIC MINES completed. Rumour says that we are going to nearly every place imaginable — quite a Cook's Tour, in fact.	
	5th	—	As above. C.R.E. visited several of the works, in particular the defensive localities, — the mined dugouts started for work	Major Nilson rejoins from hospital

Army Form C. 2118.

WAR DIARY
or
INTELLIGENCE SUMMARY
(Erase heading not required.)

23rd Feb R.E. Sheet 2

APRIL 1918

Place	Date	Hour	Summary of Events and Information	Remarks and references to Appendices
ILMINSTER CAMP.	5th (cont'd)		on these lathes, 20 carpenters from 70th (Scotland) & 77th (y R.E. have been attached to us. Owing to the distance (1½ km walk each way) between wood & lathes, both they & No 2 Section of the 6y Divn on the work, & rations are sent to them by road each night. This makes 9 full hours work to be done each day, instead of a maybe 5, which in the normal when they walk there & back.	
REIGERSBURG CHATEAU.	6th		As above. Orders for the move received. An officer of the 123rd Field Coy R.E. arrived during the afternoon to take over the work. To-night being the last night of work for this unit, as many outstanding jobs as possible were finished. WHITE MH and was completed, also PHEASANT, and the launching of DOG HOUSES, PUFF HOUSES & the maypole part of WHITETHL deep dugouts was finished. EAGLE, LOUIS, & BEAR had shell to have their portions away placed behind them. As to the trench work, DOUBLE COTTS was handed over 75% complete & PHEASANT 7/1M as 15%. Towards evening another officer, of the 201st Field Coy R.E. appeared to take over & later orders were received as to the boundaries of the two Divisions. The officer that the 30th & 39th Divisions were to taking over the 1st Guards front only.	

Army Form C. 2118.

23rd FA Corps
Sheet 3

WAR DIARY
or
INTELLIGENCE SUMMARY.
(Erase heading not required.)

Instructions regarding War Diaries and Intelligence Summaries are contained in F. S. Regs., Part II. and the Staff Manual respectively. Title pages will be prepared in manuscript.

Place	Date	Hour	Summary of Events and Information	Remarks and references to Appendices
ILMINSTER CAMP	7th	11am	Coy formed up, dismissed and to ILMINSTER CAMP proceeded via EVERZEELE	April 1918
RENGHELSBURG CHATEAU			BRIELEN (where it remained by Mtr transport to ELVERDINGHE)	
ELVERDINGHE B.15.c.5.a.			Lectured at THEDO CAMP. Bt R/gr. had a wire received that Mr. Hirchot	
			was to proceed to GODEWAERSVELDE - about there to go Dir Farm info.	
		5pm	working party, transport pulled out at 5pm taking the route STEENTJE	
			- POPERINGHE - ABEELE - BIEUVOORDE to GODEWAERSVELDE + arriving thereat	
			9pm, a being met by an advanced repost guide, with the information that the Bde	
			and RICOUR FARM between FLETRE - METERIN (a billet previously occupied by	
RICOUR FARM and METERIN			this unit for a fortnight in June 1917.) Arrived there 11pm + remained all	
			+ equivalents. Orders received for an early Start	
	8th	3.45	Transport pulled out + proceeded via CASSEL - LE BRIARDE - HAZEBROUCK -	
			MORBECQUE (where it watered) - HAVERSKERQUE (where it halted - halted for 1½ hrs)	
to			- MORBECQUE ST VENANT - ROBECQ - GUARBINGHEM to ANNEZIN.	
			Arriving at the latter place at 3.30 pm, casualty the coms being no	
			the horseman lost fashion which had had the following marches -	
ANNEZIN		7am	left ELVERDINGHE + marched to POPERINGHE via STEENTJE + ST JANS CROSS	

Army Form C. 2118.

WAR DIARY
or
INTELLIGENCE SUMMARY.
(Erase heading not required.)

23 AUGUST 1918 Sheet 4

Place	Date	Hour	Summary of Events and Information	Remarks and references to Appendices
ANNEZIN Sh.P.36.B. E.3.a.5.2.	8th (cont'd)		Entrained here by Rly. 10 a.m. Arrived TOUQUEREUX Station at 2.35 p.m. & marched to ANNEZIN. The 4 waggons accompanying the 2nd echelon got on the train to which they were billeted instead of unloading to our waggons, so came by the 11 p.m. train arriving at CHOQUES at 1 a.m.	
	9th	5.30 am	marched to ANNEZIN - arrived there about 7 am	
			Billets are very scattered, the village being about between Nº 26th & Nº J.D. HENDERSON St.	
		10 am	General parade & Divisional Salute in Marching Order - Inspection, missing advance ordered to take over work on the Right Brigade Area (2nd Div) Thursday July 7	
			Received men from the 67th Field Coy RE, 11th Durham whose at present billeted at NOTTRES - By VERMELLES (L.M.4)	
		2 pm	Lt. Coley & Gillespie marched 67th Fd. Coy RE for that purpose. Capt Carter marched ANNEQUIN to front billets, but village was full Capt Carter went to SAILLY LABOURSE & billeted the Coy in dugouts in the "TUNING FORK" line in front of the village pending the finishing of billets in the village itself. Lts Coley, Gillespie went round the line to see the work. At 1.25 pm the Coy marched out of ANNEZIN	Lt Pocock to Nº 3 Section Lt HENDERSON KM.?

WAR DIARY or INTELLIGENCE SUMMARY

Army Form C. 2118.

23rd FRENCH N.E. Sheet 5

April 1918

Place	Date	Hour	Summary of Events and Information	Remarks and references to Appendices
ANNEZIN to	10th (contd)		Through outskirts of BETHUNE to FOUQUIERES — VERQUIN — VERQUIGNEUL — LABOURSE — SAILLY LABOURSE arriving about 4pm. This route was taken because both BETHUNE & BEUVRY were being shelled with 12" H.V. guns.	
SAILLY LABOURSE L.4.a.2.6.			After a short halt, No 1 & 2 Sections moved on to a dugout in LEWIS KEEP in CAMBRIN SECTOR (36c: A.26.a.) The days trek due to live on the roads which was deep thegride & often of snow,	
	11th		Billets for the 2 back sections Hd had been found in SAILLY LABOURSE — arrived. The Coy was in process of moving on, when a warning order to move (about 2pm). Definite orders to march back to FOUQUIERES arrived at 5.40pm (at SAILLY). The forward sections arrived back at 7.30pm. Transport (which had remained at ANNEZIN on 10th) arrived at 7.45pm & at 8.15pm the Company marched back along the road we had taken yesterday, arriving in the village at 10.30pm. Billets party scattered.	
FOUQUIERES E.21.a.5.8.	12th		Transport moves from FOUQUEREUIL to FOUQUIERES to join HQ. Baths for dismounted sections. General inspections & clean up. Lt Cowley went forward to receive instructions re: work of the 2 sections who are being attached to 409th (Lowland) Field Coy RE.	

(A7883) D.D. & L., London, E.C.
Wt. W809/M1672 350,000 4/17 Sch. 52a. Form/C/2118/14

Army Form C. 2118.

WAR DIARY
or
INTELLIGENCE SUMMARY.
(Erase heading not required.)

Appendix 12
1915

23rd Aug 15 Sheet C

Place	Date	Hour	Summary of Events and Information	Remarks and references to Appendices
FOUQUIÈRES	13th	—	Most of two sections forward consisted of midnight last night. Kit inspections, particularly with reference to unrequired surplus kit. Practice in fire control — fire orders etc. Extended order drill, with practice in crossing an advance or withdrawal with fire orders. Received to send two section forward to be attached to 100th Inf Bty R.E. with Nos 2 & 4 sections moved to billets in N. ANNEQUIN via VERQUIN CAMBRIN SECTOR	
"	14th (Sunday)	—	and observed as such by H.Q. & 2 sections. 1st Coldstream, Guards. BEUVRY, leaving due at 8 a.m. Church Parade for remainder at 10 a.m. Subsequently carried out an examination of portable huts for Divn Staff, & advised collected for the same. Carpenters working on huts as above. Remainder practising the laying out of trenches — the organisation of working parties. In the afternoon the portable hut was erected & shewn to Divn Staff.	
"	15th	—	Orders for more forward received. As much kit as possible is being left at wagon lines, in case of a hasty move ; only bare necessaries taken forward. The two Elected sections are to join us on our arrival forward.	

Army Form C. 2118.

WAR DIARY
or
INTELLIGENCE SUMMARY.
(Erase heading not required.)

23rd Field Coy RE APRIL 1918 Sheet 1

Instructions regarding War Diaries and Intelligence Summaries are contained in F. S. Regs., Part II. and the Staff Manual respectively. Title pages will be prepared in manuscript.

Place	Date	Hour	Summary of Events and Information	Remarks and references to Appendices
FOUVIÈRES to N. ANNEQUIN F.24.c.0.3.	16th	—	Billets cleared up & what wagons were going forward were packed & at 1 pm the remainder of the Coy., less the MtdSection, who remain at FOUVIÈRES, marched along the same old road as before, to N. ANNEQUIN. Being billeted on the houses there, only recently evacuated by the civilian population. Naturally, there is a large amount of "loot" about but this is as far as possible being gathered into one outh. left of the houses containing it, & locked up there. The estaminet cellars have all been cleared & the wine been brought to one large barn & there guarded. Probably it will be bought by the contingent funds of the various units around & issued "rationally".	
"	17th	—	Billets cleaned up & the general débris of the recent bombardment removed. Reconnaissance of the new area by Major Wilson RE & Lt Cowley RE., and a reconnaissance of the tramway system by 2/Lts Gillespie & Henderson RE. GIVENCHY SECTOR	
"	18th	—	General confusion of rifles etc etc, and also our returns. Woke at 3.15 am to find ANNEQUIN being heavily gas shelled. Alterlarum was being given to everyone & a battery to., as our billets were on a	

D. D., P. & L., London, E.C.
(A5883) Wt. W809/M1672 350,000 4/17 Sch. 52a. Forms/C/2118/14

Army Form C. 2118.

WAR DIARY
or
INTELLIGENCE SUMMARY.
(Erase heading not required.)

23rd Field Coy RE
Sheet 8
April 1915

Place	Date	Hour	Summary of Events and Information	Remarks and references to Appendices
N. ANNEQUIN	18th (cont)		Temperature bodies, & also "up wind" of the main shelling not of very great power. Bks informed 5.30 am that "Standing by" for orders was "Standing by" for orders. Bks notified 7.30 am motorising Cy & persons till further orders. About 6 am H.F. began to shingle with shrapnel	18th WNW Coy
		21. 7.30 am orders to stand to.		That hour rcvd at 11.30 - found
		The bombardment seemed to attacking intensely		Whit duty having had
		8.30 am.		a little time in the hay long
		By orders from Brigade followed after a moment of — at 11.30 a.m. by his bicycle patrols & his garments		
		conversation with CRE Brigade to move to LETTRED [illegible] Redt		
		of a march having only a few details to guard Isolaert, Hospices etc		
		Arrived LETTRED 2pm reporting to Bde HQ then Detailed to garrison MARAIS KEEP (F.11.a.4.2)		
MARAIS KEEP F.11.a.4.2			Allowed to sum to latter date. Very hard hard accommodation must now	Also made Temporary bridge across over minor breaches.
		Coy all Rks finding 8 parties where to dig. The first job was to inform	& trouble then traverses & loopholes across
		a shake build over G by a 12'hour which had hoped the Civil Road & some other	
		Men had to improvise the woods. No 1 section commenced work immediately	
		arrival. Being relieved by No 3 at 5 pm & by dark a temporary bridge	
		was built only applied on a seven, affording only about 1/3 of the width	
		This on the enemy were responded for No 2, 4 sections to go up sector	
		having taken up communications with GIVENCHY, which was low	
		Casualties Major little bay — Wounded - buried - 2, Gnr bolstered - 3, all	
		of duty recorded, 1; burned 2. = 8, + 111.	

Army Form C. 2118.

WAR DIARY
or
INTELLIGENCE SUMMARY.
(Erase heading not required.)

23rd Fd Coy RE

April 1915

Sheet 9

Instructions regarding War Diaries and Intelligence Summaries are contained in F. S. Regs., Part II. and the Staff Manual respectively. Title pages will be prepared in manuscript.

Place	Date	Hour	Summary of Events and Information	Remarks and references to Appendices
MARAIS WEEP	19th	—	The further "distances" crossing spit was continued on the dam. The water had risen a foot or more during the night, & an inch of snow had fallen on things, were most uncomfortable. John Lily came up with the bread as a boat builder's yard. Some 12" x 2½" oak plank was taken from there & which the dam constructed about this beginning. No 1 section starting at 8 am — working till 2 pm, — No 4 section arriving till dark, finishing the dam by 6 pm. Nos 2 & 3 sections employed on working bridgehead of VAUXHALL (737 map) & WESTMINSTER (incomplete). The delay on VAUX being caused by possibility At 8 pm an urgent request came to work at MEAT FARM. No 1 section and there found bridges cut & rifle & shell holes damaged dugouts. On account of a counter attack to be made by our. All sections were withdrawn before 4 am & returned to the Keep. Very little retaliation by the Boche, our counter succeeding in regaining all enough the whole	
"	20th	—	Work on the dam continued by No 4 section (the flood water having subsided 6" during the night) at 7 am — A second subsidiary dam was made behind yesterday's main dam, & the whole work was	

Army Form C. 2118.

WAR DIARY
or
INTELLIGENCE SUMMARY.
(Erase heading not required.)

23rd Fld Co RE

Sheet 10

Place	Date	Hour	Summary of Events and Information	Remarks and references to Appendices
MARAIS WEIR	20th (cont)		pillboxes with machine guns & snipers — the gap filled with bosh from the ruined houses. No 2 Section had most of the work at 12.30 p.m. & finished the ordinary schedule & fell A' dummy bridge a small distance of water. No 4 Section on the flank was employed in machining a barricade at GIVRE to transport stores from there to MOONAR but a proper pit & portholes & sandbags were badly used up by rifle fire. Aircraft were made which took 13 men in — mostly who held (about 130 lbs per man). This would mean that an ordinary G.S. wagon load of material could be easily transported. Nos 1 & 3 were about to start for the line to take to ground when Hy Bosh fell down a barrage around & drove to attack. They took up stations by co-operating of Bttn until 10 p.m. when all being over they proceeded to the work, which was supposing of parapets & rebuilding gaps in them as the Bosh anywhere was keeping a fairly the daytime. They returned to the W.P. at 5.30 a.m. orders coming from Bn Comd.	April 14th
N. ANNEQUIN 21st			The situation having cleared, the Coy moved back to the ANNEQUIN billets for a wash & a bath, & some were needed rest. All 4 sections finished.	Sot Owen transferred to 8th HQ.
F.24.c.0.3.		7.30 p.m.	proceeded to the lines being employed as before in putting more length of barbed front lines the right the visible work having a larger extension.	

WAR DIARY
or
INTELLIGENCE SUMMARY. 23rd Feb. C.R.E.

Army Form C. 2118.

Sheet 11

Place	Date	Hour	Summary of Events and Information	Remarks and references to Appendices
MANNEQUIN	22nd	—	All A. Sections in Line N°1. Interior Cellars Defences in Moat Farm Keep. 2. Clearing out Trench facing HITCHIN ROAD (Left Flank Support) 3. Clearing out Avenue F. 4. do. Orchard Rd. Trench. N°5. do Lectures parade 7.30 pm " return to billets at 4 a.m. Each Coy they have been able to get in billets in a good night's work, only received stoppages having left the mules for Civvies.	GIVENCHY SECTOR Capt F.T.B. CARTER R.E. 2nd on leave. 2nd Lt. 233rd Fd.Coy R.E.
F.24.C.V.3.	23rd		Shelling of N. Annequin (Searching for guns?) Caused 6 Casualties including [...] 3 shot & wounded. Transport lines shelled 8 Casualties including 2 missing. 7 horses destroyed 5 wounded. 1st Batt. returned to GIVENCHY SECTOR by Mid Bde 55th Div night of 23/24. Its Coby Gillespie took its line from 7.30pm - the former fieldstrength [?] Clearing GRENADIER TR. for Left Flank Defence, the Milles [Endeavour?] took on MOAT FARM KEEP. Note :- A certain amount of wiring had been done by Coys by lifts b) carrying packs &c. by lifts. c) Transport at VAUXHALL BRIDGE much of it had been carried by Field Coy. B.M. Coy HQ ready for being taken out. Sappers have been employed on Emergency work making good Trench Covers and cabins. Fit Repairs in the Infantry not stopping it as the Infantry wants to be employed on Fatigue much greater fighting fatigue heavy casualties in Field Coy R.E. than is normal. Much handicapped by absence of pattern type pullies which could not be issued.	W.T. Beck slightly wounded (at duty) still working W. Thomas severely wounded GIVENCHY SECTOR

Army Form C. 2118.

(12)

WAR DIARY
or
INTELLIGENCE SUMMARY.

23rd Field Coy RE

(Erase heading not required.)

APRIL 1918

Place	Date	Hour	Summary of Events and Information	Remarks and references to Appendices
N. ANNEQUIN F.24.C.03.	23/4		Officers of 423rd Fd.C. CE arrive. Take over work in GIVENCHY SECTOR. See half sheet. Relief of Sector intimated – relief to simplified	
Transport Noeux les Mines L.13.d.4.6			officers took over ASM took over work, from 67 Fd C RE. W. Henderson took over cement. No previous take over. 1 me day 1 nt mal. in Day out in evening	10AM W.G. Smith takes over duties of 2IC Command – returning of 25 Fd Coy.
			L/C Gillespie taken ill 900 kandilling at	
	25/4		L/C Gillespie today gs round works preparatory to actual relief above.	
	24/4		Work in HOHENZOLLERN SECTOR began consisting of deep dugout at BART'S POST, strengthening cellars of Bde HQ and installing of water supply system.	
	27/4		Same as above.	3 Officers and 63 OR from 4th Bde attached
	28/4		Work on VILLAGE LANE (males/flatten breastw) started. Remainder of work as above. Billets shelled with Tin Gas at night. 1 man being wounded.	

Army Form C. 2118.

WAR DIARY
or
INTELLIGENCE SUMMARY.
(Erase heading not required.)

23rd Fld Coy R.E.
APRIL 1918

Place	Date	Hour	Summary of Events and Information	Remarks and references to Appendices
N. ANNEQUIN	29/4		Work on Cmfr Bde H.Q. handed over to 265th Field Coy and construction and work with 5 to 6th Welsh; the whole company being concentrated on VILLAGE LANE Posts and dug-out at BART'S POST	
Transport lines				
NOEUX-LES-MINES	30/4		Work on VILLAGE LANE Posts and BART'S POST Dug-out continued	

W. G. Smith
Capt for Major, R.E.
23rd (Fd.) Coy. R.E.

WAR DIARY or INTELLIGENCE SUMMARY

Army Form C. 2118.

23rd Field Coy RE

MAY 1918

WE 44

Place	Date	Hour	Summary of Events and Information	Remarks and references to Appendices
N. ANNEQUIN (F.23.d.9.2) Horse Lines	1		Work on Dug-out at BART'S POST and Battn H.Q. in advance of VILLAGE LINE continued.	
NOEUX-LES-MINES	2		As above. One man wounded by a stray bullet. 2nd Lt W. DOUGILL DF Tunnel Coy. in the billets at ANNEQUIN.	Major W.R. WILSON M.C. R.E. awarded French Croix-de-Guerre
	3		As above. House lines shifted to rear of NOEUX-LES-MINES owing to shelling of old lines.	
	4		Work as above continued.	
	5		Work on dug-outs and posts in advance of Village Line continued.	
	6		As above.	Sapper DYMOND and Sapper WOOLDRIDGE CLEVICK,
	7		As above. Fixing up new charges for demolition of two road bridges in ANNEQUIN. Began	TRAIT and Driver awarded the MILITARY MEDAL
Horse Lines	8		As above. Fixing of charges finished.	for sticking to dummy
moved to	9		As above. Owing to an expected Bosche attack	horses after being attacked at GIVENCHY 18.4.18
MAISNIL LES RUITZ			the Coy. moved in emergency to our H.Q. at night but returned to forenoon ANNEQUIN FOSSE A	

Army Form C.2118.

WAR DIARY
or
INTELLIGENCE SUMMARY.
(Erase heading not required.)

23rd Field Coy RE   MAY 1918

Place	Date	Hour	Summary of Events and Information	Remarks and references to Appendices
N. ANNEQUIN			A bridge on Railway leading forward from	
Hulluch Line			ANNEQUIN for demolition. A very quiet night	
MAISNIL-LES-	10		No attack having come off the company moved	
RUITZ			back in morning to its normal billets work	
			being resumed in afternoon. Work consisted of	
			pits forward of Helfaut line and digging emplace	
			Permanent charges for demolition of Railway Bridge	
			found instead of Temporary one further down.	
	11		As above	
	12		As above	
	13		As above	Lt GILLESPIE to Hospital
	14		As above	Sick
	15		As above. Took Traffic along RAILWAY across RESERVE	
	16		Line begun	
			As above	
	17		As above	

Army Form C 2118.

WAR DIARY
or
INTELLIGENCE SUMMARY.
(Erase heading not required.)

Instructions regarding War Diaries and Intelligence Summaries are contained in F. S. Regs., Part II. and the Staff Manual respectively. Title pages will be prepared in manuscript.

23 Field Coy. R.E.   **MAY 1918**

Place	Date	Hour	Summary of Events and Information	Remarks and references to Appendices
N. ANNEQUIN	18		Work on strong point forward of village line	
			and trench continued	
HOUCHIN	19		As above	
	20		As above. Tank Trap completed	Lt Gillespie rejoined.
MAISNIL-	21		As above	Hospital
LES-RUITZ	22		As above	Lt Cowley Hartshead
	23		As above	Dupuits
	24		Work as above. E. of A. on morning of 24.5.18 a	Lt Cowley D.E. and
			patrol of 10 O.B. under Lt Cowley cooperated with	3 O.R. wounded in
			K.R.R. in a raid on enemy line left to 5 under raid and evacuated
			Lt Cowley got badly cut up by own barrage. 2 O Congratulatory message
			being wounded except one Right party accepted from GOC 2nd Bde
			Their whole dugout to 3 dugouts two of well attacked. OC
			was cleared at the time and captured 2 prisoners messages were received
			Both parties covered BANGALORE TORPEDOS & left from GOC 1st Div.
			one in front of enemy support line. Letters of G.O.C. 1st Corps.

Army Form C. 2118.

WAR DIARY
or
INTELLIGENCE SUMMARY.
(Erase heading not required.)

23rd Field Coy RE   May 1918

Place	Date	Hour	Summary of Events and Information	Remarks and references to Appendices
N ANNEQUIN			Were not required as there had been	
Hinges Ridge			successfully cut by our artillery	
MAISNIL LES	25		Work on posts in MAIN LINE OF RESISTANCE	2 Casualties to Officer
RUITZ			continued. Gas Casualty see A.D.S. Log	Rest House at A.D.S
	26		As above	
	27		As above	
	28		As above. Work on Listening posts now N	
			Right Battalion HQ started. Billets at	
			ANNEQUIN shelled in afternoon, every 15	
			casualties	
	29		As above. Fitting up new Left Bn H.Q	
			begun	
	30		As above Billets heavily shelled all	
			day, several 1 ton bombs bursting close	
			O.E. One casualty (wounded in face)	
	31		Work as above continued	

Commanding 23rd Field Coy. R.E.

Copy of Message Received from G.O.C. 2nd Bde on the subject of the Raid carried out on 24th inst

O.C. 23rd Field Coy. R.E.

With reference to the raid carried out last night, I should like to express my great appreciation of the good and gallant work done by the men of the 23rd Field Coy R.E. who accompanied the raiding party.

Their presence contributed materially to the success of the enterprise, thanks to their skilful handling of the explosives, while their dash and courage in the advance to the objective was most marked.

In saying the above I am expressing the opinion of the raiding infantry, and I trust my remarks may be conveyed to the men who took part in the raid. I much regret that the casualties should have been, in the proportion to the numbers employed, so unfortunately high.

Signed. G.C. Kelly
Brigadier General
Command 2nd Inf Bde.

24. May. 1918.

Army Form C. 2118.

WAR DIARY
or
INTELLIGENCE SUMMARY.
(Erase heading not required.)

23rd Field Coy R.E.   JUNE 1918

Place	Date	Hour	Summary of Events and Information	Remarks and references to Appendices
TOURBIERES	1		Work of fitting up 2 Battalion H.Q.'s	
Fauq d 23 (GORRE SHEET)			HOHENZOLLERN SECTOR pts in Mason Line & Resistance etc continued. Efforts about to	
Horse Lines			dragging the Sam cotton in the trpf sent have	
MAISNIL-LES-RUITZ			set on fire by a flare pistol. The fire was however put out before much damage was done	
	2		No alarms	
SAILLY LABOURSE	3		Work in HOHENZOLLERN SECTOR handed over to 11th Gates RE. 2nd Lieut	
L 3 d 27			409 Field Coy RE, the company back from duty on relief into reserve at SAILLY LABOURSE.	
Usual gd	4		Training began. Work on stuffing approx. Major D R Wilson M.C. RE to H AD as O/CRE	
			in CHATEAU DES PRES taken over.	during absence of CRE
	5		Training continued	Capt Smith R.E. was granted
	6		No 2 Section marches down to BARLIN	

Army Form C. 2118.

WAR DIARY
or
INTELLIGENCE SUMMARY.
(Erase heading not required.)

Instructions regarding War Diaries and Intelligence Summaries are contained in F. S. Regs., Part II. and the Staff Manual respectively. Title pages will be prepared in manuscript.

23rd Fd Coy RE. June 1918

Place	Date	Hour	Summary of Events and Information	Remarks and references to Appendices
SAILLY LABOURSE			Summer Camp for Div H.Q. Recruiters & Company continue Training. Colonel visits H.Q. Cpl.	
L.3,a,3,7	7	M	Armstrong back at SAILLY for fatigue down Sapper COLLIER awarded	
Transport Lines			to BARLIN for new camp before 1 Section training	DCM in Birthday Honours List
MAISNIL LES	8		No 3 Section moves down to transport lines for work on Summer Camp for Div H.Q. The	
RUITZ			one section training at SAILLY LABOURSE at rifle range, walls, TBde HQ cellars etc	
			No 2 and 3 building Div H.Q. Nº 4 Training ad Nº 1 on walls.	
	9		No 4 Section moved to transport lines at GUINESPIE return	
	10		to walls on Div Summer Camp. No 1 & 2 sections from Officer's Rest returning to H.Q. Bomb and Gunnery continued house	
			as above	
	11		The Setting out practise trenches at HOUCHIN	

D. D. & L., London, E.C. (A7583) Wt. W809/M1672 350,000 4/17 Sch. 52a. Forms/C/2118/14

WAR DIARY
or
INTELLIGENCE SUMMARY.

(Erase heading not required.)

Army Form C. 2118.

JUN 1918
ROYAL ENGINEERS
[...] FIELD COMPANY

Instructions regarding War Diaries and Intelligence Summaries are contained in F. S. Regs., Part II. and the Staff Manual respectively. Title pages will be prepared in manuscript.

Place	Date	Hour	Summary of Events and Information	Remarks and references to Appendices
SAILLY- LABOURSE			Organised work of division & E.S. at SAILLY. Sapr MATHER and carpenters at work pinning out of Sec Cpl WITTY and Lc.Cpl	
Transport at			H.Q. continued work on billets at Tata H.Q. MacDonald (?) (Signaller) continued out Gas Hut at NOEUX-LES-MINES attended M.M.	
MAISNIL-LES- RUITZ			parade. One section and 1 Detachment A1 Tng Pgce 1S. Sect to 3000 Type Pulley, and two 1½ Gal cos on	
	13		As above	
	13		As above. No 1 Section moved to Le la convoy night June 1 = 3 at VAUDRIQUES	
			No 3 moving up to SAILLY.	
	14		As above. Practice trestles at HOUCHIN	
			Finished	
	15		As above	
	16		As above	
	17		As above. 2 Section and A.L. Gurling, on section to Div H.Q. Coy and go on viaduct	
SAILLY				

WAR DIARY
or
INTELLIGENCE SUMMARY.
(Erase heading not required.)

Army Form C. 2118.

233rd Fd Coy RE   June 1918

Place	Date	Hour	Summary of Events and Information	Remarks and references to Appendices
SAILLY LABOURSE	18		Two sections carrying out work at SAILLY	
Transport at	19		Camp and one on works at SAILLY	
			As above.	
MAZNIL-LES-	20		As above. No 4 Maroc St from Transport	
RUITZ			lines on Divisional Camp finished	
	21		Three sections and two details at A.1.	
			training Remainder on cooking at CHATEAU DES	
			PRES etc. Maj. Wilson rejoined.	
	22		Co alone No 1 Section marched up to	
			Transport lines.	
	23		Inspection by CRE near NOEUX-LES-MINES in	
			morning, followed by a route march and	
			on the bridges in afternoon.	
	24		Taking over works in CAMBRIN SECTOR	
			from 26th Field Coy RE began. All 4	
			Sections and A.1. training.	

WAR DIARY or INTELLIGENCE SUMMARY.

Army Form C. 2118.

Instructions regarding War Diaries and Intelligence Summaries are contained in F.S. Regs., Part II. and the Staff Manual respectively. Title pages will be prepared in manuscript.

(Erase heading not required.)

Place	Date	Hour	Summary of Events and Information	Remarks and references to Appendices
TOURBIERES	25		Company marches up to TOURBIERES billets but	
F23.d.Cent.9			reliefs and work from 26th Fd Coy RE on	
Transport line			party out working at night on dugout water	
MAISNIL-LES-				
RAILWAY EMBANKMENT near LOCK on LA BASSEE				
CANAL.				
RUITZ	26		Work on CAMBRIN SECTOR begun on	
			following Canadas without Sr RAP, drawing	
			tools for demolition charges behind	
			abutment of bridge taking LA BASSEE road	
			over COURANT de BULLY POOL in CAMBRIN	
			DEFENCES. Dugout mentioned above and	
			also one under LA BASSEE ROAD near	
			VILLAGE LINE. One section working in camp.	
	27		Camp nightly shelled.	
			No casualties. Camp again shelled.	

WAR DIARY or INTELLIGENCE SUMMARY

Army Form C. 2118.

23rd Field Coy RE

JUNE 1918.

Place	Date	Hour	Summary of Events and Information	Remarks and references to Appendices
TOURBIERES F.23.d.30.44.	28/6		Work continued on CAMBRIN defences. Forts A20.c.55.99. Brickstacks. A22.a	
	29		(as above	
	30		(as above	

Army Form C. 2118.

WAR DIARY
or
INTELLIGENCE SUMMARY.
(Erase heading not required.)

23rd Field Coy. R.E. JULY. 1918

Place	Date	Hour	Summary of Events and Information	Remarks and references to Appendices
TOURBIERES.	1.		Coy working on CAMBRIN DEFENCES. A.20.c.6.9. Repairing bridges for dismantling.	F20.C.80.3
F.23.d.6.6en.			Dugout under Railway Embankment. A.15.d.0.6. M9 dugout under LA BASSEE Road.	A.21.9.2.6
GORRE SHEET.			Clearing entrances to shelters in BRICKSTACKS. A.22.a.	
HORSE LINES.				
MAISNIL.Les ROITZ.				
	2.		Work as above. CRE. inspected line work + inspected section.	
			Billet. Major S.T.HALL proceed for a months live work.	
	3.		CAMBRIN DEFENCES. A.20.C.5.9. Platoon HQ strengthening cellar + making new entrance.	
			Repairing wire + posts. Continued work on dugout under Railway Embankment.	
			2LT. dugout under LA BASSEE Road. Started work on cellar at POINT FIXE.	F.4.d.3.6.
			Billet shelled all day. houses near No.3 dre Billet set on fire	
	4.		Work as above. No shelling.	
	5.		Work on CAMBRIN DEFENCES. Strengthening cellars, wiring posts.	

Army Form C. 2118.

WAR DIARY
or
INTELLIGENCE SUMMARY.
(Erase heading not required.)

JULY 1918

Instructions regarding War Diaries and Intelligence Summaries are contained in F. S. Regs., Part II. and the Staff Manual respectively. Title pages will be prepared in manuscript.

Place	Date	Hour	Summary of Events and Information	Remarks and references to Appendices
TOURBIERES	2.		Dugouts and Railway Embankment. Demolition tunnels in bridge nr CAMBRIN	
Fqn d sect.			LA BASSEE ROAD. Work on OP at KINGSCLEAR Tus. OP 2 Copse Keep.	
			Training vaulting horse of 1st BLACK WATCH	
Haies Line			as above	
MAISNIL LES RUITZ	4.		" as above "	
			BLACK WATCH Raid unsuccessful.	
	3.		Dugout nr Railway, demolitions charges to bridges on main BEUVRY LA BASSEE Road, improvements to collars at	
			PONT FIXE, water Supply etc continued. KINGSCLERE OP finished	
	9		As above. Work on Breastworks as stated	
	10		As above. Improvements to collars etc at MOUNTAIN LANE etc.	

Army Form C. 2118.

WAR DIARY
or
INTELLIGENCE SUMMARY.
(Erase heading not required.)

23rd Coy TC JULY 1918

Place	Date	Hour	Summary of Events and Information	Remarks and references to Appendices
TOURBIERES	11		Work on Bucharest dug-out — Railway Embankment (fitting demolition charges to bridges under LA BASSÉE road) improvements to cellars at PONT FIXE not	
House Line MAISNIL-LES-TRUITZ			MOUNTAIN HOUSE dis continued	
	12		As above, dug-out in CAMBRIN for Sunken Battery begun	
	13		As above. Dug-out for dressing clothing and PONT FIXE cellars completed. L.G. post at HERTFORD ST and SEVENTH St begun.	
	14		As above. MOUNTAIN HOUSE cellars completed.	

Army Form C. 2118.

WAR DIARY
or
INTELLIGENCE SUMMARY.
(Erase heading not required.)

223rd Field Coy RE

JULY 1918

Place	Date	Hour	Summary of Events and Information	Remarks and references to Appendices
TOURBIERES	15.		Work on oblique WOOD RAILWAY Transport of all 3	
			EMBANKMENT fixing demolition charges on Field Coys amalgamated	
HOULE LA			bridges under LA BASSEE road, L.G. Posts in under the command (temp)	
MAISNIL-LES-			HERTFORD ST and SEVENTH ST, reforming of 223 in command 26th Field	
RUITZ			proofs and holes in WILSON'S WAY, cellars Coy RE) each company	
			in CAMBRIN continued. Bridgeloads of mules (namely) Subalterns	
			(Lt GILLESPIE from 223)	
	16		As above. Demolition charges for bridges	
			completed, work on coal lorries in	
			SHAW'S CUT, SEVENTH ST and GRAFTON ST	
			begun.	
	17		As above.	
	18.		As above. L.G. Emplacement at DUPONT FIXE Major WILSON MC leave Co	
			U.K. Capt SMITH takes over Coy.	

Army Form C. 2118.

WAR DIARY
or
INTELLIGENCE SUMMARY.
(Erase heading not required.)

Instructions regarding War Diaries and Intelligence Summaries are contained in F. S. Regs., Part II, and the Staff Manual respectively. Title pages will be prepared in manuscript.

23 - Field Coy T.R.E.   July 1918

Place	Date	Hour	Summary of Events and Information	Remarks and references to Appendices
BARBIERES	19		Work on H.C. Dugout under RAILWAY EMBANKMENT cont. Covers for companies in support H.C.	
Hove huts			post and cellar at PONT FIXE strengthening	
MAISNIL -			Shelters in CAMBRIN DEFENCES continued	
LES-RUITZ	20		As above. Work at PONT FIXE completed	
	21		As above. Erection of MOIR PILLBOX near CAMBRIN Major W.R. WILSON M.C. R.E. began	attached C.R.E. 40th Div.
	22		As above. Repairs to the RUIN O.P. begun	
	23		As above	
	24		As above.	

Army Form C. 2118.

WAR DIARY
or
INTELLIGENCE SUMMARY.
(Erase heading not required.)

23rd Field Coy R.E.   July 1918

Place	Date	Hour	Summary of Events and Information	Remarks and references to Appendices
TOURBIÈRES	25		Work as in days past under RAILWAY EMBANKMENT. Erection of MOIR PILLBOX repairs to the RUIN OP. Collecting for outpost Companies and cellars.	
HOSPICE ROAD				
MAISNIL-LES-RUITZ			I/C CAMBRIN DEFENCES continued.	
	26		As above. In S.E. above at Transportation Company were Sector Infantry working on horse lines, and crown country (?) area.	
	27		Work as above continued. New post found CAPT. W.G. SMITH M.C. R.E. of reserve line began (DENNIS) and returning attached O.C. Company. 5 T.M. at one of the places in Coy(?)	
	28		Co. above. New stairway up ANNEQUIN FOSSE. H.C.G. ROBERTS R.E. began. Joins for duty.	

Army Form C. 2118.

WAR DIARY
or
INTELLIGENCE SUMMARY.
(Erase heading not required.)

23rd Fd Coy R.E.   JULY 1918

Place	Date	Hour	Summary of Events and Information	Remarks and references to Appendices
TO DRIBIERES hure line	29		Work on L.G. Dug-out inclu TAILWAY, near fire trench at TSERHILLY stairway and screening of ANNEQUIN FOSSE, posts in CAMBRIN DEFENCES	
MAISNIL-LES-RUITZ			continued. MOIR Pill-box completed.	
	30		As above.	
	31		As above.	

W.B.
Capt R.E.
O.C. 23rd Fd Coy R.E.

Army Form C. 2118.

WAR DIARY
or
INTELLIGENCE SUMMARY.
(Erase heading not required.)

Instructions regarding War Diaries and Intelligence Summaries are contained in F. S. Regs., Part II. and the Staff Manual respectively. Title pages will be prepared in manuscript.

232ⁿᵈ Field Cy R.E.   AUGUST 1918

Place	Date	Hour	Summary of Events and Information	Remarks and references to Appendices
TOURBIERES	1		Work on H.G. Post under RAILWAY EMBANKMENT	Lt D.H. GILLESPIE R.E.
			post at BEXHILL stairway and stairway to ANNEQUIN	to Vet course at No
Haarhoek			FOSSE, cellars at CAMBRIN DEFENCES, and	10 Vet Hospital.
			improvements to water supply continued.	
MAISNIL-LES-RUITZ	2		As above. BEXHILL POST completed.	
	3		As above. ANNEQUIN FOSSE stairway also completed.	
	4		As above. In Div Horse Show No 3 Tool cart	Capt W.G. SMITH M.C. R.E.
			took first prize and G.S. wagon 2ⁿᵈ prize.	to be a/Major
				Lt D.H. GILLESPIE R.E.
	5		As above. Hadwig over watch to 409 Fd Cy Rgrs.	to be a/Capt.
SAILLY	6		Company relieved by 409 Fd Cy R.E. coming	
LABOURSE			into Reserve at SAILLY LABOURSE	

Army Form C. 2118.

WAR DIARY
or
INTELLIGENCE SUMMARY.
(Erase heading not required.)

Instructions regarding War Diaries and Intelligence Summaries are contained in F. S. Regs., Part II. and the Staff Manual respectively. Title pages will be prepared in manuscript. 23rd Fld Coy R.E.

Place	Date	Hour	Summary of Events and Information	Remarks and references to Appendices
SAILLY-LABOURSE	7		Work at Sailly Regne CHATEAU DES PRES colliery dug-out for R.F.A. on SAILLY-ANNEQUIN road,	
Transport			NOEUX-LES-MINES addew bidm etc. One section	
MAISNIL-LES-			on work about Trenport lines & Sections	
RUITZ			training	
	8		As above.	
	9		As above. Tactical Scheme for officers	
	10		As above.	
	11		As above	
	12		As above.	Capt D.H. GILLESPIE returns from Vet course

Army Form C. 2118.

WAR DIARY
or
INTELLIGENCE SUMMARY.

(Erase heading not required.)

23rd Fd Coy R.E.   August 1918.

Place	Date	Hour	Summary of Events and Information	Remarks and references to Appendices
SAILLY - LABOURSE	13		One section on works on Cafard trench line, another on works around transport lines, remaining 2 training	
Transport MAISNIL - LES - RUITZ	14		As above	
	15		As above. Bridging scheme at HOUDAIN for cyclists	Lt ROBERTS proceeds on leave to U.K.
	16		As above	
	17		As above	
	18		As above	
	19		As above	

WAR DIARY
or
INTELLIGENCE SUMMARY.
(Erase heading not required.)

Army Form C. 2118.

23rd Field Coy. R.E. August 1918.

Place	Date	Hour	Summary of Events and Information	Remarks and references to Appendices
SAILLY —	20.		Work at SAILLY — Chateau des PRES continued on relais	
LABOURSE			one section working at transport lines	
Transport			Remainder of Coy. Training.	Officers from 156th Coy.
MAISNIL LES			Afternoon the 1 a.e. to MONCHY CHATEAU for	took over work.
— RUITZ.			work on DIV. H.Qrs.	120939. Sheing Smith MURNAHIE
				to 2nd Rifle Brig. at Corps Horse Show. Shot short resule.
	21.		Cyclists in Lt. DOUGH to BOYAVAL to prepare billets	
			for Coy. Work completed at CHATEAU des PRES.	
			All transport loaded & Coy. stores on rail down	
			to transport lines	
	22.		Remainder of coy. Marched to BARLIN. Bivouac	
			to BOYAVAL. Arrived at billets 11.45am.	
			Transport by road arrived 5.15 pm	
BOYAVAL.	23		Improvement of billets	
G.W.A.E.I.				

Army Form C. 2118.

WAR DIARY
or
INTELLIGENCE SUMMARY.
(Erase heading not required.)

23rd Field Coy RE   August 1918

Place	Date	Hour	Summary of Events and Information	Remarks and references to Appendices
BOUZVAL. Sheet 44.B. G.14.d.8.6.	24.		Physical training Inspection of men and kits	
	25.		Church Parade. No.1 Section rejoined.	
	26.		Physical training Brief musketry training for open warfare.	
	27.		ditto.	
	28.		ditto.	
	29.		ditto	
	30.			
	31.		Coy preparing to move in a hurry. Destination unknown	

WAR DIARY or INTELLIGENCE SUMMARY

Army Form C. 2118.

23 yr Coy RE

23rd Field Coy. Sept 1918

Place	Date	Hour	Summary of Events and Information	Remarks and references to Appendices
ARRAS	1st		Coy. less transport arrived at Tipon, having left BOYAVAL at 5:15 p.m. on 31st Aug. Marched to ANVIN. Train to ARRAS. Coy. moved up to forward billets in GUEMAPPE. Transport by Rd from BOYAVAL stopped for night at Savy on main St Pol - Arras road. (31st-1st). Arrived ARRAS midnight 1st-2nd. Tool carts stood around power Coy same night at GUEMAPPE.	St Pol, moved for 48 hours leave. Shirt. LENS "
	2nd		Sections moved up to consolidate tanks at DURY in support of attack by Canadian Corps. Transport moved forward to WANCOURT. Hdqrs. to STRIKE Copse on main ARRAS - CAMBRAI Road. (on as attached)	61st Bde.
	3rd		Coy. less one section & transport moved to RIENCY. work on forward roads. Transport moved to FEUCHY-CHAPELLE.	ditto
	4.			"
	5.			"
	6.			
	7.			

Army Form C. 2118.

WAR DIARY
or
INTELLIGENCE SUMMARY.
(Erase heading not required.)

23rd Field Coy R.E.   SEPT. 1918.

Instructions regarding War Diaries and Intelligence Summaries are contained in F. S. Regs., Part II. and the Staff Manual respectively. Title pages will be prepared in manuscript.

Place	Date	Hour	Summary of Events and Information	Remarks and references to Appendices
ARRAS	8th		Coy moved back by bus to "Y" huts at ETRUN on ARRAS - St. Pol main road. Transport rejoined coy.	Sheet
Sector	9th		ditto.	LENS 11
"	10a.		Coy complete entrained at MARŒUIL at 10/km	
"			Arrival at MARCELCAVE. detrained & marched to MORCOURT.	Sheet AMIENS 17.
ST. QUENTIN Sector	11.		Coy at MORCOURT. Transport by road to BRIE.	
	12.			
	13.		Coy by bus to billets on PEVISE - MERANCOURT road. Transport rejoined coy. - Officers inspected site of bridge at CAULINCOURT CHATEAU	Sheet St QUENTIN 18
	14.		Two nissen erected next to demolished bridge CAULINCOURT Chateau at W.5d.1.8. Sheet 62° S.E. Coy moved by road to Billets on Tertry TERTRY - CAULINCOURT Road. W 4 A 2.3.	

Army Form C. 2118.

WAR DIARY
or
INTELLIGENCE SUMMARY.
(Erase heading not required.)

23rd Field Coy R.E.   SEPT. 1918.

Place	Date	Hour	Summary of Events and Information	Remarks and references to Appendices
Sht 62c SE. W4a.2.3	15.		Two sections on Bridge W.5.d.1.8.	
	16.		ditto.	
	17.		Coy. less transport moved up to LEAF WOOD. No 1 Section attached to 1st Batt. (S. Hudson No 3) Lt. Roberts & party checked out Assembly areas for troops forming up for the attack. One section working on bridge at W.5.d.1.8 Another on bridge at VERMAND. Foot Carts & Pack animals with attackers.	
	18.		Coy. stood by in morning to be required to consolidate ground won by 1st and 2nd Bdes but morning worked on bridges at VERMAND in afternoon. 1 Section working in line with 12th Bde.	
	19.		C.O. above Coy H.Q. shifted to small wood W.6.d.8.8.	
	20.		Work on 5 bridges between CAULAINCOURT & VERMAND cont.	

Army Form C. 2118.

WAR DIARY
or
INTELLIGENCE SUMMARY.
(Erase heading not required.)

Instructions regarding War Diaries and Intelligence
Summaries are contained in F. S. Regs., Part II.
and the Staff Manual respectively. Title pages
will be prepared in manuscript.

Place	Date	Hour	Summary of Events and Information	Remarks and references to Appendices
CADLINCOURT	20		Work on bridges as above continued. No 3 Section working	Lt POCOCK
W.6.d.3.8			Rue with 1st Bde	leave to U.K.
(Sheet 62C)				
	21		As above	
	22		Work on bridges leaded over to 409 Fd Coy R.E. 3 Sections employed on construction of forward Bde H.Q. S of MAISSEMY. 1 Section doing work in Rue with 1st Bde.	
	23		Two sections working on forward Bde H.Q. Lt HENDERSON and ROBERTS taped out line of assembly for 2-3 Bde during night.	
MARTEVILLE	24		Coy moved up to position of assembly in Railway Bde east of MARTEVILLE in TR 33 on the section with 1st Bde adjoining attd of 2nd and 3rd Bdes being successful the whole company attd of Bdes	

Army Form C. 2118.

WAR DIARY
or
INTELLIGENCE SUMMARY.
(Erase heading not required.)

Place	Date	Hour	Summary of Events and Information	Remarks and references to Appendices
	25		at night in consolidation of ground won by 2nd Bde between PONTRUET and GRICOURT. Two posts to field and platoon areas were constructed in all.	
	26		Work of consolidation of 2nd Bde's line continued, all 4 sections again being out.	
			Work of consolidation continued.	
	27		One section with 2nd Bde working on 25 strong posts. Remainder standing by.	
	28		One section with 2nd Bde Remainder working on bridges between CAULINCOURT and VERMAND.	
	29		Enjoy standing by during successful attack on	

Army Form C. 2118.

WAR DIARY
or
INTELLIGENCE SUMMARY.
(Erase heading not required.)

Place	Date	Hour	Summary of Events and Information	Remarks and references to Appendices
			WINDENBURG LINE. One section working on tub track in evening. Section previously with 2" Bde attached to 3" Bde.	
BERTH	August 30		Coy (less 1 Section with 3" Bde) moved up to dug outs in HUGNET WOOD near BERTHAUCOURT. One section working to Adv D. H.Q. at MAISSEMY in afternoon. Transport lines moved to HATTENCOURT.	
			W² Burgoyne	
			Major RE	
			O.C. 23rd Fld Coy RE	

WAR DIARY
or
INTELLIGENCE SUMMARY.

Army Form C. 2118.

23rd Feb Coy R.E. OCTOBER 1918

Place	Date	Hour	Summary of Events and Information	Remarks and references to Appendices
BERTHAU COURT	1		1 Section with 3rd Bde, 2 sections working on Div HQ Transport at MAISSEMY.	
at MARTEVILLE	2		As above	
	3		As above	Sergt HARRIS, Cpls PILCHER, OREN and NEWSHAM and Sapper SEWELL awarded M.M.
	4		As above	
	5		One section working on water point at PONTRU. Remainder on above (1) with 3rd Bde rejoined.	
MARTEVILLE	6		Coy moved back to billets at transport lines MARTEVILLE in RAILWAY EMBANKMENT near MARTEVILLE	
	7		One section working at Bde HQ VERMAND	

WAR DIARY
or
INTELLIGENCE SUMMARY.

Army Form C. 2118.

Place	Date	Hour	Summary of Events and Information	Remarks and references to Appendices
MARTEVILLE	8		The whole company practised platoon in attack	Capt GILLESPIE leave to U.K. M.C. awarded to Rev A W M CASSAN C.F. (attached)
			OMIGNON near VERMAND	
BEAUCOURT	9		Coy moved up complete to billets in dug outs etc in old GERMAN Front line near BEAUCOURT.	
	10		Coy training	
	11		Coy at above	
MERICOURT	12		Coy moved to billets in German huts at MERICOURT	
	13		Coy employed on FRESNOY - MONTBREHAIN & MONTBREHAIN - BRANCOURT roads and water pt at DOON MILL	
	14		Coy working on MONTBREHAIN - FONTAINE road & DOON MILL water pt	

WAR DIARY
or INTELLIGENCE SUMMARY.
(Erase heading not required.)

Army Form C. 2118.

23rd Field Coy   OCTOBER 1918.

Place	Date	Hour	Summary of Events and Information	Remarks and references to Appendices
MERICOURT.	15		Coy working on FRESNOY - MONTBREHAIN Mile water point.	2nd Lieut HENDERSON returned M.C.
	16		Coy above. No 2 Section moved to BOHAIN for attachment to 1st Bde.	2nd Lt HENDERSON Reported U.K.
VAUX-ANDIGNY Transport at BOHAIN.	17		Company moved in afternoon to billets VAUX ANDIGNY in case required during unsuccessful attack by 1st and 2nd Bdes. Transport remained at BOHAIN.	
	18		Coy standing by at VAUX ANDIGNY. Lt GATES killed in afternoon while out reconnoitering in WASSIGNY	
LA VALLEE MULATRE	19		Coy moved complete to LA VALLEE MULATRE	

WAR DIARY
or
INTELLIGENCE SUMMARY.

Army Form C. 2118.

Place	Date	Hour	Summary of Events and Information	Remarks and references to Appendices
LA VALLEE MULATRE	20		No. 2 Section rejoined from 1st Bde. One section employed in putting old German Trenches at VAUX-ANDIGNY in working order. Remainder of Coy. working on roads along N edge of ANDIGNY FOREST and repairs to wells in LA VALLEE MULATRE	1 Lt GATES formed at VAUX-ANDIGNY cemetery
	21		Work on roads and repairs to billets at VALLEE MULATRE continued.	
	22		As above	
	23		As above	Lt ROBERTS evacuated H.C.
	24		As above. O.C. elements of Coy. to 1st Bde H.Q.	Lt DOUGILL came to Y.K.
	25		As above	

Army Form C. 2118.

WAR DIARY
or
INTELLIGENCE SUMMARY.
(Erase heading not required.)

23rd Field Coy October 1918.

Place	Date	Hour	Summary of Events and Information	Remarks and references to Appendices
VALLEE	26		Coy working on LA TONNELLE – WASSIGNY and WASSIGNY –	Capt Gillespie returned from leave to U.K.
MUATRE			BLANCS FOSSES – LA VALLEE MULATRE roads and repairs to billets &c.	
"	27		As above. Wire field removed from R.35.c.7.8 sheet 57 3 S.E.	
"	28		as above.	
"	29		Coy working on roads as above. repairs to billets & wells. Making barrel pier bridges for launching on canal. Lt Roberts made reconnaissance of SAMBRE Canal.	
	30		Work on LA TONNELLE – WASSIGNY road. Barrel piers. erecting shelters at 1st Bde. HdQrs	
	31		Work as above. Two forts watering points started in Vallee.	

Army Form C. 2118.

WAR DIARY
or
INTELLIGENCE SUMMARY.

(Erase heading not required.)

23rd Field Coy. RE   Nov. 1918.

Place	Date	Hour	Summary of Events and Information	Remarks and references to Appendices
VALLEE	1.		Coy. preparing Pontoon Bridges, landing ladders, work continued on water points.	
MULATRE	2.		As above. Demonstration of bridging to G.O.C. etc.	
	3.		Coy. finished preparing Pontoon Bridges. Coy. moved up to R.36. at 18.30hrs. to prepare Bridges for launching on following morning.	
	4.		1st Div. attacked this morning & over Bridges successfully launched	

Army Form C. 2118.

WAR DIARY
or
INTELLIGENCE SUMMARY.
(Erase heading not required.)

Instructions regarding War Diaries and Intelligence Summaries are contained in F. S. Regs., Part II. and the Staff Manual respectively. Title pages will be prepared in manuscript.

23rd Field Coy. R.E.   Nov 1916

Place	Date	Hour	Summary of Events and Information	Remarks and references to Appendices
LA VALLEE	1.		Coy employed repairing bridges & landing ladders. Work continued on water points	
MULATRE	2		As above	
	3.		Demonstration of bridging to G.O.C.	" Lt. HONESTONE Joined Coy
			Coy finished preparing bridges. Coy moved up to canal bank South of CHATILLON. Work during night assembling bridges & cutting track to stream on W. side of canal	
	4.		Coy launched bridges. The canal bank was reached at ZERO + 5 min. Sgt. Cook of No 4 section charged a post of 6 Germans with a machine gun. All 4 bridges were across the canal by ZERO + 10 min	ZERO 05:45

Awards for Bridging Canal — November 4th 1918.

40.19659 Sapr. J. Sewell M.M.	Bar to the Military Medal.
28836. L.Cpl (T/Cpl) J.R. Bostock.	Military Medal
223512. Sapr. A. Hocking	"
374414. " T. Williamson	"
134284. " E.C. Evans.	"
166424. " J. Lewis.	"
36861. Dvr. (L.Cpl) Ja. Elliott.	"
26179. Sapr. (L.Cpl) J.P. Trussler.	"
25740. Corporal. G. Adamson.	"
16448. Cpl. (T.Sgt) E. Banham	"
154940. Sapr. F.W. Kirby	"
30439. Sapr. A.G. Watkins.	"

Authority IX Corps No. H.R./416 dt 21.11.1918

Army Form C. 2118.

WAR DIARY
or
INTELLIGENCE SUMMARY.
(Erase heading not required.)

23rd Field Coy RE   Nov. 1918.

Place	Date	Hour	Summary of Events and Information	Remarks and references to Appendices
LA VALLEE	5.		Coy. Resting at billets. minor work on water troughs &c.	
MULATRE	6.		Coy. less one section marched to FRESNOY LE GRANDE. One section left at VALLEE MULATRE for work on horse watering point in WASSIGNY.	
FRESNOY LE GRANDE	7.		See Returned to Coy. Remainder employed repairing existing lock.	
"	8.		Coy at rest. work on billets & 1st Bde. Hd. Qrs.	
	9.		as above	
	10.		above	
	11.		Coy employed packing surplus iron stores for removal to BOHAIN	
	12		as above	

Army Form C. 2118.

WAR DIARY
or
INTELLIGENCE SUMMARY.
(Erase heading not required.)

23rd Field Coy RE   Nov 1918.

Place	Date	Hour	Summary of Events and Information	Remarks and references to Appendices
FRESNOY LE GRANDE	13.		Coy moved by bus to GRANDE FAYT. Transport by road.	
GRANDE FAYT.	14.		Cleaning weapons &c. Arms & equipment inspected	
	15.		Coy moved by march route to SARS POTTERIES.	
SARS POTTERIES.	16.		Coy moved by march route to GRANDRIEU, BELGIUM. Road very bad craters at crossroads &c.	
GRANDRIEU.	17.		Route march to CASTILLON. Coy employed en route removing mines from roads & bridges.	Lt GREGOR from Army standard reconnaissance with call to front of firing zone.
CASTILLON.	18.		Route march to FRAIRE.	Lt FITZ HENRY from 2nd Field joined.
FRAIRE.	19.		Route march to YVES GOMEZEE, big reception by inhabitants.	Lt GREEN joined Coy.

Army Form C. 2118.

WAR DIARY
or
INTELLIGENCE SUMMARY.
(Erase heading not required.)

23rd Field Coy RE   Nov 1918

Place	Date	Hour	Summary of Events and Information	Remarks and references to Appendices
YVES COMEZÉE	20th		Coy employed cleaning wagons. Inspection of Brett. from below.	
"	21.		as above.	
"	22.		as above. Inspection by CRE	Lt (A/t-Major) W CARROT O.C. 23rd Field Coy RE
"	23.		Route march to COREENE.	
COREENE	24		Route march to RATEEN SOMMIÉRE.	
RATEEN SOMMIÉRE	25.		Coy Resting. Inspection & cleaning harness.	
"	26		do.	
"	27		do.	
"	28		do.	
"	29		do.	
"	30		do.	D H Ellis Major RE Commanding 23rd Field Coy RE

Army Form C. 2118.

23rd Field Co. RE

WAR DIARY
or
INTELLIGENCE SUMMARY.

(Erase heading not required.)

DECEMBER 1918.

Place	Date	Hour	Summary of Events and Information	Remarks and references to Appendices
ROSTENNE -SOMMIERE	1/12/18	—	March to LAVIS and DINANT	The Field Coy. is still moving with Group of the Division
LAVIS	2.12.18	—	Move to FURZEE	
FURZEE	3.12.18	—	Halt FURZEE. Work unloading	Reconnaissance of large towns to be carried out by offr
"	4.12.18	—	Troops due to leave FURZEE	
"	5.12.18	—		
"	6		Troops on ek of Com	
"	7		Train	
"	8		Cleaning Harness, Saddlery	
"	9		March to NOISEUX. Men in barns	
NOISEUX	10		March to MAGOZ through DURBUY	
MAGOZ	11		March to OZO	
OZO	12		12 noon	
"	13		March to KRENT-ST-PONT	
KRENT-ST-PONT	14		March to BECHEE	
BECHEE	15		Rest	
"	16		March to THOMMEN	

Army Form C. 2118.

WAR DIARY
or
INTELLIGENCE SUMMARY
(Erase heading not required.)

23rd Field Co. RE

DECEMBER 1918

Instructions regarding War Diaries and Intelligence Summaries are contained in F.S. Regs., Part II. and the Staff Manual respectively. Title pages will be prepared in manuscript.

Place	Date	Hour	Summary of Events and Information	Remarks and references to Appendices
THOMMEN	17th		March to ANDLER via ST VITH	
ANDLER	18		" KRONENBURG	
KRONENBURG	19		" BLANKENHEIMERDORF	
BLANKENHEIM -DORF	20		Refit - Army of Occupation lectures	
"	21		March to EICHERSCHEID	
EICHERSCHEID	22		March to STOTZHEIM	
STOTZHEIM	23		March to NIEDERDREES	
NIEDERDREES	24			

Army Form C. 2118.

23rd (Aux) Coy RE
DECEMBER 1918

WAR DIARY
or
INTELLIGENCE SUMMARY.
(Erase heading not required.)

Instructions regarding War Diaries and Intelligence Summaries are contained in F. S. Regs., Part II. and the Staff Manual respectively. Title pages will be prepared in manuscript.

Place	Date	Hour	Summary of Events and Information	Remarks and references to Appendices
HELLEBECQ	26		Physical Drill Training & Games	
	27		Training & work on death.	
	28		Training. School leave & Return of Capt D.H. Gillespie MC — on leave to UK.	
			Lectures.	(to 11/1/19 Dec 1918)
	29		Church Parades	Reinforced Draft of 1 NCO & 9 OR
	30		Training. Hockey, Football	
	31		Work & General Fatigues.	A new pattern D.T. of Lamps was issued during October.
			Construction of hot air.	

Army Form C. 2118.

WAR DIARY
23 (A) Dv. R.E.
or
INTELLIGENCE SUMMARY.
JANUARY 1919

(Erase heading not required.)

Instructions regarding War Diaries and Intelligence Summaries are contained in F. S. Regs., Part II. and the Staff Manual respectively. Title pages will be prepared in manuscript.

WO 95/5

Place	Date 1919	Hour	Summary of Events and Information	Remarks and references to Appendices
NIEDERDOLLEN	1	—	New Year Day - Church Service	
"	2	—	Military musketry training	Russ visit now to be paid to Bonn
				CO Lectures
				to begin lectures to JR's in English
				Members as specified Nov & Dec
				S/T. 7E 13 instn
"	3	—	—	
"	4	—	Played football match	
"	5	—	Lost 3 cricket ty stores	
"	6	—	Military Education & Training	Div working Coys scheme in on cc
				Major E. will be O.R. in Bonn
				Pet of 2 Corps Officers etc. Cornet Comm
				to made up for attend in Div area
"	7	—	Musketry Range Practice	
"	8	—	Training	A keyman of R.E. Rigs around
"	9	—	Infantry Training	Div Education Sch
				Lt Dougill proceeds in 12 day's leave in the
"	10	—	Training	U.K. & on return

Army Form C. 2118.

WAR DIARY
or
INTELLIGENCE SUMMARY.

83 (Cdn) Bn JANUARY 1919

(Erase heading not required.)

Place	Date	Hour	Summary of Events and Information	Remarks and references to Appendices
Camp at NIEDERKRÜCHTEN	Jany 1919 11		Summary	Remark
"	11		Sunday — no work	1st CO Parents leaving for CAN FURL
"	12		Battn parades - works, upkeep, rifle	
"	13		Works. Transport inspected by A.D.V.S. for conjection of general standing & horses units fit for war	
"	14		Works. Rifle drill & drill Plan	
"	15		Ordinary	Officers J. THATCHER M.C. G/Capt E.J. 2 in command
"	16		C contests re election debate	Lieut THATCHER M.P. & SKELDING.P. arrive on command from CEF
"	17		Work	
"	18		Sunday — no work	5 men reinforcements came from base
"	19		Works Sunday no work	
"	20		Conducts & bathing	
"	21		Works	Church Parade attended by Belgian Ethnic with music

23rd (F.) Coy R.E.   WAR DIARY   JANUARY 1919
INTELLIGENCE SUMMARY

Army Form C. 2118.

Place	Date	Hour	Summary of Events and Information	Remarks and references to Appendices
NIEDER DREST	Jan 1919 22	—	Works	
"	23	—	Works + recreation training	
"	24	—	Works 4cc?	R/Sgt 1 off + 5 O.R. transfer to R.E. Records L'pool —
				Dining & Hotel
				Lt. G. G. Roberts M.C. to BRIDGING SCHOOL, MARLOW CHATEAU (Re Repat. officers) (23/1/19)
"	25	—	Works	2/Lt G.D.E. Gibbs to Dep't Staff School, Rotherham 43 R.U
				(Re Repat officers) (sent 24/1/19)
"	26	—	Voluntary Church parade	Maj. W.G. Smart DSO. MC to hand lecture
"	27	—	Works – Loading rubber stove, coal hut 9ft × range cooker, furniture ladle	Capay to hang forward
"	28	—	Works. Reloading rubber stove	Maj. W.G. Smart DSO. MC to S.M.E. CHATHAM (Re Repat. officers)
"	29	—	Works	
"	30	—	Works	
"	31	—	Works	

N.F. Harman Capt.
O/C 23rd (F) Coy R.E.

Army Form C. 2118.

WAR DIARY
or
INTELLIGENCE SUMMARY.

23 (Field) Coy. R.E.

Feby 1919.

Vol 53

(Erase heading not required.)

Instructions regarding War Diaries and Intelligence Summaries are contained in F. S. Regs., Part II. and the Staff Manual respectively. Title pages will be prepared in manuscript.

Place	Date	Hour	Summary of Events and Information	Remarks and references to Appendices
NIEDERDREIS	Feby 1	—	Company Drills & Games	
"	2	—	Voluntary Church Parade	
"	3	—	Works	
"	4	—	Works + recreation	
"	5	—	Works	
"	6	—	Games + works	
"	7	—	Works	
"	8	—	Drills	
"	9	—	Sunday	
"	10	—	Bath: sheet day: games	
"	11	—	Works: Rides: Mounted Infantry Training	
"	12	—	Works	

Army Form C. 2118.

WAR DIARY
or
INTELLIGENCE SUMMARY.
(Erase heading not required.)

23(Cub)DG R.
Feby 1919

Instructions regarding War Diaries and Intelligence
Summaries are contained in F. S. Regs., Part II.
and the Staff Manual respectively. Title pages
will be prepared in manuscript.

Place	Date	Hour	Summary of Events and Information	Remarks and references to Appendices
MEDJEZ-EL-BAB	13			
	14			
	15			
	16			
	17			
	18			
	19			
	20			
	21			
	22			
	23			
	24			

Army Form C. 2118.

WAR DIARY
or
INTELLIGENCE SUMMARY. Feby 44
(Erase heading not required.)

Instructions regarding War Diaries and Intelligence Summaries are contained in F. S. Regs., Part II. and the Staff Manual respectively. Title pages will be prepared in manuscript.

Place	Date	Hour	Summary of Events and Information	Remarks and references to Appendices
MI-DAR-es-SALAM	25			
"	26			
"	27			
"	28		Here to 1 APPEND to diary	

J. Hauler Taylor
Major R.A.
Commanding 23rd (Fd.) Coy R.E.

Army Form C. 2118.

WAR DIARY
or
INTELLIGENCE SUMMARY.
(Erase heading not required.)

23rd (Field Coy R.E.) WC 54

Instructions regarding War Diaries and Intelligence Summaries are contained in F. S. Regs., Part II. and the Staff Manual respectively. Title pages will be prepared in manuscript.

Place	Date March	Hour	Summary of Events and Information	Remarks and references to Appendices
IPPLENDORF (HOCHERSDORF)	1	—	Settling into new billets.	
	2	—	Sunday	
	3	—	Work on & about billets, building cart-lingses, shelters re painting vehicles.	
	4	—	as above	
	5	—	as above	2/Lt Thatcher N.P. admitted to hospital
	6	—	Work- painting vehicles - etc	6 Horses & Mules (Class Z) despatched. Report to refer off escorts to move to release dep't
	7	—	as above	
	8	—	as above + recreational training	

WAR DIARY
or
INTELLIGENCE SUMMARY.
(Erase heading not required.)

Army Form C. 2118.

23rd Field Coy RE

MARCH 1919.

Place	Date	Hour	Summary of Events and Information	Remarks and references to Appendices
WICKRIEDSDORF	9	—	Sunday — Voluntary church parade.	
	10	—	Painting vehicles &c	
	11	—	Ser Int cert inspections. 4.15 class	2/Lt THATCHER W.P. to and from Hospital
	12	—	Work in area, military training	Men to Hucal Colognes - 3 day leave
	13	—	as above — check gate tools	
	14	—	Men in Coy Aft fairy to prepare for area at Cologne	2/Lt HENDERSON R.D. to PHQ - 2 class
			Trunning Month area — Month Leave out	
	15	—	Half — cate	
	16	—	Sunday. Vol. Ch. Parade.	

Army Form C. 2118.

WAR DIARY
or
INTELLIGENCE SUMMARY.
(Erase heading not required.)

237 (Coy) R.E.

MARCH 1919

Instructions regarding War Diaries and Intelligence Summaries are contained in F. S. Regs., Part II. and the Staff Manual respectively. Title pages will be prepared in manuscript.

Place	Date	Hour	Summary of Events and Information	Remarks and references to Appendices
Waldneyesberg	17	—	Work on vehicles. Training	First Gauge bath given for use as Divisional Baths — Ref. 9/17
	18	—	ditto	Seven first interviews held
	19	—	" Inspection by D.A.D.O.S. of mechanical equipment	7 Pnrs (Class Z) sent to Armee Colberg St Cologne Depot
	20	1.		2/Lt SHIELDING Kegles demobilized + A.O.R
	21	1	Work — branches welder + breakdown military training	Capt A.E. Gunn + Lt Doyle proceed to Cologne for course of language 2nd Army College 4 O.R. Demob. 30 O.R. Reinf. from 504 (FA) Coy. Transferred to 75th (YA) Coy R.E.
	22		ditto	
	23		ditto	Demob Suspended 24 O.R. Return from Como Camp due to Educational Strikes
	24			Demob Resumed 9 O.R. Demob

Army Form C. 2118.

WAR DIARY
or
INTELLIGENCE SUMMARY.
(Erase heading not required.)

23 (FD) Coy R.E.

March 1919

Place	Date	Hour	Summary of Events and Information	Remarks and references to Appendices
			Summary. Remarks	
Wormersdorf Germany	25		Few available Sappers employed in Renovating & cleaning Waggons &c	17. O.R. Demob. & 24. O.R. Releivable men transferred to 409 (FD) Coy R.E. Coy have now only 6. O.R. for Demob before reaching Cadre Strength as laid down in Demob Regs. Transfer 10 (X) Class Mules to 75 (FD) Coy R.E. " 2 (Z) " " 76 " "
	26		Ditto	10 (Y) Class Horses } Handed over to Conducting 2 (X) " " } Party from 1st M.G. Batt. at OBERDREES X Roads
	27			Coy now have only 4 Horses above cadre Strength
	28			
	29			Mr Henderson returns from Paris leave.
	30			All Horses & Mules Medical (Y & Class) being examined as every animal for [signature]
	31			

Army Form C. 2118.

WAR DIARY
or
INTELLIGENCE SUMMARY.
(Erase heading not required.)

Instructions regarding War Diaries and Intelligence Summaries are contained in F. S. Regs., Part II. and the Staff Manual respectively. Title pages will be prepared in manuscript.

Place	Date	Hour	Summary of Events and Information	Remarks and references to Appendices
Wormersdorf Germany			April 1919 Summary	23rd (ya) Coy RE
	1		Clean Arms inspection for whole Coy	11th Stacked to 409th Coy RE
	2		Works, cleaning wagons etc	
	3		Works and Recreational Training	
	4		Works	
	5		Works & Recreational Training	
	7		Works, packing wagons and erecting jumps	
	8		Works & Recreational Training	
	9		Works, packing wagons Company tools checked	
	10		April meeting of 23rd D Field Coy. Works	
	11		Works, continuing packing	

Army Form C. 2118.

WAR DIARY
or
INTELLIGENCE SUMMARY.

(Erase heading not required.)

Instructions regarding War Diaries and Intelligence Summaries are contained in F. S. Regs., Part II. and the Staff Manual respectively. Title pages will be prepared in manuscript.

Place	Date	Hour	Summary of Events and Information	Remarks and references to Appendices
			April 1919	
Wiesdorf Germany	12		Works etc	
	14		Sports meeting with 26th Fld Coy RE	
	15-16		Ditto	
	17-19		Works, clearing speaking wagons	Att Brigade to act as leave (19.4.19)
	20		Ditto	
	22-26		Works, clearing wagons etc. Divisional Parade	Maj Nevton to 206 W Tunl. Coy. Coy practically as Cadre A strength
	28		Driven to Coln and home	
	29		Works etc	Horses to U.K.
	30		Officers mess for May 1 Celebrations	

www.ingramcontent.com/pod-product-compliance
Lightning Source LLC
Chambersburg PA
CBHW080804010526
44113CB00013B/2324